THE POLITICS OF POST-9/11 MUSIC:
SOUND, TRAUMA, AND THE MUSIC INDUSTRY IN
THE TIME OF TERROR

The Politics of Post-9/11 Music: Sound, Trauma, and the Music Industry in the Time of Terror

JOSEPH P. FISHER
The George Washington University, USA
and
BRIAN FLOTA
Oklahoma State University, USA

ASHGATE

Published by
Ashgate Publishing Limited
Wey Court East
Union Road
Farnham
Surrey, GU9 7PT
England

Ashgate Publishing Company
Suite 420
101 Cherry Street
Burlington
VT 05401-4405
USA

www.ashgate.com

British Library Cataloguing in Publication Data
The politics of post-9/11 music : sound, trauma, and the
  music industry in the time of terror. – (Ashgate popular
  and folk music series)
  1. Popular music – 2001–2010 – History and criticism.
  2. Music – Social aspects – United States – History – 21st
  century. 3. September 11 Terrorist Attacks, 2001 – Influence.
  I. Series II. Fisher, Joseph P. III. Flota, Brian.
  306.4'842'0973'09051–dc22

Library of Congress Cataloging-in-Publication Data
The politics of post-9/11 music : sound, trauma, and the music industry in the time of terror
/ [edited by] Joseph P. Fisher and Brian Flota.
    p. cm. — (Ashgate popular and folk music series)
  Includes index.
  ISBN 978-1-4094-2784-1 (hardcover : alk. paper) — ISBN 978-1-4094-2785-8
(ebook) 1. Popular music—United States—Political aspects. 2. September
11 Terrorist Attacks, 2001—Songs and music—History and criticism. 3. War on Terrorism,
2001–2009—Songs and music--History and criticism. I. Fisher, Joseph P. II. Flota, Brian.
  ML3918.P67P655 2011
  781.640973'09051—dc23

2011021370

ISBN 9781409427841 (hbk)
ISBN 9781409427858 (ebk)

Printed and bound in Great Britain by the
MPG Books Group, UK.

Contents

General Editor's Preface   vii
Notes on Contributors   ix
Foreword   xi
Acknowledgments   xvii

Introduction—Greet Death: Post-9/11 Music and the Sound of Decay   1
Joseph P. Fisher and Brian Flota

PART I   ELECTRIC DREAMS: THE MEDIUM AND THE MESSAGE

1   Rock, Enroll: Music and Militarization since 9/11   13
       Samuel Dwinell

2   Music, Terrorism, Response: The Conditioning Logic of Code and
       Networks   31
       Benjamin J. Robertson

3   Technostalgia and the Resurgence of Cassette Culture   43
       Craig Eley

PART II   HAIL TO THE THIEF: POST-9/11 EXPERIMENTAL MUSIC

4   Why Protest Albums Can't Teach Dissent: The Emergent
       Complexity of Post-9/11 Protest   57
       Conrad Amenta

5   On a Maddening Loop: Post-9/11 Rubble Music   69
       Isaac Vayo

6   Terrorism and the Politics of Improvisation   79
       Rob Wallace

7   Nine Inch Nails' Year Zero and the Biopolitics of Media Convergence 93
       Katheryn Wright

**PART III   WHAT'S GOING ON, AGAIN?: PROTEST AND
             NOSTALGIA**

8   Casualties of War: Hip-Hop and the Old Racial Politics of the
      Post-9/11 Era   107
      Aisha Staggers

9   That Was Now, This Is Then: Recycling Sixties Style in
      Post-9/11 Music   115
      Jeffrey Roessner

10   A New Morning in Amerika: Conservative Politics and Punk Rock
      in the 2000s   129
      Matthew Siblo

11   "Agony & Irony": Indie Culture's Sardonic Response to
      America's Post-9/11 Devolution   145
      S. Todd Atchison

**PART IV   IDLE AMERICAN, AMERICAN IDOL:
             MAINSTREAM MEDIA AND IDEOLOGY**

12   Post-Dixie Chicks Country: Carrie Underwood and the
      Negotiation of Feminist Country Identity   161
      Molly Brost

13   Walking the Great Line: Underoath and Christian Fundamentalism
      in Punk Rock after 9/11   173
      Gerrit Roessler

14   War Is Heavy Metal: Soundtracking the US War in Iraq   185
      Steve Waksman

Index   *207*

General Editor's Preface

The upheaval that occurred in musicology during the last two decades of the twentieth century has created a new urgency for the study of popular music alongside the development of new critical and theoretical models. A relativistic outlook has replaced the universal perspective of modernism (the international ambitions of the 12-note style); the grand narrative of the evolution and dissolution of tonality has been challenged, and emphasis has shifted to cultural context, reception and subject position. Together, these have conspired to eat away at the status of canonical composers and categories of high and low in music. A need has arisen, also, to recognize and address the emergence of crossovers, mixed and new genres, to engage in debates concerning the vexed problem of what constitutes authenticity in music and to offer a critique of musical practice as the product of free, individual expression.

Popular musicology is now a vital and exciting area of scholarship, and the *Ashgate Popular and Folk Music Series* presents some of the best research in the field. Authors are concerned with locating musical practices, values and meanings in cultural context, and draw upon methodologies and theories developed in cultural studies, semiotics, poststructuralism, psychology and sociology. The series focuses on popular musics of the twentieth and twenty-first centuries. It is designed to embrace the world's popular musics from Acid Jazz to Zydeco, whether high tech or low tech, commercial or non-commercial, contemporary or traditional.

Professor Derek B. Scott
Professor of Critical Musicology
University of Leeds

Notes on Contributors

Conrad Amenta: Writer; *Cokemachineglow.com*

S. Todd Atchison: University of North Carolina at Greensboro

Molly Brost: University of Southern Indiana

Samuel Dwinell: Ph.D. candidate; Cornell University

Craig Eley: Ph.D. candidate, American Studies; University of Iowa

Ryan Randall: Ph.D. candidate, Visual and Cultural Studies; University of Rochester

Benjamin J. Robertson: Instructor, Department of English; University of Colorado, Boulder

Gerrit K. Roessler: University of Virginia

Jeffrey Roessner: Mercyhurst College

Matthew Siblo: Ed.M.; Ph.D. Candidate in Counseling; The George Washington University

Aisha Staggers: Assistant Director, Center for Public Policy & Social Research; Central Connecticut State University

Lloyd Isaac Vayo: Defiance College

Dr. Rob Wallace: Research Associate; Improvisation, Community, and Social Practice; University of Guelph

Steve Waksman: Associate Professor, Music and American Studies; Smith College

Katheryn Wright: Florida State University

Foreword

The Earth Still Is Not a Cold Dead Place:
A Conversation with Chris Hrasky

In late August 2001, the instrumental rock band Explosions in the Sky released their second record *Those Who Tell the Truth Shall Die, Those Who Tell the Truth Shall Live Forever*. The album's cover art depicted an angel flying above a group of soldiers in silhouette, a plane flying in the distance. Ominously, the declaration "This plane will crash tomorrow" was inscribed on the inside of the sleeve. Roughly two weeks after the album's release, the events of September 11, 2001 unfolded to the world's horror.

The uncanny, almost unthinkable, coincidence set off a barrage of speculation about the group's prescience. Did they know? How could they know? Are they joking? Were they involved? Indeed, the band's bassist, Michael James, was deemed a threat to security and was detained in an Amsterdam airport when authorities discovered that he had the words "this plane will crash tomorrow" written on his guitar (Chamy).

Two years later, the band released what many critics have seen as their masterwork: the gorgeous *The Earth Is Not a Cold Dead Place*. More restrained than its exceedingly loud predecessor, *Earth* journeys through passages of deep melancholy on its way toward a triumphant conclusion in its final track—the soothing, reassuring "Your Hand in Mine." Writing for *Pitchfork*, Hartley Goldstein was correct to call the record "about as close as indie rock gets to an intentionally 'post-9/11' album."

A long four years after that – during which America's Gulf Coast suffered the tragedy of Hurricane Katrina, and, of course, during which the country became increasingly mired in wars in Iraq and Afghanistan – Explosions in the Sky followed up with the equally poignant *All of a Sudden I Miss Everyone*. Startlingly, the album's cover art displayed a lone man in a rowboat holding a lantern, gazing at a distant city almost entirely submerged in water.

Ask any music writer to name the most important band of the contemporary era, always a shifting designation, and you better cancel your dinner reservations. In the course of compiling this volume, we, the editors, have missed many dinners. However, no matter what our disagreements were about what bands to represent, what trends to survey, what albums to include, we continually returned to Explosions in the Sky, believing them to hold an absolutely central position in the culture of post-9/11 America. Whether or not their connections to the current sociopolitical moment are accidental has no bearing on the fact that they have remained consistently relevant throughout a decade of pronounced cultural turmoil.

Therefore, we contacted the band to see if they would be willing to lend a voice to this volume—to frame it, as it were. Drummer Chris Hrasky (CH) graciously accepted our invitation and kindly offered some of his time to talk about the process—and politics—of writing music in the post-9/11 American landscape. One of the most striking themes that emerged over the course of our conversation concerned the ways in which, both from a creative and consumer standpoint, the shifts during the decade since 2001 in the production and dissemination of music have, possibly, sapped the act of listening of its potential to foster communal connections—despite the omnipresent language of file*sharing*. This issue is explored in the chapters that follow and, we contend, represents a significant inquiry about the connections between music and politics in the Time of Terror. If music is the universal language, what happens if it is primarily heard in relative cultural isolation? This question becomes even more charged when we consider that, despite the premium that many musicians, critics, and fans place on the Internet as the utopian space for community, that particular community is implicitly constructed as Western, if not primarily American. After all, not every country in the world has unfettered access to music or to the Internet. We are grateful to Chris for his assistance with this project.

Q: So here we are, nearly ten years out from 9/11 and the release of *Those Who Tell the Truth Shall Die, Those Who Tell the Truth Shall Live Forever*, and we are back to talking about the band in the context of the September 11th attacks. Is this surprising—or irritating—to you in any way?

CH: At this point, it doesn't really bother us, because it really hasn't come up in several years. When [9/11] happened, and we had just put that record out the week before, it was pretty much the main topic of our interviews—not that we were doing a ton of interviews back then. The phrase "This plane will crash tomorrow" is written in the liner notes, and, for some reason, some rumor started that the record came out on September 10th, which was completely untrue; it came out two weeks before that. So there would be interviewers who would ask us if there was some connection between that phrase and 9/11. It's as if they were looking for us to say something like, "We knew it was going to happen" or that we had premonitions or something. We would tell them that [the album's] artwork [by David Logan] and liner notes were completed six months prior to September 11, and some journalists seemed disappointed with that answer. Also, at the time, college radio wouldn't play us because of the band name. We sort of understood everyone was in this weird panic state, having this totally new experience we'd never really been through as a country, so maybe people weren't thinking very clearly about things. It was just very, very strange. It went on for a full year like that. [Interviewers] would say things like, "You guys are from Texas and George Bush is from Texas. Can you comment on that?" They were trying to make up these weird connections that didn't even make any sense. One of the guys in the band is Pakistani [guitarist Munaf Rayani], so they would talk about that sometimes. Again, this was the first time we'd ever been interviewed for anything—so it was kind of a strange trial by fire, I guess.

Q: Did that experience inform the way you envisioned your subsequent records at any level?

CH: I don't know if it really ever had the effect where it framed how we would write the next record. Even in some of your questions, you mentioned *The Earth Is Not a Cold Dead Place* and asked if some of the songs were a reaction to 9/11. As far as I remember—we wrote that record eight years ago—that never came up in the conversation about what these songs were about, or how these songs should be, or even what they should be called.

Q: So-called "indie" music is all the rage in academic circles these days. Any thoughts on how your role in this anthology might establish a connection between Explosions in the Sky, the tragedy of September 11, and the realm of "academic" writing?

CH: I wonder if the band's intention is even important. I do feel like once you've made something and put it out there, it develops a life of its own; the audience seems to make of it what they will. If there are people who make the connection [to 9/11], I think it's valid. Just because we didn't consciously make the connection doesn't mean it doesn't exist in some way. We didn't write any songs about 9/11. That just didn't happen. But if people look at it as though "this song is about 9/11," then that connection exists for them.

Q: Are you OK with our anthology spinning the music in a political way?

CH: If that's how people relate to it or that's how it's interpreted, I certainly don't have a problem with it. Politics is not something that comes up when we're writing songs or titles or artwork—at least not on the surface. That title, *The Earth Is Not a Cold Dead Place*, came from this idea of life being very confusing. It was a dark time, and the record is sort of about trying to hang on to the beauty in the world. So I guess in some sense that could be considered political. As far as making these connections between our music and politics: just because it's not present for the four of us in the band doesn't invalidate the argument. It comes back to how people view the record[s] themselves.

Q: To force the issue a bit, we should discuss the genre of music the band performs. Since your music is entirely instrumental, one can leap to the conclusion that it is apolitical. However, the titles of the tracks on your two post-9/11 albums seem to direct listeners to ways in which they are meant to be listened. Tracks like "First

Breath After Coma," "Memorial," "Your Hand in Mine," "Welcome, Ghosts," and "Catastrophe and the Cure" all suggest both personal and collective reactions to crises. As such, do you think of your music as political in any way? If so, how is this politics directly related to the emotional quality of your music?

CH: When we write a song, it comes down to asking how we know when [it] is finished. Do we find it moving in some way? Is it evocative of something? The last thing we want [our songs] to be is background music, which is always a risk with instrumental music. The fundamental goal is always for it to be evocative in some way or, as cheesy as it sounds, to let the listener create the narrative of what the song is about. What does it mean to them, if anything at all? It's kind of an intangible thing for us: "Well this works. This sounds cool. This feels good. This makes me feel something. Why does this drum beat or this guitar note make us kind of bored?" So it's really more about emotional responses. We generally don't think of our music as political.

[However], we were wondering how the artwork for *All of a Sudden I Miss Everyone* [by Esteban Rey] was going to be received. [That record] came out in early 2007, and we thought for sure that this image of a flooded city and this guy on his own in a rowboat ... we just thought for sure people were going to connect it to New Orleans and Katrina. Even if that wasn't something we were necessarily trying to convey, it was something we were OK with. [Ironically], no one—no fan, no interviewer—has ever brought that up. To us it seems very obvious. We were actually worried that people were going to say we were exploitative or too heavy-handed: "Oh my God, this is so literal. It's a flooded city and this lonely guy on this boat." We were working on one of the songs on that record in August 2005. That was the one time we were actually talking about an event while we were writing a song and trying to connect the two. It ended up being [the song] "It's Natural to Be Afraid." We never actually refer to the songs by their actual titles when we talk about [them]. We always refer to them as what we were calling them when we were writing them. That song, in our minds, is just called "New Orleans." It still is. If anyone brings that song up, we say, "Remember that part in 'New Orleans.'" That's sort of the one instance where there was a very direct connection to an event.

Q: Along those same lines, the title of *All of a Sudden I Miss Everyone* comes from an awkward scene in John Cassavetes' 1974 film *A Woman Under the Influence* in which an eccentric mother, waiting for her children at a bus-stop, publicly displays signs of her mental health in the process of disintegrating. Would you say that the music on that album (or any of the band's other albums) is about the loneliness of being alienated when one most needs help?

CH: All of us have seen that movie five or six times over the past ten years. That's definitely one of my top five movies of all time. I was watching the movie again after the record had come out, and that line came up, and I just thought, "Holy shit!" That's not how we came up with that title—which is totally crazy because I remember the scene. I totally know the line. The way she's saying it is pretty much exactly how we were thinking of what the title and the record meant. It's sort of about going about your daily life and your routine and feeling really isolated. Not isolated where you're stuck up in a research station in the North Pole, but literally at your job, hanging out with your friends, your family, but still that feeling of just utter, "Why do I feel so alone? And even though I'm surrounded by everyone, why does it feel like I miss everyone all the time?"

Q: What do you think of the recent resurgence of vinyl collecting? Do you think your records are more properly experienced when listened to on vinyl, on CD, or in another digital format? Do you think the "return to vinyl," especially for younger listeners reared in the age of the CD, represents a nostalgic return to "simpler times"?

CH: Obviously, things are so much faster now. You don't have to dig very deep. You can listen to ten-second snippets and say "I don't like it. I don't care." It makes me kind of sad because that's not how I grew up listening to music. It was a much more communal thing. It was like, "Someone got the new Dinosaur Jr. record. Come over and we'll all listen to it." That was a big part of growing up for me. That was a regular thing.

   I'm very curious to see how it will be for us when we put our new record out.[1] Our digital sales are increasing, but percentage-wise, our physical sales are still really strong. We put a lot of work into the artwork, so maybe that's [the reason]. It makes me hope that people have this connection to us and that they want to have this artifact of what we do. The artwork for our next record is the most elaborate we've done, which is interesting because it's at a time when most record and CD formats just come out pretty basic. If there are people who are spending the time to go to the record store or waiting for it to be shipped to them from the label, then we would like to give them something worthwhile. Sure, [anyone] can go to iTunes and get it instantly. I do that a lot. But there's nothing cool to look at, and it's an underwhelming experience. Our hope is that you're rewarded with a cool package and cool artwork. And because the artwork has always been so important to us, almost as important as the music, we'll always think about it that way. At the same time, there is something positive about being able to find good music easily.

   [If we think about the role of] technology—how are things like social networking changing the way we experience our lives? What will the repercussions of that be twenty years from now? This weird isolation and anonymity of online socializing; the "wired" life—it's certainly easier not to be a part of society in a physical sense. I don't even really buy anything in a store. I get stuff [online] if I want a CD, book or a movie. It's cheaper and I don't have to drive. That whole experience of

---

1   Their fifth album, *Take Care, Take Care, Take Care*, was released April 18, 2011.

purchasing goods and consuming has totally changed for me. Things are certainly easier, but it also makes me sort of disappointed in myself.

Q: Explosions in the Sky hail from Texas; the band scored a film about football; the band's name, from what we've read, was inspired by a fireworks display; the band is framing an anthology about 9/11. Does all of this make the band, at its core, an American band? Does this distinction even matter? Is it one that you've already embraced?

CH: We're comfortable with that statement [that we're an American band], but we're definitely not the love it or leave it type.

Works Cited

Chamy, Michael. "Born on the Fourth of July: To the Moon and Back with Explosions in the Sky." *The Austin Chronicle*. Oct. 24, 2003. Web (accessed Jan. 5, 2011).

Goldstein, Hartley. Review of *The Earth Is Not a Cold Dead Place*, by Explosions in the Sky. *Pitchfork*. Nov. 30, 2003. Web (accessed Jan. 5, 2011).

Logan, David. Cover art. *Those Who Tell the Truth Shall Die, Those Who Tell the Truth Shall Live Forever*. Temporary Residence Limited, 2001. LP.

Rey, Esteban. Cover art. *All of a Sudden I Miss Everyone*. Temporary Residence Limited, 2007. LP.

Acknowledgments

The editors: Thanks to Gayle Wald, Robert McRuer, and Jeffrey Cohen for their support and advice from the very beginning of this project. Also, thank you to Heidi Bishop, who has been a fantastic managing editor all throughout the production of this volume.

Joseph P. Fisher: Thanks to Explosions in the Sky, Chris Hrasky in particular, for inspiring this project and for remaining willing to be involved in it the entire way. I also owe a word of thanks to Alexander Tieberg-Bailie for introducing me to *The Disintegration Loops*. Like so many of my students, Alex has taught me more than he will ever know. As always, I am grateful for the love and support of my parents, Patricia and Paul Fisher, and my brother, Kevin Fisher—all of whom have patiently endured my incessant music listening and collecting habits for longer than anyone else could. Finally, thank you to my wife Kelly for her unconditional patience and love. This publication, like so many of my other projects, would not have reached completion had Kelly not been touching it from a distance since day one.

Brian Flota: I thank Joe Fisher for asking me to help him work on this project, which has been very rewarding for me. I would also like to thank the English Department at Oklahoma State University for allowing me the time and concentration needed to work on this book. I would especially like to thank Carol Mason for suggesting Steve Waksman as a scholar who would be suitable for contributing to this collection. I am also grateful to my online communities at *RateYourMusic.com* and *PoMo Jukebox* for keeping me aware of exciting new music. Of course, I am thankful to our contributors, who have put up with our criticisms and suggestions with grace. It has been an honor to work with all of them. Last, but not least, these acknowledgments would be incomplete without mentioning the love and support of my parents, Sandra L. Simmons and Bradley T. Flota.

Conrad Amenta: I would like to thank the staff at *Cokemachineglow*, one of the smartest communities of music writers working today.

S. Todd Atchison: I would like to thank Caitlin Saraphis and Alice Mitchell for their insightful edits of earlier chapter drafts.

Molly Brost: I would like to thank Ben O'Dell, Oana Popescu-Sandu, Melinda York, David O'Grady, and Mark Krahling for their feedback on an early draft of my essay.

Samuel Dwinell: My initial interest in this topic was developed in conversation with members of the group Iraq Veterans Against the War. I wish to thank Judith Peraino, Nick Salvato, and Amy Villarejo for their insightful comments at various stages of this project. Particular thanks also goes to Shelley Feldman and Chuck Geisler for organizing the "Accumulating Insecurity" workshops at Cornell University in 2008. These events proved formative for my interest in aspects of militarization. My greatest debt of thanks is to Rachel Lewis, without whose bibliographic dexterity, theoretical acumen, and willingness to read drafts I would never have undertaken this project.

Craig Eley: Thanks to Rob Latham's seminar on subcultures at the University of Iowa, where the idea for my chapter developed under encouragement and valuable feedback. Also, a special word of thanks to David Z. Morris, with whom I recorded my first cassette release. Thank you, David, for being a great bandmate, friend, and intellectual sparring partner.

Benjamin J. Robertson: Thanks to Paul Youngquist and numerous students for their conversations about media, music, and more; mash-up artists everywhere for challenging conventions of music production, consumption, and distribution; and Lori Emerson for being Lori Emerson.

Gerrit Konrad Roessler: I am indebted to my supervisor at the University of Dortmund, Professor Walter Grünzweig, for his support at the earliest stages of both my academic career in general, and the chapter in this volume in particular. I owe thanks to my friends and colleagues Kelly Gross, Brett Martz, Gabriel Cooper, and Matt Lockaby for reading rough drafts, listening to ideas, and debating them on many occasions. Finally, I express my most heartfelt gratitude and love to my partner, Allison Sommers, for supporting me in all my endeavors, be they academic or otherwise.

Jeffrey Roessner: Thanks to Christy Rieger, always my first and best reader. And special acknowledgment to Erich Hertz for the ongoing, always compelling conversation about music. The essay would not have been possible without such wonderful support.

Matthew Siblo: I would like to thank everyone who agreed to be interviewed for my chapter, Lori for her inestimable patience and understanding throughout the writing process, and Tom for his priceless guidance and long-winded explanations. My chapter is dedicated to my brother who, despite his protests that punk rock loses something on the page, continues to be the most important reader of my work.

Aisha Staggers: I would like to thank my family and friends for their love and support, Teba Henderson for introducing me to hip-hop at the age of ten, and my father, Ronald Staggers, for teaching me to appreciate good music. I dedicate this to Amaya Elle, Ira Davis, Marvin and Tammi.

Isaac Vayo: Thank you to my dissertation committee (chair Ellen Berry and members Cynthia Baron, Rob Sloane, and Don McQuarie) for their guidance in helping me to refine the ideas in my chapter in this volume, and to my wife Lauren for bearing with my unending discussions of its content.

Steve Waksman: Thanks to the editors, and especially Brian Flota, for inviting me to be part of this project and for their patience as I toiled through the writing process. Also, big thanks to Carol Mason, my friend and colleague from afar, for connecting me with Brian and opening the way to my contribution to this book.

Rob Wallace: Thanks to Joe Sorbara, Jesse Stewart, Simon Rose, and members of the ICASP reading group at the University of Guelph for their feedback. Thanks also to Curtis Bahn and Tomie Hahn for alerting me to the different, but related history of IEDs (improvised electronic devices).

Katheryn Wright: I would like to thank Amit Rai for his encouragement. Without Clinton Bryant's continual support and encyclopedic knowledge of all things related to popular music, I could not have completed this chapter.

Introduction—Greet Death:
Post-9/11 Music and the Sound of Decay[1]

By Joseph P. Fisher and Brian Flota

> The music was dying. I was recording the death of this sweeping melody. It was very emotional for me, and mystical as well. Tied up in these melodies were my youth, my paradise lost, the American pastoral landscape, all dying gently, gracefully, beautifully.
>
> William Basinski

In August 2001, avant-garde composer William Basinski began transferring a series of analog tape loops, which he recorded in the early 1980s, to digital file format. Early in the process, Basinski realized that the tapes themselves were disintegrating. As the composer watched the old magnetic tape gliding through his recording equipment, he noticed that particles of tape material were flaking off, irreparably altering his initial recordings, and capturing, in literally gritty detail, the sound of decay.

The added significance of this narrative is a matter of context: Basinski completed this project in September 2001, and at the time, he was residing in Brooklyn, New York. On the morning of September 11, 2001, Basinski watched the destruction of the World Trade Center from his rooftop as he played his newly archived tape loops over and over again in the background, providing an eerily relevant soundtrack for what remains, perhaps, the most significant day in post-millennial American history.

When Basinski released these loops commercially, he did so as an expansive four-CD set entitled *The Disintegration Loops*. Though hardly as popular or as well-known as other "9/11 albums"—like Bruce Springsteen's *The Rising* or, perhaps more esoterically, Godspeed You Black Emperor!'s *Yanqui U.X.O.*—The *Disintegration Loops* have achieved a modest amount of critical praise. Most notably, as the obligatory best-of-the-decade music lists began to be compiled at the end of 2009, Basinski's name gained a fair amount of public prominence, at least among music bloggers. The music magazine *Resident Advisor* ranked *The Loops* as the 86th best album of the '00s. Similarly, the music site *Pitchfork* listed

---

[1]   Joseph P. Fisher thanks Sarah Zupko for allowing him to adapt two of his *PopMatters* blog posts for use in this chapter. Those posts are as follows: Fisher, Joseph P. "Greet Death: William Basinski, Hospitality, and the Sound of Decay" (*PopMatters*, 16 July 2010. Web); Fisher, Joseph P. "Losing My Religion: Revealing the Hollow Reality of Lo-Fi" (*PopMatters*, 23 July 2010. Web).

the set as the 196th best release (out of a possible 200) of the 2000s, while the website *Tiny Mix Tapes* placed *The Loops* in the number 10 spot—two slots above, it should be noted, *Merriweather Post Pavilion* (2009) by indie favorites Animal Collective.

It is certainly possible that the dramatic backdrop which adorns *The Disintegration Loops* is the reason for the set's enduring relevance. After all, Basinski's subsequent releases have not garnered the same attention, critical or popular, as *The Loops*. Regardless of the set's contextual ties to the 9/11 attacks, *The Disintegration Loops* arguably still stand as the most significant musical artifacts of the so-called Time of Terror. As a group of recordings that chronicle the process of auditory and material decay, *The Loops* metonymically embody the sonic fixations of much post-9/11 music: concerns with fidelity, the tensions between "outmoded" recording techniques and digital media, the connections between "reality" and physicality, and a nostalgic gaze on the past. As Basinski writes in the liner notes to *The Disintegration Loops*, he witnessed the death of his past as his compositions physically and auditorily disintegrated. Along those lines, the writers in this volume probe, from a variety of angles, and through discussions of a variety of contemporary music genres, the ways in which the post-9/11 musical landscape, particularly in North America, has been shaped by artistic and technological attempts to deconstruct the split between the past and the present—the split between pre-9/11 temporality and post-9/11 temporality. Furthermore, these writers question the political import of such attempts, particularly when they are often dependent on an idealized, frequently pastoral, vision of the past—a vision that, many of our writers argue, only fragments and disintegrates the more that it is revisited, looped, reimagined.

In his slim meditation on the 9/11 attacks, *Welcome to the Desert of the Real!*, Slavoj Žižek argues that "the ultimate and defining moment of the twentieth century was the direct experience of the Real as opposed to everyday social reality—the Real in its extreme violence as the price to be paid for peeling off the deceptive layers of reality" (5–6). By drawing on examples as diverse as Hollywood disaster movies, hardcore pornography, and the endless recycling and rebroadcasting of the 9/11 news footage (the last of which has become a ritual, at least in the United States, on each anniversary of the attacks), Žižek excavates what he sees as a central irony in the drive to experience the Real: it "culminates in its apparent opposite, in a *theatrical spectacle*" (9; emphasis in original). Indeed, it is telling that the 9/11 attacks were notoriously described—by political pundits, news broadcasters, and the public more generally—as being "like a movie." While the extreme, potentially pornographic video coverage of 9/11 attacks was meant to reveal and transmit the reality of the attacks, it also worked to configure 9/11 as a spectacle, an event that was, in its utter realness, also unreal—too real to be conceived beyond the trappings of theatrical performance.[2]

---

[2]   Eerily, Khalid Sheikh Mohammed, the proclaimed mastermind of the 9/11 attacks, is quoted in *The 9/11 Commission Report* as having originally imagined a plot in which ten

Though Žižek, and many other critics who have written on 9/11, primarily configures the spectacle of the attacks in visual terms, it is quite easy—and necessary—to appropriate his remarks to examine 9/11 as a kind of auditory spectacle.[3] While a sizeable majority of 9/11's (eye)witnesses encountered the attacks visually, through various visual news media, the comments relayed by the firefighters from FDNY Engine 7, Ladder 1 (the first firefighters to respond to the World Trade Center attacks) suggest that 9/11, as an event, was initially an auditory one. "And then we heard a plane come over; and in Manhattan, you don't hear planes too often, especially loud ones," one of the firefighters stated upon hearing American Airlines Flight 11 fly overhead before seeing it crash into the North Tower (quoted in *9/11*).

To be clear, resituating 9/11 as an auditory event is not meant as an attempt to prioritize one set of sensory impressions over another, though it should be noted that conceiving of the attacks solely in visual terms, which has been the dominant paradigm to date, ignores the sensory impressions of, at least, blind and visually impaired witnesses. Rather, moving 9/11 from a visual register to an auditory one is meant to highlight the various ways that the attacks were preceded by—even in the final seconds before them—noise. The 9/11 Commission writers describe, in a chapter titled "The System Was Blinking Red," the enormous amount of "chatter" that was dominating defense channels all throughout 2001. (The first subsection of this chapter is even titled "The Drumbeat Begins.") Even more telling are the comments from the firefighters of FDNY Engine 7, Ladder 1, because, as the documentary that chronicles their rescue work bears out, American Airlines Flight 11 roared above New York City, making an almost otherworldly racket which predicted the destruction that followed. Jacques Attali's famous analysis of noise is, of course, relevant here: "*Noise is violence*: it disturbs. To make noise is to interrupt a transmission, to disconnect, to kill" (26; emphasis in original). Setting aside the chaos that ensued after the World Trade Center and Pentagon were attacked—interruptions in telecommunication service, the seemingly endless distribution of misinformation via the mass media, the horrifying sound of the collapsing towers—it is arguably the primordial, disruptive howl of AA 11 that, perhaps, signifies everything about 9/11: it bespeaks the massive global disorder that followed it.

An intriguing musical parallel to the events of September 11, 2001 was the resurgence, later that very month, of low-fidelity (or lo-fi) rock. Merely two weeks after 9/11, New York City's The Strokes released their debut album *Is This It* to widespread critical acclaim. In his article "Maim that Tune: The Moldy Peaches

---

planes were to be hijacked, nine of which were to crash into various targets on the east and west coasts of the United States. Mohammed would then have landed the tenth plane, killed all of the male passengers, and delivered an anti-US speech through the mainstream media. *The Commission* writers are perceptive in their description of this plan: "This is theater, a spectacle of destruction with KSM as the self-cast star—the superterrorist" (154).

[3] See also Baudrillard, Borradori, Spivak.

and the Apotheosis of Lo-Fi," Mark Desrosiers praised the album's engineering for being "perfect in its imperfection." Likewise, Desrosiers gushed that lead singer Julian Casablancas' voice sounded "raw," while "the band's grooves crackle like vinyl." Though time has seen The Strokes' star fall a bit, the importance of *Is This It* remains as high as ever: *Rolling Stone* named it the second best album of the decade in its "50 Best Albums of the Decade" list (Fricke et al.). It is no surprise, then, that the remainder of the naughties, as clever music scribes have called the first ten years of the new millennium, saw countless bands marketing themselves, or being marketed as, lo-fi. And many of these bands also hailed from New York City: Yeah Yeah Yeahs, TV on the Radio, LCD Soundsystem, The Dirty Projectors, A Place to Bury Strangers, and Sleigh Bells, just to name a few, have arguably brought more attention to New York City's music scene than at any time since the heyday of the city's legendary punk movement in the mid- to late-1970s. Thus, in many ways, the sound of post-9/11 New York has become just as prominent and relevant as the sight of it.

Though written in 2002, a few years before many of these bands would hit their commercial and critical peaks, Desrosiers does a wonderful job of detailing the renewed appeal of rougher, unpolished sounds. "'High fidelity' ... is now a lie," he quips. The truth? Reality, the Real. "Real life is analog," Desrosiers argues. This claim in many ways paraphrases Attali's description of music: *"Music is a channelization of noise"* (26; emphasis in original). For Attali, and for Desrosiers, noise precedes music because it exists prior to the organizational controls that channel it and ultimately render it musical, melodic even. As such, noise—as heard in the crackle of vinyl, the imperfections of the human voice (before Autotune, of course), the scuzzy distortion that is part and parcel of any electric music—disrupts the fabricated fiction of high-fidelity recordings, the kinds of recordings that are traditionally considered "music." In other words, music is fiction, whereas noise is real—the essence of real life, of reality as we know it.

It is fitting, then, that William Basinski would see the death of his youth, which he links to the American landscape, in the disintegration of his analog tapes. As those tapes flaked and fragmented, the physicality of his past, which, for him, had bound itself magnetically to his recordings, gradually crumbled into ruin. The only evidence that such a past ever existed emerges sonically on his digitized recordings as disruptive lacunae that repeatedly violate the melodic flow of the original loops. On *The Disintegration Loops*, we hear the jarring noise of death and decay. We hear the sound of loss, the sound of destruction, the sound of an America that has been unalterably changed by the spectacle of the Real—a spectacle of aural catastrophe.

Given that noise embodies the potential for cultural disruption, and given that so much post-9/11 American music has deliberately—and spectacularly, we might say—appropriated the affectations of lo-fi, it is puzzling to note that the past decade has seen very little, if any, overtly political music, particularly in light of the deep turmoil that has characterized American politics, domestically and abroad, ever since. While much has already been said about musical responses to 9/11 such as

Paul McCartney's "Freedom," Alan Jackson's "Where Were You (When the World Stopped Turning)," Toby Keith's "Courtesy of the Red, White, and Blue (The Angry American)," and Sleater-Kinney's *One Beat*, as well as various musical coincidences around the time of the attacks that seemed in poor taste, much less has been written about the post-9/11 surge in patriotic music, which saw older albums by country musicians Lee Greenwood (*American Patriot* and *Super Hits*) and Charlie Daniels (*A Decade of Hits* and *Super Hits*) climb up *Billboard*'s Top Pop Catalog charts ("Top Pop").[4] One of the goals of this collection is to reveal the implicit as well as explicit connections between the tragic events of that day, their geopolitical aftermath, and the myriad changes within the music industry that followed in its wake.

For instance, in the hours before the terrorist attacks on Tuesday, September 11, 2001, new releases by Jay-Z (*The Blueprint*), Bob Dylan (*"Love and Theft"*), Slayer (*God Hates Us All*), and Dream Theater (*Live Scenes from New York*) hit record store shelves. This brief list is remarkable for a few reasons. The albums by Jay-Z (as Aisha Staggers observes in her essay) and Bob Dylan have subsequently been regarded as classics, each possessing a release date relegated to an eerie but otherwise insignificant role in its critical reception. However, the releases by Slayer and Dream Theater did not escape such a fate, as both were marked by controversy based solely on the arbitrary (and coincidental) date of their release. The title alone for Slayer's album, *God Hates Us All*, either seemed outrageously blasphemous or entirely appropriate depending on one's religious beliefs in the aftermath of the attacks. Its original cover art, depicting nails driven into a blood-soaked Bible, did not help quell the controversy. Similarly, the cover art for Dream Theater's live album depicts a "Big Apple" on fire, with images of the World Trade Center inside its flames; the cover image was quickly pulled with a new, less offensive image put in its place. As these examples suggest, the simple affiliation of the date September 11, 2001 with these releases has served to shape their legacy in complex ways these artists could have never imagined.

More widely recognized than anything that Slayer or Dream Theater have recorded since 2001 (or ever) has been the massive popularity of the televised talent show *American Idol*, which debuted in the United States in 2002. *Idol* has not only given Fox Television its highest Nielsen ratings ever for an episodic show but also has made stars out of previously unknown singers such as Kelly Clarkson, Carrie Underwood (who is the subject of Molly Brost's contribution to this volume), Clay Aiken, Jennifer Hudson, Chris Daughtry, and Adam Lambert,

---

[4]   A sampling of these coincidences include the appearance of the track "NYC Cops" on The Strokes' *Is This It* with the lyric "New York City cops, they ain't so smart," the cover art for Explosions in the Sky's album *Those Who Tell the Truth Shall Die, Those Who Tell the Truth Shall Live Forever*, announcing, "This plane shall crash tomorrow" (which is discussed at length in the Foreword to this volume), and The Coup's original artwork for *Party Music*, designed before 9/11, which included an image of a giant fireball emanating from the World Trade Center.

among others. More importantly, it returned the solo vocalist to a level of popular cultural dominance not seen since the heyday of Whitney Houston, Mariah Carey, and Michael Jackson in the early 1990s. Though it is fairly commonplace for solo performers—singers and songwriters—to be configured as icons of pop music, those figures also reflect the conventions of folk music, wherein the individual vocalist has historically sung songs of social protest. This elongated, liberal history is, of course, never recognized by the notoriously conservative *Idol*. Nevertheless, this volume, in part, excavates those historical connections while asking if something as hi-fi—as fabricated—as *American Idol* can actually be more politically aware than it would seem at first glance.

Another seemingly apolitical post-9/11 musical trend has been the wide popularity of mp3 downloads. The (illegal) downloading of music seriously began to complicate the music industry's enforcement of copyright violations; as such, it was implicitly configured as a kind of consumer terrorism against entrenched distribution models. One offshoot of this trend was the production of recordings known as mash-ups, which fuse two or more previously recorded tracks into an entirely new one. Combined with the increasing affordability of music editing software programs like ProTools and Garageband, amateur acts as well as popular DJs began reworking some of popular music's sacred cows. As Benjamin Robertson discusses in his chapter, the most highly publicized mash-up recording was *The Grey Album*, produced by Danger Mouse in 2004. On it, he cleverly fused Jay-Z's *The Black Album* (2003) with The Beatles' self-titled double LP (1968), more commonly referred to as "The White Album." Because of obvious copyright violations, the album was never officially released. However, an internet campaign known as "Grey Tuesday" (February 24, 2004) reportedly resulted in 100,000 downloads of the album, and there was nothing the record industry could do about it (Rimmer 133). The popularity of *The Grey Album* opened the doors for mash-up artists such as Girl Talk while also prompting a collaboration between Jay-Z and the nu-metal act Linkin Park. Eventually, as Conrad Amenta and Katheryn Wright note later in this collection, major acts like Radiohead (with their 2007 album *In Rainbows*) and Nine Inch Nails (2008's *The Slip*) would eventually forsake tactile forms of their music almost completely, offering their albums as online accessible mp3 files.[5] In Radiohead's case, they offered their fans a "pay what you want" model, while Nine Inch Nails released their album for free under a Creative Commons agreement. These gestures, whether occurring top-down, from artist to consumer, or bottom-up, from consumer to artist, all imply a collective rage against the machinery of old media—the noisy disruption of so many worldly shoplifters uniting to take over.

Ironically, however, just as tactile music media seemed ready to be pitched into the proverbial dustbin of history, the album was institutionalized as an artistic medium. Prior to the terrorist attacks, Congress passed the National Recording

---

[5]   Both albums would eventually get "proper," tactile releases several months after their initial release online.

Preservation Act of 2000, sponsored by California Representative William M. Thomas. As a result, the National Recording Registry was begun in 2002. Three albums were included in the first registry: Frank Sinatra's *Songs for Young Lovers* (1954), Miles Davis' *Kind of Blue* (1959), and Bob Dylan's *The Freewheelin' Bob Dylan* (1963). Twelve albums were eventually included as part of the registry for 2003. Coinciding with this official sanctioning of the album was the trend of long-popular musical acts performing their most famous albums in their entirety in a concert format. One of the first groups to do this was, interestingly enough, Slayer, who performed their 1986 classic *Reign in Blood* at a handful of shows in 2004 from start to finish. Many artists, such as Patti Smith, Sonic Youth, Van Morrison, and the Flaming Lips, followed suit and began organizing concerts and tours based around performances of their older albums: *Horses*, *Daydream Nation*, *Astral Weeks*, and *The Soft Bulletin* respectively. Not coincidentally, the decade since 2001 has also seen a resurgence in vinyl record production and sales. In 2008, for example, the purchase of vinyl records nearly doubled, inching up 89 percent, and in 2010 vinyl sales reached their highest volume since Soundscan began tracking these numbers (in 1991), totalling 2.8 million copies (Roberts; Harding). Though this resurgence is often seen as a backlash against the ever-widening reach of the Internet and digital media, which is a point that Craig Eley makes in his chapter about cassette culture, it is also possible to hear William Basinski's words echoing in the background of that backlash: vinyl, for many, embodies the paradise of the past.

One of this volume's core claims is that this backward glance to the days when music was distributed, and generally consumed, on physical media in long-playing format—it is worth noting here that a popular live album concert series carries the ironic name Don't Look Back—implies a nostalgic longing for the prelapsarian time before the 9/11 attacks. A major focal point of this nostalgic gaze has been on the sounds of pre-9/11 popular music. For instance, in the latter half of "the naughties," heavy metal, a topic that Steve Waksman discusses in his contribution, largely transcended the "nu-metal" trappings of the early 2000s and returned to the genre's more "traditional" sounds, as deployed by bands as diverse as Dragonforce, Mastodon, Wolfmother, Boris, and Sunn O))). Similarly, the popular new wave sounds of the 1980s returned to the forefront, as groups like The Killers, Franz Ferdinand, Interpol, and LCD Soundsystem produced highly acclaimed and well-selling albums. Likewise, many disbanded groups from the 1980s and 1990s reunited, toured, and, in many cases, recorded new music throughout the same period. Many of these groups—The Pixies, Pavement, Dinosaur Jr., Mission of Burma, and, in particular, Guided By Voices—were early purveyors of lo-fi music, which suggests that, despite the obvious monetary motivation behind these reunions, their music carries a social currency that extends beyond entirely commercial contexts.

Finally, despite the fact that you, dear reader, are currently holding this bound book in your hands, the way that audiences of all kinds receive music criticism has changed substantially in recent years. As all print media have continued to decline in sales, longtime pop-music print stalwarts like *Rolling Stone*, *Spin*, and *Alternative Press* have had to bolster their online presence to keep up with Internet upstarts such as *Pitchfork*, *PopMatters*, and *Stereogum*, as well as user-generated content sites like *RateYourMusic* and the online encyclopedia *Wikipedia*. Many of these sites allow user comments, which have served to democratize music criticism. Just as news crawlers became staples of televised newscasts after September 11th, 2001, ostensibly in an attempt to provide viewers constantly with new information, music aficionados used the World Wide Web to their advantage, creating their own media outlets to disseminate news about their favorite musical acts. Oftentimes, these outlets have made use of blogging platforms such as *tumblr*, *CafePress*, and, of course, *Blogger* to enact a grassroots, potentially countercultural campaign against the towering old media monoliths.

The Politics of Post-9/11 Music is divided into four sections. The first, "Electric Dreams: The Medium and the Message," consists of essays that explore the impact of the increasing digitization of music over the decade after 2001. Samuel Dwinell focuses on the various ways in which the militarized rhetoric of the post-9/11 era has penetrated the domestic sphere in the form of video games, websites, mp3 files, movie trailers, and *YouTube* clips. In his piece, Benjamin J. Robertson observes how mp3s and iPods have rendered the very activity of listening to music a far more individual experience than it was in twentieth-century periods of warfare. Lastly, Craig Eley looks at the "technostalgia" craze and the recent revival of cassette culture, especially among lo-fi and noise rock acts.

The second section, "Hail to the Thief: Post-9/11 Experimental Music," features work that examines subversive responses to the tragedy of September 11, 2001 from the underground (like Lloyd Isaac Vayo's piece on the controversial "rubble music" of Cassetteboy, especially their song "Fly Me to New York," which fuses a narrative of the 9/11 terrorist attacks from the perspective of the terrorists with iconic and unauthorized samples from the long-cherished back-catalog of the American icon Frank Sinatra) and the ways in which (African-)American improvised music—particularly jazz—has entered itself into the lexicon of military jargon (as Rob Wallace explores in his contribution, which deconstructs the frequent use of the term "improvised explosive device," or IED, in media accounts of the US war in Iraq). Lastly Conrad Amenta and Katheryn Wright look at two popular groups who experimented with the way their albums were disseminated, rendering the act of music consumption an act of protest. Amenta convincingly observes, for instance, that Radiohead's obvious anti-Bush leanings on their 2003 album *Hail to the Thief* are less provocative as contemporary protest than their more ambiguous 2007 follow-up, *In Rainbows*, which was distributed through the Internet as mp3 files with a pay model that circumvented the traditional financial structure of the major labels. Similarly, Wright discusses Nine Inch Nails' multimedia experiment *Year Zero* (2007), and how frontman Trent Reznor's dystopic vision rejected major label interference and expanded the physical boundaries of the album.

"What's Going On, Again?: Protest and Nostalgia," our collection's penultimate section, confronts head-on the perception that 60s-style protest has been largely absent in the Time of Terror. In her essay, Aisha Staggers argues that mainstream hip-hop since 9/11 has shirked the political engagement it proudly displayed during the Golden Age of Hip-Hop. Jeffrey Roessner challenges the assertion that protest music was vital during the 1960s, and subsequently looks at how contemporary "freak folk" acts like Grizzly Bear and Fleet Foxes have sonically evoked an apolitical 60s sound in their post-9/11 music. Matthew Siblo looks at the rise of conservative punk around the time of the 2004 US Presidential Campaign. Siblo also looks back at punk's past, interviewing figures such as Ian MacKaye and Mark Anderson. Similarly, S. Todd Atchison observes how punk theorizes protest through irony and sarcasm, focusing on late-punk groups Alkaline Trio and Green Day's responses to the Time of Terror.

The final section of the book, "Idle American, *American Idol*: Mainstream Media and Ideology," broadly examines how the rhetoric of American patriotism has been fused – or, rather, confused – with constructions of femininity, masculinity, and religion. Molly Brost and Steve Waksman's pieces make compelling cases about how American gender constructs are *meant* to reinforce an unflappable American idealism, yet also reveal how they are problematized by the very constructs which maintain these cultural-national projections. Gerrit Roessler similarly observes how two seemingly contradictory cultures, punk and Christianity, exert outsider identities, yielding unexpected relationships. Molly Brost focuses on country singer Carrie Underwood and how her tougher brand of country femininity might not have been possible without the example of the Dixie Chicks, who, to the detriment of their career, infamously criticized George W. Bush onstage at a show in England in 2003. Roessler looks at the unexpected mainstream success of the Christian, screamo punk band Underoath. Lastly, our volume concludes with Steve Waksman's contribution, which examines how heavy metal music is deployed in five films about the Iraq War experience, all of which contest and substantiate the claim in the title of his essay that "War is Heavy Metal."

Works Cited

The 9/11 Commission Report: Final Report of the National Commission on Terrorist Attacks Upon the United States. New York: W. W. Norton and Co., 2004. Print.

9/11: The Filmmakers' Commemorative Edition. Dir. Jules and Gideon Naudet. Paramount, 2002. DVD.

Attali, Jacques. *Noise: The Political Economy of Music*. Trans. Brian Massumi. Theory and History of Literature, Vol. 16. Minneapolis: U of Minnesota, 1985. Print.

Basinski, William. Liner Notes. *The Disintegration Loops*. 2062, 2001. CD.

Baudrillard, Jean. *The Spirit of Terrorism and Other Essays*. London: Verso, 2003. Print.

Billboard, "Top Pop Catalog." *Billboard*. Sept. 29, 2001: 60. Print.

Borradori, Giovanna. *Philosophy in a Time of Terror: Dialogues with Jürgen Habermas and Jacques Derrida*. Chicago, IL: University of Chicago, 2003. Print.

Desrosiers, Mark. "Maim That Tune: The Moldy Peaches and the Apotheosis of Lo-Fi." *PopMatters*. Mar. 6, 2002. Web. Jan. 2, 2011.

Fricke, David, et al. "50 Best Albums of the Decade." *Rolling Stone*. Dec. 24, 2009: 47–56. *Academic Search Premier*. Web. Jan. 2, 2011.

Harding, Cortney. "Vinyl Posts 14% Sales Gain in 2010." *Billboard*. Jan. 5, 2011. Web. Jan. 15, 2011.

Pitchfork. "The Top 200 Albums of the 2000s: 200–151." *Pitchfork*. Sept. 28, 2009. Web. Dec. 31, 2010.

Resident Advisor. "RA Poll: Top 100 Albums of the '00s." *Resident Advisor*. Jan. 25, 2010. Web. Dec. 31, 2010.

Rimmer, Matthew. *Digital Copyright and the Consumer Revolution: Hands Off my iPod*. Cheltenham: Edward Elgar Publishing, 2007. Print.

Roberts, Randall. "Nielsen Soundscan 2008 Sales Figures Released: LP Sales Up 89 Percent – And Neutral Milk Hotel Breaks the Top Ten." *LA Weekly*. Jan. 5, 2009. Web. Feb. 22, 2011.

Spivak, Gayatri Chakravorty. "Terror: A Speech After 9-11." *boundary 2* 31.2 (2004): 81–111. Print.

Tiny Mix Tapes Staff. "Favorite 100 Albums of 2000–2009: 20–01." *Tiny Mix Tapes*. Feb. 2010. Web. Dec. 31, 2010.

Žižek, Slavoj. *Welcome to the Desert of the Real!: Five Essays on September 11 and Related Dates*. New York: Verso, 2002. Print.

PART I
Electric Dreams:
The Medium and the Message

Chapter 1

Rock, Enroll:
Music and Militarization since 9/11[1]

Samuel Dwinell

> What role will we assume in the historical relay of violence, who will we become
> in the response, and will we be furthering or impeding violence by virtue of the
> response we make?
>
> Judith Butler

Introduction

There has been a curious lack of attention to forms of popular music that advance politicized interventions in US contexts since September 11, 2001. It has become commonplace to decry the apparent lack of American "protest music" in comparison with the enthusiasm with which an earlier generation of artists took up issues such as the Vietnam War or "Third World" poverty.[2] Carefully sutured into the newly turbo-charged machine of "post-9/11" US nationalism, it would seem, popular music artists now all sing from the same jingoistic hymn sheet that political scriptwriters quickly provided to the Bush administration in the immediate aftermath of the 9/11 tragedy. Voices from below either failed to penetrate the hegemonic grasp of censored, corporate media networks, or never sound in the first place. Such was the extent of popular support for the newly named "war on terror." This chapter does not seek to deny the power of the new politics of security to disallow or, as David Palumbo-Liu writes, make appear "treasonous," positions of "skepticism, doubt, and critical thinking" with respect to the "war on terror" (124). Rather, I attempt to demonstrate how the new state of (being at) "war on terror" includes spaces for, and even encourages, certain forms of protest music. How has the "post-9/11 world," theorized so powerfully by Slavoj Žižek as an example of what Giorgio Agamben refers to as a bio-political "state of exception," been achieved over the last ten years? (140–1). I discuss related examples of post-9/11 popular music that advocate on behalf of

---

[1]   An early version of this study was presented at the "Popular Culture and (World) Politics" conference, held at the University of Bristol, United Kingdom, on September 11–12, 2008, and organized by Christina Rowley.

[2]   See, for example, Reebee Garofalo's article "Pop Goes to War." Scholars of theater and performance, however, have noted what Chris Megson refers to as "upsurge in political theatre" in Western contexts since 9/11 (369).

both "pro-" and "anti-war" causes, arguing that North American protest music of different political stripes in fact contributes to the maintenance of what Bülent Diken calls the new, everyday "normality" of the post-9/11 "war on terror" (82). In other words, popular culture in the "digital age" becomes inseparable from everyday life, and, in turn, inscribes the militarized into the commonplace. We must understand these connections between global violence and daily life in order to imagine alternatives to militarized cultural production.

This chapter is thus concerned with ascertaining how, since September 11, 2001, the media technologies that we use every day become complicit with the discourse of the "war on terror," not least by stripping meaningful dissent of validity. With respect to popular music since 9/11, I ask how militarized networks of different media work both to represent and to constitute the conditions of everyday life. In the first section, I summarize how others have theorized significant changes to culture and society brought about by the tragedy of 9/11. Next, I discuss two important case studies of militarized cultural production in the years immediately following 9/11: the video game *America's Army*, released by the US Army as a recruitment tool in 2002, and the song "(America's Army) Die Jugend Marschiert" (2005), an "anti-war" response to the game from the Canadian punk-rock band Propagandhi. I argue that both these texts function as important precursors to the type of "militarization of everyday life" enacted through the text that I discuss in the final, largest section of this chapter: "Citizen/Soldier," a recent music video and song that was produced through an ostensible act of collaboration between the US Army National Guard and the popular American rock act 3 Doors Down. Here, rock music and military recruitment converge in perhaps surprisingly direct ways. As the first example of the hybridization of music video and military recruitment commercial, "Citizen/Soldier" (2007) not only represents the confluence of these two distinct and historically important genres of audio-visual cultural production, but also must be understood, I argue, within its contemporary, multimedia environment.[3] This seemingly ubiquitous distribution relies on established patterns of media interactivity, thereby allowing connections to be forged between what Judith Butler refers to as the post-9/11 "relay of violence" and the practices of everyday life (187).

Militarization since 9/11

The common theoretical distinction between military and police force, whereby the latter exert power within the nation-state and the former outside it, has of course often been breached in recent US and world history by various iterations of military

---

[3]   For an important and rare discussion of "music as new media," see Lister et al., 191–7. They write that, in today's digital environment, "[i]t is almost impossible to talk about music without almost immediately considering the means by which it is consumed" (191). See also Coates.

power in civilian life. Since the birth of the studio system, Hollywood films, for example, have not only routinely defined visual pleasure through the use of military themes, but also regularly entered into financial and artistic collaborations with sections of the US military.[4] By 2000, moreover, media studies scholar Tim Lenoir could speak productively of what he called the "military-entertainment complex" in the US (238). Yet, as many commentators have argued, 9/11 precipitated a period of redoubled discourses of US nationalism—one during which militarized cultural production in the US became less the exception than the rule. Many commentators have pointed perspicuously to the ways in which, partly as a result of the Bush administration's prompt delivery of mediatized, rhetorical effusions, the razing to the ground of the World Trade Center (and the concomitant, indefensible loss of life) became emblematic of a US "national" tragedy. That is, discursive operations in the immediate aftermath of 9/11 successfully produced the "Twin Towers" as a synecdoche for, specifically, the US nation-state. Such post-9/11 US nationalism thus worked performatively to (re)produce what Benedict Anderson famously referred to as a national "imagined community."[5] This renewed US nationalism, one that cohered around feelings of fear and retribution, soon provided a nodal point through which support could quickly be garnered for the US-led invasion of Afghanistan in October 2001 and the ensuing military offensive, "Operation Enduring Freedom." Furthermore, alongside the Afghan theater of war, the new "war on terror" later came to include the 2003 invasion of Iraq, as well as sweeping changes to US policy, such that, in addition to the military operations in the Middle East, a new part of both the discourses and force of US defense became "homeland security"—a "state of exception," perhaps, characterized by a redoubled, militarized focus on both the borders of the US nation-state and many of those within them.[6] As James Thompson, Jenny Hughes, and Michael Balfour explain, "[A] war declared on an abstract noun ['terror'] has permitted global powers to construct a shifting series of objects as targets of offensive operations" (276). This "relay of violence" expanded and increased to fever pitch.

---

[4]   Most helpful among the extensive literature has been Springer, Doherty, and Slocum.

[5]   For a highly useful account of the ways in which, immediately following 9/11, "the US populace ... are routinely interpellated into varying degrees of subjection by [the Bush administration's] discourse," see De Genova 149. I am grateful to Nicholas De Genova, Bülent Diken, Deborah Cowen, and Amy Siciliano for sharing drafts of their work, and with further insight through discussion, with me and other participants, at the "Accumulating Insecurity" workshops at Cornell University in Fall 2008, organized by Shelley Feldman and Chuck Geisler.

[6]   See the Special Issue of *Social Text* edited by Brent Edwards et al. entitled "911—A Public Emergency" (20/3, Fall, 2002), and, in particular, contributions by Zillah Eisenstein ("Feminisms in the Aftermath of September 11"), Muneer Ahmad, ("Homeland Insecurities: Racial Violence the Day after September 11"), and Jasbir Puar and Amit Rai, as well as Parris N. Glendening's "Governing after September 11th: A New Normalcy."

The redoubling of US nationalism after 9/11, it seems, has provided commentators with urgent occasions to theorize new complicities between our daily consumption of mass media in the US and the violence enacted globally under the aegis of the "war on terror." One of Butler's key insights regarding this global aftermath of 9/11, which also refers to a "cycle of revenge," is the way in which she connects large-scale "retributive" projects, such as the US-led military operations in the Arab Middle East, and the seemingly more mundane aspects of the "war on terror," such as the kinds of discursive violence relayed, broadcast, and transmitted via mass media, particularly newspapers and cable television news (188). Since 2001, other prominent scholars, such as Slavoj Žižek, Douglas Kellner, and Patricia Mellencamp, have provided more extensive accounts of the processes by which the mass media in the US has worked to forge connections between military offensives in the Middle East and everyday life at "home," such that not only do scenes and sounds of global violence now seem commonplace, but also, and more importantly, a broad consensus of public opinion is formed in support of the "war on terror" (Žižek 54). As we have come to realize, the "'war on terror' is a war that has indeterminate and shifting borders as well as an unprecedented global reach and is being fought in the spaces of language, mainstream media and alternative digital mediascapes as much as on the frontiers of Afghanistan and Iraq" (Thompson, Hughes, and Balfour 276–7). Thus, today, the politics of security, Diken writes, has become the "most important factor of sociality": not something that can be extracted from contemporary social relations, but that which forms them (81).

As we will see with the music video and US National Guard recruitment film "Citizen/Soldier," cultural production in the years since 9/11 has played an important role in constituting and maintaining the imbrication of the "war on terror" in the everyday. Aggregating an array of public and private mediatized sites to the extent that it becomes ubiquitous in popular culture at a particular historical moment, "Citizen/Soldier," and other examples of militarized multi-media cultural production, partake in that which commentators such as Henry Giroux, Marita Sturken, and Zillah Eisenstein have persuasively referred to as the post-9/11 "militarization of everyday life." In this chapter, I employ this term to name the processes by which the post-9/11 politics of security become naturalized through our variously everyday activities, such as the types of practices associated with consuming popular music in the "digital age."

A significant body of scholarship now attests to the significance of American popular music within post-9/11 discourses of US nationalism. The overall picture presented by scholars such as Martin Cloonan, Suzanne Cusick, J. Martin Daughtry, Reebee Garofalo, Jonathan R. Pieslak, Kip Pegley, Susan Fast, and Martin Scherzinger is one, perhaps, in which the cultural context of the post-9/11 world powerfully, and almost without exception, demands that contemporary, American popular music be expressive of, and largely complicit with, militaristic US nationalism. For example, Cusick's recent work on music and torture reveals both that forms of "no touch torture," such as the types of sensory deprivation that results from the use of music as torture, has formed part of the US military's "oral tradition" since at least the Cold War, and, more significantly, that the post-9/11 "war on terror" has witnessed a profound change in how such torture is received in contemporary US culture ("Music as Torture"). Today, a range of mediatized sites—from online public chat forums, to the portable media players of US soldiers, to the high-decibel speakers of the Guantánamo Bay interrogation rooms—delineates a global network of music as torture that is specific to the post-9/11 "war on terror," one which spans military and civilian cites globally ("Music as Torture"). "Provok[ing] no public outcry" ("You are in a place" 4), Cusick describes how this bespeaks a new habituation on the part of the US public for aspects of post-9/11 militarization ("You are in a place" 17–18). These studies of music since 9/11 represent an invaluable intervention in the field of musicology. Popular music studies of the last few decades of the twentieth century were perhaps too preoccupied with refuting the Frankfurt School's claims regarding the capacity of the "culture industry" to create, maintain, and deceive a passive consuming public. A return in the years following 9/11 to scholarly engagement with what Gage Averill uncompromisingly refers to as the "nefarious uses to which the power of music is put [in the context of the 'war on terror']" works powerfully to revise this institutional privileging of popular music's anti-establishment potential. This scholarship provides a vital context for understanding new, post-9/11 developments in popular culture, such as the militarization of everyday entertainment enacted by the US Army National Guard's "Citizen/Soldier" recruitment campaign.

The "War on Terror" and the Bedroom

"Citizen/Soldier" was in fact not the first example of the US military's production of innovative, hybridized forms of popular entertainment and recruitment in the years following 9/11. Although there has been a long history of the collaboration between software technology industries and military agencies, the video game *America's Army* represents the first instance of US state-sponsored production and distribution of a video game for the purposes of military recruitment (Nichols 39–40). Free to play online, *America's Army* was released by the US Army as a recruitment tool on July 4, 2002—not by coincidence, one assumes, the date of the first US Independence Day after 9/11—and remained popular for several years, before being superceded by later versions of the game. The game includes hyperlinks that guide players to the US Army's primary recruitment tool, the *Go Army* website. In turn, the site makes it easy for its visitors to chat online with recruitment officials and to leave personal contact information. In other words, while playing *America's Army*—a game not unlike many other popular "First-Person Shooter" video games—players are encouraged to connect with state power in perhaps surprisingly direct ways. *America's Army* channels the diversionary energy of video gaming toward US military recruitment.

America's Army represents an important, innovative, post-9/11 example of the US military's committed appropriation of established forms of entertainment, but its spaces of distribution, and the audiences it reached, nevertheless remained limited. To be sure, players of the game range from active duty servicemen and women across the world to civilian teenagers and young adults. Yet, as we will see with the 2007 "Citizen/Soldier" recruitment campaign for the National Guard, examples of the militarization of entertainment in the US in subsequent years attained a far greater purchase on the terrain of everyday life than *America's Army*. The 2002 video game was only playable on personal computers, and thus remained largely confined to private, domestic locations, such as the bedroom or living room; players of the game consisted mainly of the particular demographics mentioned in Palumbo-Li's account: those already playing video games. Although the game occasionally encourages players to return to the US Army's recruitment website, it functioned relatively straightforwardly as a vehicle with which the US Army could connect with young people—and do so in predominantly domestic, private spaces.

Significantly, the seeming simplicity of the US Army's approach to recruitment with *America's Army* also provided an opportunity for opposition to the game within the realm of popular culture. The song "(America's Army) Die Jugend Marschiert" by the Canadian, activist punk-rock band Propagandhi, responds directly to the video game. It begins with twenty seconds of a grainy, Third Reich-era recording of the Hitler Youth song "Die Jugend Marschiert" (The Youth Are Marching) before abruptly launching into a thrashing, punk-rock invective about the supposed indoctrination of children brought about by *America's Army*. The game is referred to in the song—albeit in exuberantly riotous screams that render most of the lyrics unintelligible—as a "Trojan Horse that you living idiots paid for and actually rolled into your own kids' rooms." This edited collage of sound, by which the seemingly distant strains of an unaccompanied children's chorus are juxtaposed uncompromisingly with punk-rock "noise," remains the most significant sonic aspect of the song. Since it depends upon previously recorded material, it renders the song impossible to perform live. In other ways, too, the form of the song, as well as its subject matter of the video game-*cum*-recruitment campaign *America's Army*, seems to play with its own mediatization. As well as its inclusion on Propagandhi's album *Potemkin City Limits* (2005), the song appears on www.americasarmy.ca, one of the band's websites. This URL is of course a reference to www.americasarmy.com, the official website of the US Army's video game, and represents an aggressive form of "digital activism" on the part of Propagandhi. This URL helps to expand the circulation of the song to users who mistype the much more widely known official website of the *America's Army* video game. Whereas the US Army used *America's Army* to appropriate video gaming as a tool in military recruitment, Propagandhi responded by reversing this tactic. Through the innovative use of the URL, the band attempts, on behalf of an "anti-militarization" politics, to take over the same area of cyberspace in order to advance the outlandish analogy between contemporary American society and Hitler's Third Reich.

Given the band's wholehearted involvement since the mid-1990s with a number of progressive political issues, we should take seriously the extent to which the satirical elements of "(America's Army) Die Jugend Marschiert" make a politicized appeal to parents in the form of advocating on behalf of removing militarized culture and entertainment from the private space of "kids' [bed]rooms." The relatively limited distribution of *America's Army* to precisely these spaces perhaps justifies, and inspires, such an approach. Indeed, the song represents a response to the video game, one that, in Judith Butler's terminology, attempts to "impede," rather than "further," the post-9/11 relay of violence. Like much North American protest music since the 1960s, such as that associated with the Vietnam War, "(America's Army) Die Jugend Marschiert" adopts an oppositional stance toward the perceived wrongs of a specific, current development. The song's political message, despite its willfully childish invocation of the Third Reich, seeks to restore the sanctity of young people's domestic spaces and to return the military or the militarized to its "proper" place—outside the borders of the nation-state, or at least the boundaries of the private home.

However, such an attempt to "undo" the incursion into the everyday of the militarized fails to recognize the extent to which, in the years since 9/11, practices of everyday life have in fact become constitutive of the "war on terror." From 2005, for example, the US Army released many different versions of *America's Army*, including those for arcade machines, mobile phones and other portable devices and game consoles. Many different types of interactive entertainment, and, more importantly, many different types of both private and public spaces, thereby became infiltrated by the video game. In other words, although Propagandhi responded aptly to the first version of *America's Army*, the type of protest they developed, one that makes a demand for the restoration of usual conditions, does not provide the grounds on which to challenge the new "normality" of the politics of security. The band's brand of "anti-war" protest music cannot conceive of ways by which we can learn to live within the "state of exception." In this sense, "(America's Army) Die Jugend Marschier," despite its highly innovative use of sound collage and digital activism, remains complicit with the "war on terror," since, by failing to challenge head-on the connections between everyday life and post-9/11 militarization, it fails to acknowledge the naturalization of the "war on terror."

We must recognize two important and related aspects of Propagandhi's intervention into cultural politics with this song: first, that the years since 9/11 have by no means been bereft of concerted attempts to create and distribute "anti-war" protest music, and, second, that by employing a model of protest more suited to eras in which militarization was the exception rather than the rule, such music permits what Diken refers to as the "business as usual" of the "war on terror" to continue unabated (81). The following section closely examines the various elements of the US National Guard's 2007–2008 recruitment campaign,

"Citizen/Soldier." I delineate the ways in which both the text and the context of the campaign contribute to the militarization of everyday life in ways that surpass the relatively limited context of the original *America's Army* video game. Since the purportedly anti-war rhetoric of Propagandhi does not adequately challenge the militarization of the everyday, we need more than ever to understand how the post-9/11 world requires that we respond to the "relay of violence" in such a way that we remain cognizant of how the "war on terror" implicates the everyday and determines the limits of our response.

Music Video and the Everyday

The US Army National Guard's recruitment campaign, "Citizen/Soldier," represents a highly significant example of the ways in which popular culture in the age of digital media becomes inseparable from the practices of everyday life, and, in turn, allows discourses of securitization in the post-9/11 period to become naturalized within the commonplace. In the first instance, at the time of its release in late 2007, "Citizen/Soldier," in a similar way to the unprecedented conflation of video game and military recruitment tool undertaken by *America's Army*, became the first convincing hybridization of music video and US military recruitment advertisement. Second, the project has proven influential in the years since its release; in 2008, the National Guard and the southern rock luminary Kid Rock released the video "Warrior," a similar hybridization of music video and recruitment advertisement that draws in discourses and practices of everyday life. To be sure, however, rock and heavy metal music have been used before as the soundtrack to US military recruitment commercials, even though, as Jonathan R. Pieslak suggests, such recruitment ads before 2002 usually featured the types of rich orchestral scoring more typical of Hollywood movie soundtracks (27). Pieslak argues that "The Creed," a recruitment commercial for the New Jersey National Guard released in 2006 with a song-length, heavy-metal soundtrack, remains "one of the first complete songs in a popular music style specifically commissioned for the purposes of military recruiting" (30). An *ad hoc* band assembled only once in the US military-run Section 8 Studios performed the song. Upon its release in movie theaters, the video confused some audience members. They wanted to know why, unlike with practically every other music video, they could find no information regarding the band performing in "The Creed."[7]

In contrast to "The Creed," "Citizen/Soldier" works repeatedly to reassure its audiences that a well-known band performs the featured song. We should not discount this as a musical or mediatized form of advocacy, one by which the members of 3 Doors Down seek to encourage support for nationalist discourses

---

[7]   See responses to the video using the "comment" function on various postings of the video on *YouTube*. For example, "artoftheninja" asks, "hey,what [*sic*] song is this and what band?"

of security. Within the general scheme of popular music in the US, 3 Doors Down have provided a reliably conventional output of rock. Since 2001, they have eschewed the trend to incorporate timbral elements of electronica, while riding the wave of the garage rock revival. As Philip Auslander has shown, much rock music performance, whether live, recorded, or filmed, has been preoccupied with maintaining a governing aesthetic of "authenticity." Although the majority of shots in "Citizen/Soldier" show scenes featuring US military operations (including extravagant historical "reenactments" of the Revolutionary Wars, "D-Day," and the Vietnam War, all worthy of any Hollywood major studio), frequent cuts to shots of the band performing "Citizen/Solider" work to identify the popular band 3 Doors Down as the song's performers. In addition, the sonic elements of the song—especially the distinctive timbre of lead singer Brad Arnold's voice— are consistent enough for any rock fan to identify the performers of the song as 3 Doors Down (and this is despite an unusual tom-tom beat that underscores most of the track, perhaps rather topically suggesting war-drums, gunfire, or an adrenaline-fueled heartbeat). Indeed, by the time the "Citizen/Soldier" video was released in 2007, 3 Doors Down, hailing from Escatawpa, Mississippi, had been popular for nearly a decade. The band's brand of "post-grunge" southern rock speaks broadly to a rural, American, blue-collar "authenticity," an impression that has been bolstered by their live appearances alongside such other southern rock luminaries as Lynyrd Skynyrd and Tantric. In sum, both the moving image and musical elements of "Citizen/Soldier" reinforce the impression that the video is at least in concert with the work of a well-known rock band, a band noted, moreover, for its cultivation of an "authentic," individual voice. The video strives, it seems, not by any means to disguise the militaristic elements of the project, but rather to express a spirit of collaboration between the National Guard and 3 Doors Down.

One important effect of emphasizing the influence of a well-known rock band on the "Citizen/Soldier" project is that it becomes recognizable to audiences as a largely unproblematic example of a music video. With this form, as Pieslak explains, the "preexisting song governs the duration of the video and the images are set within the structure of the music" (30–31). This description aptly characterizes the "Citizen/Soldier" video, the song of which, while not exactly predating the video's exhibition in movie theaters, was released in audio formats simultaneously. The video's production style also played an important role in its generic identification. Instead of the military-run Section 8 Studios, Antoine Fuqua, director of famous music videos for artists such as Prince and Queen Latifah, was enlisted to help produce "Citizen/Soldier," according to a National Guard press release in *Business Wire*. Indeed, "Citizen/Soldier" features the type of fast-paced editing that has typified music video since the launch of MTV in the early 1980s (Vernallis 27). In this case, exhilarating crane and tracking shots cover fully armored servicemen making jumps from helicopters; hand-held camera-work seemingly captures the urgency of coming almost face-to-face with opposing forces in what appear to be the darkened alleyways of a ruined urban landscape; and mortar and rifle explosions are timed carefully with the music. As Michel Chion has argued, this kind of "play" with sound and image has become typical of music video and represents some of the ways in which examples of the genre often reject the more naturalistic demands of narrative Hollywood cinema (167). Through its liberal use of the audio-visual "evidence" of a well-known rock band performing the song, as well as more formal features such as artistic editing, "Citizen/Soldier" reads unequivocally as an example of the genre of music video to the extent that is unprecedented for a US military recruitment advertisement. The importance of this for understanding how "Citizen/Soldier" partakes in the post-9/11 militarization of everyday life rests on patterns of distribution and reception of music video today.

Rarely any longer broadcast in full on their original home on cable television channels such as MTV, music videos today, like music in audio formats, circulate predominantly in digital form online, and, increasingly, in ways that do not violate copyright restrictions (Austerlitz 221–3). Recording companies and other media corporations are keen to encourage the wide distribution of music videos and have been particularly successful in shifting people toward digital or new media (Dickey and Sullivan 10). They can be readily accessed and exhibited in a plethora of settings, including personal computers in the home, office or school, and mobile phone devices in an even wider range of locations (Beebe and Middleton 1–3). Video streaming websites such as *YouTube* (launched in 2005), according to Jean Burgess and Joshua Green, have become among the most visited sites on the Internet. In this way, technology and patterns of distribution have changed the ways in which audiences receive music video. At least according to many theorizations of new media, such as those advanced by Lev Manovich, these changes represent the ways in which forms of "interactivity" have largely replaced the "passivity" of what Andrew Goodwin referred to in 1992 as the "distraction factory" of music television. Today, such online "interaction" with music video includes searching for videos online, commenting on them, embedding them in blogs and social media profiles, and creating amateur "response" videos.[8] In one particularly established pattern of interactivity with music videos, audiences often search for an appealing video online after seeing a short clip of it on TV or in other spaces of exhibition (Cha et al.). This user-directed journey through various media platforms—from TV to *YouTube*, for example—exemplifies what Henry Jenkins has influentially referred as the "convergence culture" of new or digital media: a blurring of the boundaries, or a "flow of content," between forms and technologies of mediatization (2). "Citizen/Soldier" weaves itself seamlessly into established patterns of media interaction on the part of its audiences, positively embraces a novel culture of online video streaming, and aggressively competes with any of the highest budget music videos for other popular artists.

The point to recognize here is that, in the first decade of the twenty-first century, music video has perhaps become all but ubiquitous in everyday interaction with multiple forms of online media. Yet, the networks of distribution of music videos such as "Citizen/Soldier" extend beyond the types of Internet browsing described

---

[8]   On the latter, see Salvato.

above. As I will discuss below, the music video "Citizen/Soldier" functioned as the central point for an even wider network technological platforms and entertainment formats. Like many examples of contemporary popular music, the song itself circulated digitally in purely audio formats, for example; moreover, the most important way in which the National Guard increased circulation of the "Citizen/Soldier" video well above that expected of a high-budget music video from a well-known artist was to exhibit it in movie theaters. In sum, music video proved a highly suitable genre for a high-budget military recruitment film such as "Citizen/Soldier," the primary aim of which, one presumes, was not dollar profit but maximum distribution. Thus where music video intersects with advocacy in support of the "war on terror," it is a wide range of everyday practices and spaces that become inundated by post-9/11 discourses of security. The following section attempts to delineate the everyday life of post-9/11 militarization, at least as it emerges in relation to the "Citizen/Soldier" campaign. Although seemingly ubiquitous, distribution of the video is in fact selective and functions as an instrument of exclusion; certain members of society are expressly *not* interpolated by the video's address, while conservative definitions of the family are further reified. New or digital media, routinely praised for their supposedly democratizing capacities, can just as readily serve as technologies of propaganda that work to imbricate nationalist discourses of post-9/11 security into exclusionary concepts of the citizen and the family.

Militarization and Everyday Life

Both the audio and visual aspects of the "Citizen/Soldier" video itself, and its patterns of distribution, demonstrate that the recruitment campaign functions through particular, ideological constructions of a post-9/11 US citizenry. For example, the campaign targeted the pre-feature film slot of a wide range of movies, including the post-apocalyptic science-fiction movie *I Am Legend*, the holiday-themed family comedy *Fred Claus*, and the Disney musical *Enchanted*. A longer version of the video was also included on the DVD-extras for a range of Hollywood movies. A "blanket release" to Hollywood movies such as this resulted in "Citizen/Soldier" achieving a very wide audience, including young children and parents who do not form part of the target demographic for recruitment ("National Guard"). This apparent "militarization of the family," an aspect, perhaps, of what Deborah Cowen and Amy Siciliano have referred to as the contemporary "securitization of childhood," needs to be placed in the context of the ways in which such so-called "blanket distribution" passes over sites of non-Hollywood film, including the niche markets of non-Anglophone and queer cinemas. This works to naturalize and further reify conservative definitions of the family against non-US and queer alternatives.[9] Furthermore, the broad connotations of the music

---

[9]   On the latter, see, for example, Halberstam.

also continue in this vein. Steve Waksman persuasively traces a genealogy of such contemporary rock music to the hypermasculine performance of early electric guitar "hero[es]" such as Jimmy Page and Led Zeppelin (238). Waksman explores how a particular performance style of rock music, one that seems to combine self-absorption with a brash robustness, has become coded as both white and masculine. Rock music, such as that by 3 Doors Down, becomes an "occasio[n] for doing 'identity work,'" in this case of accomplishing, perhaps, a white, heterosexual, male identity (Walser 116).

However, the cinematic imagery of the video, edited to accompany the song, perhaps provides the clearest indication of the ways in which the post-9/11 militarization of everyday life enacted by the "Citizen/Soldier" recruitment campaign entails a subtle redefinition of the US citizenry. Much of the video contains historical scenes, including lavish "reenactments," but a scene toward the end of the video revisits more recent history. Shot among dusty, urban wreckage, the setting reminds us of the scenes in lower Manhattan on September 11, 2001. There then appears the didactic text, "I stepped forward when the towers fell." Next, in the midst of what we must take to be a depiction of a "domestic" humanitarian disaster such as 9/11, we see a black National Guardsman return a blond-haired boy to his distressed mother. Finally, the video closes with a freeze frame of the URL of the National Guard's recruitment website. Here, we should note the ways in which this sequence assigns particular duties to different members of a seeming multicultural, national utopia (one in which Arab ethnicities are tellingly absent), but, with its redolence of Christian wisdom (like in the "Story of Solomon"), the scene works to reawaken strong American nationalist myths concerning the cohesion of the citizenry, the feminization and vulnerability of the US nation, and the primacy of social reproduction. Jasbir Puar, for example, writes how, since 9/11, the "body [of the terrorist] must appear improperly racialized (outside the norms of multiculturalism) and perversely sexualized in order to materialize as the terrorist in the first place" (38). Much in this video suggests how it likewise works to renew and redefine both codifications of multiculturalism and the nuclear, "national family", in order to produce a seemingly coherent citizenry against such an absent figure of the terrorist (Puar and Rai, 136).

However, the "goal" of the video, signaled not least through the largely chronological order of the scenes of historical reenactment, seems to emerge as the final freeze frame: the URL of the National Guard recruitment website. In some versions, the shot of the rescued boy proceeds directly via a match cut to the text of the URL. By galvanizing its audiences into action by the urgency and apparent heroism of its message, and by thrilling them with stunning, fast-paced sequences on the big screen "and in surround-sound" that demand to be revisited, the "Citizen/Soldier" video steers its audience online towards the National Guard's official website. Of all the video's many locations, formats, and technological platforms, moreover, the only one at which contact with a military recruitment bureau can take place remains the National Guard's official recruitment website. Similar to the promotion of the US Army's website through the video game

America's Army, GoGuard.com allows instant, online chatting between a recruiter and a visitor to the site, as well as many ways in which visitors can leave their contact details for National Guard recruiters. For the duration of the video's run in movie theaters, "Citizen/Soldier" enjoyed a pride of place on *GoGuard.com*. It was played in full-screen, high-quality graphics. In addition, the National Guard website allowed free mp3 downloads of the song, thus taking advantage of, rather than seeking to diminish, the widespread culture of music file-sharing. In such a network of mediatized sites, online video streaming sites and digital audio-file sharing become not the official National Guard website's competitors, but rather its means of widespread promotion. These features of the site, alongside the ways in which the video itself places emphasis on the freeze-frame shot of the site's URL, establish *GoGuard.com* as the center of the wide, digital expanse created by various versions of the song and video. The goal of the video's apparent ubiquity, and the ways in which it operates as an aspect of the post-9/11 "militarization of everyday life," clearly centers on the official recruitment website.

It is important to draw attention to the ways in which the digital environment's apparently free "flow of content," its multiple sites, technologies, and capacity for "user-generated content," can nevertheless serve the purposes of state propaganda, and thus assist in the post-9/11, global "relay of violence." The purportedly democratizing technologies of new media—such as *YouTube*, whose motto, after all, is "Broadcast Yourself"—in fact play a key part in this militarization of everyday life. Music video spans multiple sites of audio-visual media across the erstwhile divisions between public and private exhibition, as well as what are ostensibly "corporate" and "user-generated" media. As it does so, it can become the conduit for the post-9/11 militarization of everyday life. Yet, as we have seen, the ultimate destination of the "Citizen/Soldier" video, including its patterns of distribution, remains the official National Guard website; the "media journey" from the movie theater to the Internet, for example, emerges as the basis for the entire recruitment project. Rather than precisely a "free flow of content across multiple platforms," as Jenkins describes a typical new media environment, the direction of "flow" in this case is highly managed. When the user lands on the National Guard's official recruitment website, he or she has completed this over-determined journey that began with the music video, delivered through multiple platforms, technologies, and modes of spectatorship.

Conclusion

The "Citizen/Solider" recruitment campaign, in its encompassing of cable TV, broad swaths of cyberspace, FM radio, multiplex movie theaters, cell phones, and portable media players, emerges as an important example of the relentless, contemporary "militarization of everyday life." In both video and audio format, "Citizen/Soldier" appears and reappears at multiple sites of distribution/reception that span public and private spheres; and, as it does so, it engages audiences in different forms of spectatorship and interactivity. The campaign employs the genre of music video, and the ways in which popular culture in the "digital age" becomes inseparable from practices of everyday life, in order to inscribe militarization into the commonplace and thereby to strip arguments condemning the "war on terror" of validity. One thing that these examples of militarization in the popular cultural sphere since September 11, 2001 can perhaps remind musicians and of scholars is the extent to which protest music remains an important feature of the "post-9/11 world." We must recognize, in other words, the sincerity with which the members of 3 Doors Down no doubt engaged in the collaborative project with the US Army National Guard, "Citizen/Soldier." For this reason, the band's efforts are importantly thought alongside those of Propagandhi, whose politics attempt to oppose precisely the cause of US nationalism for which 3 Doors Down have long been campaigning. In Propagandhi's work, the vehement plea to remove *America's Army* from the private spaces of young people's homes neglects to take account of the ways in which post-9/11 politics of security already interpolate the child, the family, and the nation as important constituents of the discourse of the "war on terror." Unlike Propagandhi, we must ask, "What can I do with the [militarized] conditions that form me?" (Butler 187). As Jacqui Alexander writes, we must "move away from theorizing resistance as reactive strategy to theorizing power as interwoven with, and living alongside, marginalization" (229). Cultural production that truly undermines the militarization of everyday life must begin by acknowledging that the "war on terror" is here to stay.

Works Cited

Alexander, M. Jacqui. "Not Just (Any)*body* Can Be a Patriot: 'Homeland' Security as Empire Building." *Interrogating Imperialism: Conversations on Gender, Race, and War.* Ed. Robin L. Riley and Naeem Inayatullah. New York: Palgrave Macmillan, 2006. 207–240. Print.

Anderson, Benedict. *Imagined Communities: Reflections on the Origin and Spread of Nationalism.* New York: Verso, 1991. Print.

Artoftheninja. Comment. "The Creed." Army National Guard. *YouTube.* June 1, 2006. Web. Feb. 13, 2011.

Auslander, Philip. *Liveness: Performance in a Mediatized Culture.* 2nd ed. New York: Routledge, 2008. Print.

Austerlitz, Saul. *Money for Nothing: A History of the Music Video from the Beatles to the White Stripes.* New York: Continuum, 2007. Print.

Averill, Gage. "Soundly Organized Humanity." *ECHO: A Music-Centered Journal* 3.2 (2002): n.p. Web. Jan. 10, 2008.

Beebe, Roger and Jason Middleton. *Medium Cool: Music Videos from Soundies to Cellphones.* Durham, NC: Duke UP, 2007. Print.

Burgess, Jean and Joshua Green. *YouTube: Online Video and Participatory Culture.* Malden, MA: Polity Press, 2009. Print.

Butler, Judith. "Explanation or Exoneration, or What We Can Hear." *Social Text* 20.3 (2002): 177–88. Print.

Cha, Meeyoung, et al. "I Tube, You Tube, Everybody Tubes: Analyzing the World's Largest User Generated Content Video System." Proceedings of the 7th ACM SIGCOMM Conference on Internet Measurement. Oct. 24–26, 2007. San Diego. Proceedings.

Chion, Michel. *Audio-Vision: Sound on Screen.* Trans. Claudia Gorbman. New York: Columbia UP, 1994. Print.

Coates, Norma, "Sound Studies: Missing the (Popular) Music for the Screens?" *Cinema Journal* 48.1 (Fall, 2008), pp. 123–30. Print.

Cowen, Deborah and Amy Siciliano. "Surplus Masculinities and Security," forthcoming in *Antipode.* Unpublished manuscript.

Cusick, Suzanne G. "Music as Torture/Music as Weapon." *TRANS—Transcultural Music Review* 10 (2006), article 11. n.d. Web. March 12, 2010.

———. "'You are in a place that is out of the world...': Music in the Detention Camps of the 'Global War on Terror.'" *Journal of the Society for American Music* 2.1 (2008): 1–26. Print.

De Genova, Nicholas. "Spectacle of Security, Spectacle of Terror." *Accumulating Insecurity: Violence and Dispossession in the Making of Everyday Life.* Ed. Shelley Feldman, Charles Geisler, and Gayatri Menon. Athens: University of Georgia. 141–65. Print.

Dickey, Jeff and Jack Sullivan. "Generational Shift in Media Habits." *MediaWeek* 17.7 (2007): 10. Print.

Diken, Bülent. "From Exception to Rule: From 9/11 to the Comedy of (T)Errors." *Irish Journal of Sociology* 15.1 (2006): 81–98. Print.

Doherty, Thomas, *Projections of War: Hollywood, American Culture, and World War II.* New York: Columbia UP, 1990. Print.

Garofalo, Reebee. "Pop Goes to War, 2001–2004: US Popular Music after 9/11." *Music in the Post-9/11 World.* Ed. Jonathan Ritter and J. Martin Daughtry. New York: Routledge, 2007. 3–26. Print.

Glendening, Parris N. "Governing after September 11th: A New Normalcy," *Public Administration Review* 62, Special Issue: *Democratic Governance in the Aftermath of September 11, 2001* (Sep. 2002): 21–3. Print.

Goodwin, Andrew. *Dancing in the Distraction Factory: Music Television and Popular Culture.* Minneapolis: University of Minnesota Press, 1992. Print.

Halberstam, Judith, "Forgetting Family: Queer Alternatives to Oedipal Relations." *A Companion to Lesbian Gay, Bisexual, Transgender, and Queer Studies.* Ed. George E. Haggerty and Molly McGarry. Malden, MA: Blackwell Publishing, 2007. 315–24. Print.

Jenkins, Henry. *Convergence Culture: Where Old and New Media Collide.* New York: New York UP, 2006. Print.

Lenoir, Tim. "All but War Is Simulation: The Military-Entertainment Complex," *Configurations* 8.3 (Fall, 2000): 289–335. Print.

Lister, Martin, et al. *New Media: A Critical Introduction.* 2nd ed. New York: Routledge, 2009. Print.

Manovich, Lev. *The Language of New Media.* Cambridge, MA: The MIT Press, 2000. Print.

Megson, Chris. "'This Is All Theatre'": Iraq Centre Stage." *Contemporary Theatre Review* 15.3 (2005): 369–71. Print.

"National Guard Launches Innovative Film Campaign in Theatres Nationwide, Announces LM&O Marketing Inc." *Business Wire.* Nov. 29, 2007. Web. Dec. 17, 2008.

Nichols, Randy. "Target Acquired: America's Army and the Video Games Industry." *Joystick Soldiers: The Politics of Play in Military Video Games.* Ed. Nina Huntemann and Matthew Thomas Payne. New York: Routledge, 2010. 39–52. Print.

Palumbo-Liu, David. "Multiculturalism Now: Civilization, National Identity, and Difference before and after September 11th." *boundary 2* 29.2 (2002): 109–127. Print.

Pieslak, Jonathan R. *Sound Targets: American Soldiers and Music in the Iraq War.* Indianapolis: Indiana UP, 2009. Print.

Puar, Jasbir, *Terrorist Assemblages: Homonationalism in Queer Times.* Durham, NC: Duke UP, 2007. Print.

—— and Amit Rai. "Monster, Terrorist, Fag: The War on Terrorism and the Production of Docile Patriots." *Social Text* 20.3 (2002): 117–48. Print.

Salvato, Nick. "Out of Hand: YouTube Amateurs and Professionals." *The Drama Review* 53.3 (Fall, 2009): 67–83. Print.

Slocum, J. David (ed.) *Hollywood and War, The Film Reader.* New York: Routledge, 2006. Print.

Springer, Claudia. "Military Propaganda: Defense Department Films from World War II and Vietnam." *Cultural Critique* 3 (Spring, 1986): 151–67. Print.

Thompson, James, Jenny Hughes, and Michael Balfour. *Performance in Place of War.* Calcutta: Seagull Books, 2009. Print.

Vernallis, Carol. *Experiencing Music Video: Aesthetics and Cultural Context.* New York: Columbia UP, 2004. Print.

Waksman, Steve. *Instruments of Desire: The Electric Guitar and the Shaping of Musical Experience.* Cambridge: Harvard UP, 2001. Print.

Walser, Robert. *Running with the Devil: Power, Gender, and Madness in Heavy Metal Music.* Middletown, CT: Wesleyan UP, 1993. Print.

Žižek, Slavoj. *Welcome to the Desert of the Real.* New York: Verso, 2002. Print.

Chapter 2
Music, Terrorism, Response: The Conditioning Logic of Code and Networks

Benjamin J. Robertson

Writing for the music website *Pitchfork* in 2009, Eric Harvey suggested that "it's possible the past 10 years could become the first decade of pop music to be remembered by history for its musical technology rather than the actual music itself." While artists continue to make notable music, Harvey may be correct: these days, music is secondary to the technology that subtends it. In the context of the present volume, this claim can be modified as follows: in the twenty-first century, music no longer effectively speaks in its capacity as music—on the level of its content, that is. There are, of course, still artists whose music acts as a form of explicit political and social commentary. However, those statements are beholden to codes beyond the musical, to the logic of the technologies through which they are distributed, on which they are heard, and with which they are produced. Music in the twenty-first century does not exist for popular culture if it is not online, nor amenable to the iPod. As a result, the political battles music once fought with lyrics, notes, and chords are now fought according to another code entirely.

I refer here to two very different conceptions of *code*, a difference that manifests according to two different understandings of networks. On one hand, *code* structures the political, gives order to the disordered, and allows culture to become Culture. According to Jacques Attali, "Codification of this sort gives music a meaning, an operationality beyond its own syntax, because it inscribes music within the very power that produces society" (25). This "code" corresponds to a homogenous, total network—society as such.

On the other hand, *code* refers to the logic that conditions the functionality of objects and actors within manifold networks. In this context, the code that affords functionality in one network does not afford the same functionality in another. Moreover, code does not always and forever allow for the same functionality within a single network, as the codes that govern one network are themselves open to revision by codes from other networks with which the first overlaps. For example, law may govern the architecture of the Internet, but the law and the Internet are not the same network (even if they connect with one another). Internet architecture allows for certain transactions, but not for others. Law may either allow or forbid these transactions as well, regardless of architectural affordance. Finally, the Internet itself is not homogeneous. Its code varies in numerous ways: servers in one country may allow certain content, while servers in another do not;

TCP, UCP, HTTP, and FTP are part of the Internet Protocol Suite, but operate within different layers of that suite, according to different architectures. Friedrich Kittler questions whether code, thus conceptualized, adequately addresses the numerous contexts in which it is deployed. Claiming that the "notion of code is as overused as it is questionable," he nonetheless argues, "If every historical epoch is governed by a leading philosophy, then the philosophy of code is what governs our own, and so code—harking back to its root, 'codex'—lays down the law for one and all" (45). As the governing concept of the twenty-first century, code determines our actions within society's multiple, heterogeneous networks.

To make sense of this development and its importance, I must return to Attali, who defines a series of three consecutive networks that order society and music's place within it: sacrifice, representation, and repetition. Each corresponds to a different moment in the development of capitalism. A fourth network, composition, will exist at some point in the future according to Attali's somewhat romantic argument. He writes, "In each network, as in each message, music is capable of creating order. Speaking generally and theoretically, in the framework of information theory, the information received while listening to a note of music reduces the listener's uncertainty about the state of the world" (33). In the first three networks, music produces order, but only according to the requirements of older codes, codes involved with systems of exchange, symbolic or otherwise. Music partakes of ceremony in sacrifice, exists as a flow of information in representation, and appears as an instantiation of a pre-existing recording in repetition. In each case, "A network can be destroyed by noises that attack and transform it, if the codes in place are unable to normalize and repress them" (Attali 33).

For Attali, both a society's political apparatus and its music belong to a self-similar network. That is, the network is homogeneous throughout and provides a foundation upon which politics and music interact. Change to the network comes about as a result of noise, which enters the network from outside and which the network and its codes cannot parse. Noise can destroy the network and thereby destroy extant power relations; it may thus create the necessary conditions for a new society: "The presence of noise makes sense, makes meaning. It makes possible the creation of a new order on another level of organization, of a new code in another network" (Attali 33). To be clear, however, noise must find some purchase within the network. Even if it is new, it must dovetail with some extant part of society if it is to operate as a force of change. Attali's notion of the musician provides a concrete example of this model: "Poet laureate of power, herald of freedom—the musician is at the same time within society, which protects, purchases, and finances him, and outside it, when he threatens it with his visions" (11). The musician must be inside the network to affect it, but the noise with which he or she affects must come from outside the network if it is to change society.

Attali's network/outside may allow for the alien, but the alien comes from an ill-defined "beyond"—subject to no rule but capable of instigating rule as it enters the network itself. Following Attali's logic, al Qaeda comes from the outside to disrupt the United States and to, perhaps, reorder that society through the deployment of its alien codes. Similarly, music by artists such as Eminem, Green Day, and Nine Inch Nails makes noise from beyond society that, at best, ultimately heralds the destruction of that society's codes and the replacement of such with the codes that arise from noise. Obviously, both al Qaeda and these artists already exist within society to some extent, else they would not be able to penetrate it.

The issue is that, no matter what, in Attali's theory, there is only ever one network—the one that exists that can only ever be replaced, but never supplemented or bifurcated. Writes Attali: "All music, any organization of sounds is then a tool for the creation or consolidation of a community, of a totality" (6). Because of this singularity, music can interact with societal structures and redefine them. However, this singularity requires Attali to explain noise in terms of an outside and thus produce a binary that buttresses a dialogical model of musical activism in which music responds to politics to debate the future form of society.

Even if we accept the doctrine of the outside in this context, we cannot accept the idea of the single total network. Society is not a network/inside facing a non-network/outside. There is no Network; there are only networks. We can see at least three of these numerous networks at work in the context of this anthology: the sociopolitical network of the United States, the al Qaeda terrorist network, and a network of music and musicians. These networks surely connect with one another, but they are neither reducible to each other nor to a single meta-network to whose rules they all conform.

Thus, networks are everywhere. Further, these networks themselves are neither self-similar nor coherent. In 2007's *The Exploit*, Alexander Galloway and Eugene Thacker argue that "networks never claim to be integral whole objects in the first place. To name a network is to acknowledge a process of individuation ('the Internet,' 'al Qaeda'), but it is also to acknowledge the multiplicity that inheres within every network ('the Internet' as a meta-network of dissimilar subnets, 'al Qaeda' as a rallying cry for many different splinter groups)" (12). Whatever the agents within these networks express, in the years since Napster and 9/11 (at least), that expression has become less significant than the technologies through which these expressions circulate.

With that in mind, we must acknowledge that music in the twenty-first century cannot be understood as political speech simply in its capacity as music—as an ordering of lyrics, notes, chords, etc.—that comes from outside politics in order to face them and, ideally, change them. Rather, we must account for music: 1) within a series of networks that sometimes overlap with one another; and 2) according to the codes that allow (or do not allow) it to move between these networks.

The remainder of this essay is divided into two parts. The first implicitly extends my discussion of Attali by addressing the notion of a culture/counter-culture divide within which contemporary music continues to situate itself. The second discusses two of the various technologies that condition music in the twenty-first century, the mp3 and the iPod, in the context of what Gilles Deleuze calls "control," a progression beyond the discipline described by Michel Foucault. In the course of this argument, I largely eschew a specific discussion of the two topics of this volume: 9/11 and music. Rather, I make a few specific references to the actual events of 9/11 or to the music that follows in its wake. This lacuna is intentional. I argue here that such specifics are less important than the environment that surrounds them. 9/11 provoked numerous musical reactions: loss, anger, confusion, and so on. Whatever the reaction, however, close reading—answering questions like "What are they saying?" or "How does this song express itself?" — itself does not provide tools adequate to address the questions "How does music function in the context of twenty-first-century politics?" or "How does activism manifest and operate in the wake of events such as the terrorist attacks of 9/11/01?" The various musical responses to post-9/11 US domestic and foreign policy offer an opportunity, rather, to come to terms with the fact that "traditional," often 60s-styled activism and dialogue no longer make sense as tactics or strategies in a world governed by control.

Music and Activism In and After the 60s: Discipline

In the wake of the political fallout of the terrorist attacks of 11 September 2001—the USA PATRIOT Act, the Department of Homeland Security, the National Threat Level, the fearmongering of the Bush Administration, and so on—numerous musicians expressed their discontent. Eminem released "Mosh" via the Guerrilla News Network on the eve of the 2004 election. The song called into question Bush's motivation for the Iraq War, and speculated that the terrorists had succeeded in what they set out to do to the US. Less specific was Green Day's *American Idiot*, a rock opera/concept album that described the cultural and political landscape of the post-9/11 United States through the character Jesus of Suburbia, a discontented youth who travels to the big city where he witnesses firsthand an American population that has allowed its own mindlessness to come to pass. Similarly, as Katheryn Wright's addition to this volume discusses, Nine Inch Nails' *Year Zero* offers a sci-fi critique of the year 2022, a time when a fully theocratic state controls all forms of communication and, thereby, thought.

In each of these examples, we can see artists challenge power by making statements that counter power. Such statements become a soundtrack to a historical moment by creating countercultural consciousness. Music in this context *is* the protest. The notes, chords, and lyrics of popular songs face power with alternative statements. When power states, "War!" "Capitalism!" "Empire!" "Neoliberalism!" or something similar, music offers a response, an expression of something else.

This model, of course, reached its mythical apotheosis during the 1960s, a period in which political activism—the resistance to conformity and technocracy—became indistinguishable from the music of the era. Sit-ins and chants, Woodstock and The Beatles: in our cultural memories, the events of the decade play out juxtaposed with a music that has come to stand in for them. This confluence of music and politics allows for an understanding of music as speech, as a statement that responds to politics. This understanding has been with us ever since. The 1990s even tried to outdo the 60s with not one but two Woodstocks and a presidential inauguration headlined by REM. After 9/11, albums such as *American Idiot* and *Year Zero* likewise offered further proof that we consider music political only according to what it says and to whom it says it.

However, even if we accept this 1960s understanding of communication between power and resistance as tenable in that decade, the post-9/11 world reveals its problematic nature (even if people still believe in its viability). By the mid-1990s, if not earlier, forward-thinking activist groups had begun to realize that the nature of communication had changed, that the very environment in which power operates had become something else altogether. If there was a time when protests and other direct confrontations with power worked, then it had passed by the middle of Clinton's administration and existed as nothing but romance by the middle of Bush's. Critical Art Ensemble (CAE), for example, laments activists' inability to recognize the changing landscape on which political battles are fought, criticizing those who still believe in older forms of protest and therefore "see no need to invent new approaches" (10). They write, "Nostalgia for 60s activism endlessly replays the past as the present, and unfortunately this nostalgia has also infected a new generation of activists who have no living memory of the 60s" (10). CAE does not refer to music, but we can easily locate music within this narrative as a soundtrack to events and as speech itself. And while more recent activist events, such as the Seattle World Trade Organization protests in 1999, become interesting in light of the ways in which they use new methods and technologies such that CAE demands, the "hell no, we won't go"-style chants that characterize them and their endorsement by musicians render them as but slightly revised versions of the activism CAE describes. They remain (attempts at) direct confrontations with power, primarily concerned with content, with comprehensible statements that express displeasure, anger, and disgust with the current organization of society. Thus music has what Attali calls an ordering effect: it comes from outside the network of society (even while existing within that network) in an attempt to alter the codes according to which that network operates. It positions two groups against one another, in dialogue: power and resistance, claim and counterclaim. And while this model does not ignore the question of technology out of hand, it assumes that power can be located, can be addressed, and, most importantly, will be able to (or is willing to) hear counter-statements as they are uttered. In other words, it assumes a single network, a totality, within which all codes are the same code, or at least parse according to the same logic.

Eminem's "Mosh" provides a perfect example of this understanding. The song was released shortly before the Bush/Kerry election in late October 2004 as a music video available at the Guerrilla News Network website. Although it would appear on Eminem's album *Encore* (released 16 November 2004), "Mosh" was not a conventional single; its online form was its only official release. Despite the nature of its distribution, "Mosh" buys into the conventions of 60s-style protest. The song is a call to arms, a demand that people come to political awareness and vote Bush out of office. The video is more explicit still in its belief in a dialogical form of protest. Eminem reads headlines about Bush's tax cuts for the wealthy, the war in Iraq, bin Laden's continuing freedom, and so on. In response to these headlines, he states his opinion and then marches through the streets and raps in front of crowds, gathering unto himself an army of the dispossessed and disaffected who proceed to a voting precinct to register their discontent through the franchise. A subsequent version of the video, released after the election and entitled "The Mosh Continues," features the same crowd storming what appears to be Bush's State of the Union address. The protesters confront Bush, Cheney, the Supreme Court (whose ruling gave Bush the election in 2000), and a crying John Kerry with signs that demand that troops be brought home and other such sentiments. Save for the style of the music, an activist from the 60s would recognize the scene without any trouble whatsoever.

While much of the video for "Mosh" implies a coming violence, in the end it reads very much like a civics textbook: read the newspaper, craft a response, enter the debate. Both versions conclude with Eminem inviting dialogue and suggesting the possibility of reconciliation between longstanding political opponents galvanized by 9/11. If words are not enough, the individual must appear in front of those with whom he or she should speak.

However, the failure of such dialogue does not result from a problem with dialogue per se, but rather from the medium through which speech travels and the protocols that medium imposes upon it. In a passage specifically about civil disobedience, but which can stand in for any mode of political activism that relies on direct confrontation with an opponent on what is perceived to be common ground, CAE writes that traditional civil disobedience "has no effect on the core of organization" because it assumes that the power center of an organization can be located (13). Civil disobedience assumes a "head" of power and thus the possibility of dialogue. Within the networked environment of the late twentieth and early twenty-first centuries, however, there exists no single position of power:

> For an oppositional force to conquer key points in physical space in no way threatens an institution. Let us assume that a group of dissidents managed to occupy the White House. It might prove embarrassing for the administration in power and for the Secret Service, but in no way would this occupation actually disrupt the effective functioning of executive power. The presidential office would simply move to another location. The physical space of the White House is only a hollow representation of presidential authority; it is not essential to it. (CAE 13–14)

Facing one's opponent does not suffice to produce political change. Communication—whether in words or lyrics, text or music, images or sounds— is, in and of itself (to borrow CAE's term) dead capital. The network in which the activist speaks may not be the network in which the opposite power lives. To move between networks and to shift society from one form to another does not require convincing arguments; it requires amenability to the network form. Music in this context is no longer noise coming from beyond promising a new code, but itself must always already be encoded in such a way to afford its movement within the network and across the networks.

And here is the crux of the issue: technological environments were very much what activists in the 1960s understood themselves to be fighting. To give in to the logic of the network was to lose one's individuality and accept conformity to a hostile logic. The title of Theodore Roszak's *The Making of a Counter Culture: Reflections on the Technocratic Society and its Youthful Opposition* explicitly describes a dialogical relationship between power and resistance, between a conformity-inducing culture and a counterculture that championed individuality. Likewise, it reveals what power is to Roszak and his generation—what we might call that society's network form. Roszak writes:

> By the technocracy, I mean that social form in which an industrial society reaches the peak of its organizational integration. It is the ideal men usually have when they speak of modernizing, up-dating, rationalizing, planning. Drawing upon such unquestionable imperatives as the demand for efficiency, for social security, for large-scale co-ordination of men and resources, for ever higher levels of affluence and ever more impressive manifestations of collective human power, the technocracy works to knit together the anachronistic gaps and fissures of the industrial society. (5)

Technocracy conditions society as a totality, draws together and orders individuals into a logical, bureaucratic whole. It does not do so through force or literal violence: "In the case of technocracy, totalitarianism is perfected because its techniques become progressively more subliminal" (Roszak 9). Roszak continues: "While possessing ample power to coerce, [technocracy] prefers to charm conformity from us by exploiting our deep-seated commitment to the scientific world-view and by manipulating the securities and creature comforts of the industrial affluence which science has given us" (9). Technocracy thus induces totality by positing and maintaining an ideal—efficiency, rationality—and then by rewarding individuals who live up to that ideal.

Although the techniques Roszak describes (economic reward, security) are very different than those Michel Foucault enumerates in his discussion of discipline (drills, exercise), we can nonetheless see in Roszak's claims a disciplinary society. For Foucault, discipline involved the creation of "docile" bodies—bodies conditioned to behave, to conform to a standard. While discipline has its roots in the prison, it exists in any number of social institutions—the family, the school, the church, the military—and manifests according to spaces specific to those institutions. While the child does not learn the same discipline in the schoolhouse as in the home, he or she nonetheless learns discipline broadly across these spaces and thus becomes amenable to the act of disciplining. This amenability is the signature of a useful member of society:

> Discipline increases the forces of the body (in economic terms of utility) and diminishes these same forces (in terms of political obedience). In short, it dissociates power from the body; on the one hand, it turns it into an "aptitude," a "capacity," which it seeks to increase; on the other hand, it reverses the course of the energy, the power that might result from it, and turns it into a relation of strict subjection. (Foucault 138)

Whatever power disciplinary exercise might provide to the individual in terms of resistance (in terms, that is, of individuality) immediately turns around to become means of subjection. Similarly, whatever rewards the technocracy offers, they always serve to advance the technocracy rather than individual interests. Capital always requires a market. Such markets require a rational logic. Such logic serves the technocracy.

I do not mean to suggest that Foucault and Roszak make the same argument. They part ways, for example, over the issue of subjectivity. Contra to Foucault's claim that one is always subject to one power or another, Roszak implicitly endorses a state of freedom that technocracy precludes. However, these differences are of minor concern to my discussion, which describes societies that seek to turn all people into a part of a total system, to make individuals cogs in the machine. Even if each individual becomes a different cog, they all serve a functionalism and become part of a technology. In such a network, music as response makes sense and offers a vehicle for change (perhaps); but once society no longer demands conformity, music finds that there is nothing to which it might respond.

Music and Technology in the Twenty-First Century: Control

Here we return to the claim by Eric Harvey with which I began this essay—that the first decade of the twenty-first century will be better remembered for the technologies that surround music than for the music itself. While Harvey focuses on the mp3, his argument applies to other technologies with which music has become involved since the 1990s. These other technologies, especially the iPod, I argue, operate and form an environment of control that stands in distinction to the disciplinary network of the past.

The mp3 has, along with the iPod, achieved the status of Kleenex or Thermos, a genericized name that serves as metonym for an entire class of objects: FLAC, Ogg Vorbis, AAC, WMA, and so on. The objects within this class are not so much things as they are codes, or codecs (coder-decoders), which render content amenable to the technologies that play, distribute, or manipulate it. They came into existence as standards by which media content could be made amenable to network distribution. In 1988 by the International Organization for Standardization charged The Moving Picture Coding Experts Group with the task of digitizing films for purposes of efficient portability. A hacker would eventually make the audio layer of their product available to the general public. As a result, the mp3 began its ascendancy in 1992.

By the late 90s, the mp3 became the de facto standard format for musical content. However, the mp3 was not simply or even primarily a medium for the transmission of content. Rather, it was a logic; it conditioned what music was, could be, and did. Jonathan Sterne writes, "The mp3 is a crystallized set of social and material relations. It is an item that 'works for' and is 'worked on' by a host of people, ideologies, technologies and other social and material elements" (826). Sterne also notes that, despite the mp3's specific characteristics, its specific encoding and position within a series of other codes causes most "writers still [to] represent the mp3 itself as a mute, inert object that 'impacts' an industry, a social environment or a legal system" (827). Sterne does not analyze what we mean when we say, "I got this mp3 from iTunes." That is, when he writes "mp3" he does not mean "song." Rather, he means the technology itself and its particular networked relationships, which touch, but are distinct from its musical content (itself only one aspect of the sum of those relationships).

A history of the mp3 as technology would include discussion of: the foundation of Napster; the debuts of iTunes, the iPod, and the iTunes music store; the release of significant mash-up albums such as Danger Mouse's *The Grey Album* and The Kleptones' *A Night at the Hip-Hopera*; the release of popular singles (such as Nine Inch Nails' "The Hand that Feeds") as Garageband (AIFF) files for remixing by fans; and the fact that artists now account for the technical aspects of the mp3 when they master their recordings. Such a history might continue for some time, as whatever there was of music outside the multiple networks these events imply are made amenable to those networks and are enfolded within them.

Such a history is the history of power in the twenty-first century, whose logic does not conform to the dialogical structure implied by such binaries as network/outside, culture/counterculture, and homogeneity/individual. Reading Foucault, Gilles Deleuze argues that these oppositions may still exist in some contexts, but that the homogenizing technologies of discipline have largely been replaced by personal technologies of control. On the concept of discipline, Deleuze writes, "Disciplinary societies have two poles: signatures standing for *individuals*, and numbers or places in a register standing for their position within a *mass*" (179). By contrast, control societies replace the signature with "codes indicating whether access to some information should be allowed or denied. We're no longer dealing with a duality of mass and individual. Individuals become '*dividuals*,' and masses becomes samples, data, markets, or '*banks*'" (180). Thus, whereas discipline *molds* individuals such that they fit into the dominant side of the binary, control *modulates* the person such that the means of subjection become immanent to him- or herself. The person becomes a "dividual," a term Deleuze does not define specifically, but one that implies the manner in which someone can be internally divided (or, again, modulated) through the application of technologies that limit action or thought on a personal basis. The dividual is the person who must exist simultaneously in multiple networks and according to multiple codes.

The transformation of the individual into the dividual results from a technology that has become autonomous and specific. Passwords allow access without behavioral conditioning and track movement without panopticism. These networks are no longer total or totalizing. Within their multiplicity, the activist can no longer achieve an outsider's position. One can no longer escape the Network; one can merely move to another.

In other words, under control, songs can no longer be expressions of an individualistic, anti-technocratic opposition. Music can no longer scream "No!" as it faces that which it refuses. It has become fully imbricated in the very logic of power, and it becomes secondary to the technology that was at one time merely its support. Thus Steve Jobs can speak, without irony, of cultural change in terms of a technology that debuted shortly after 9/11: the iPod. He cites his own experience with musical counterculture in the 60s and 70s and then notes that "music is really being reinvented in this digital age, and that is bringing it back into people's lives. It's a wonderful thing. And in our own small way, that's how we're working to make the world a better place" (quoted in Goodell). These comments illustrate both the difference between older forms of cultural resistance and a blindness to that difference. Jobs buys into the narrative of music-as-soundtrack-to-cultural/political-events *and* offers the iPod as a means by which to return to that previous moment, when music mattered, when music was the driving force behind making the world a better place. If the music of Bob Dylan, Jimi Hendrix, The Beatles, et al. healed the psyche of a nation (or at least the youth of that nation) torn apart by Vietnam, assassination, and other scandal, the iPod itself can do the same in the twenty-first century for whatever ailments currently face the US.

In *The Perfect Thing*, Steven Levy defines these ailments as the loss he felt after 9/11. He asks, "How could you devote your energies to documenting the Internet, cool gadgets, and the future of music when all this darkness was afoot?" (19). Unwittingly perhaps, Levy lists here, along with "music," aspects of the technocracy against which the 60s counterculture would have rebelled. The result of this convergence of culture and counterculture? For Levy, and presumably for millions of others, nothing but the return of music as a soundtrack for life:

> One day sitting in the subway, I plugged in the iPod and the world filled up with the Byrds singing "My Back Pages." The faces around me suddenly became characters in a movie centered around my own memories and emotions. A black-and-white moment of existence had sprung into Technicolor. I held my iPod a bit tighter. Something odd began to happen. As the days passed and I bonded with my iPod, my spirits lifted somewhat. (18)

Levy goes further to imply that he feels a connection with George W. Bush, whose own iPod became news in 2005. Levy writes, "I wasn't exactly *forgetting* about 9/11, but I was getting excited—once more—about technology and its power to transform the world" (18). Similarly to Jobs, Levy demonstrates a romantic understanding of technology as that which can overcome some sort of personal or interpersonal rift. For Jobs this fragmentation might take the form of ideological opposition. For Levy, it is within the self: the wound opened by unexpected violence.

However, if Jobs and Levy's terms are romantic, we must recognize in them something fundamentally opposed to the romanticism of the 1960s: music is no longer centered in itself, but rather in the device on which it plays. In an interview for the book *The Cult of iPod*, Michael Bull states: "One of the interesting things is that with vinyl, the aesthetic was in the cover of the record. You had the sleeve, the artwork, the liner notes. With the rise of the digital, the aesthetic has left the object—the record sleeve—and now the aesthetic is in the artifact: the iPod, not the music. The aesthetic has moved from the disc to what you play it on" (quoted in Kahney 26). In so doing, the concept of music-as-expression becomes secondary to the networks in which it travels. Cyberpunk writer Bruce Sterling describes this pivotal technological transition: "Not for us the giant steam-snorting wonders of the past ... eighties tech sticks to the skin, responds to the touch: the personal computer, the Sony Walkman, the portable telephone, the soft contact lens" (346). Technology no longer dwarfs the individual subject with the threat of assimilation into an inhuman system. Technology now exists for the individual. The iPod and all of its attendant applications, devices, and accessories is such a technology, the management of which in turn manages its user. Tellingly, in Levy's account "My Back Pages" is an entirely personal soundtrack, heard by him alone. It can never serve as a metonym for that moment within a community.

By way of conclusion, I offer two points. The first comes from theorist Paul Virilio, who argues in *Ground Zero* that "the tragic events in New York in September 2001 showed us the alarming situation of an overpowerful state suddenly brought up short against its own consciousness—or, rather, against its *techno-scientific unconsciousness*: in other words, against the Gnosticist faith on which it is founded" (65). For Virilio, 9/11 resulted from a scientific rationality that prohibits prohibition, that does not say "no" to progress, ever. While this claim comes in a context somewhat different than that of the present argument, it nonetheless underscores my central point that there is a conditioning logic of technology, that the rational systems through which we move daily found our existence and allow or disallow our actions. Such is the case whether we refer to music or to terrorism: the network and its codes engender the object or event.

My second point comes from Deleuze, who, like the present argument, does not claim that this system is all powerful. He writes: "It's not a question of worrying or of hoping for the best, but of finding new weapons" (178). Whatever these weapons are, they will not be the weapons of the past.

Works Cited

Attali, Jacques. *Noise: The Political Economy of Music.* Trans. Brian Massumi. Minneapolis: U of Minnesota, 1985. Print.

Critical Art Ensemble. *Electronic Civil Disobedience and Other Unpopular Ideas.* Brooklyn, NY: Autonomedia, 1996. Print.

Deleuze, Gilles. *Negotiations.* Trans. Martin Joughin. New York: Columbia UP, 1995. Print.

Eminem. "Mosh." *Google Videos.* n.d. Web. March 25, 2010.

——. "The Mosh Continues." *YouTube.* n.d. Web. March 25, 2010.

Foucault, Michel. *Discipline and Punish: The Birth of the Prison.* Trans. Alan Sheridan. New York: Vintage, 1979. Print.

Galloway, Alexander and Eugene Thacker. *The Exploit: A Theory of Networks.* Minneapolis: U of Minnesota, 2007. Print.

Goodell, Jeff. "Steve Jobs: The *Rolling Stone* Interview." *Rolling Stone.* Dec. 25, 2003. Web. March 25, 2010.

Harvey, Eric. "The Social History of the MP3." *Pitchfork.* August 24, 2009. Web. Mar. 25, 2010.

Kahney, Leander. *The Cult of iPod.* San Francisco: No Starch P, 2005. Print.

Kittler, Friedrich. "Code." *Software Studies.* Ed. Matthew Fuller. Cambridge, MA: MIT, 2008. 40–47. Print.

Levy, Steven. *The Perfect Thing: How the iPod Shuffles Commerce, Culture, and Coolness.* New York: Simon & Schuster, 2006. Print.

Roszak, Theodore. *The Making of a Counter Culture: Reflections of the Technocratic Society and its Youthful Opposition.* Garden City, NY: Doubleday, 1969. Print.

Sterling, Bruce. "Preface from *Mirroshades.*" *Storming the Reality Studio: A Casebook of Cyberpunk and Postmodern Science Fiction.* Ed. Larry McCaffery. Durham, NC: Duke UP, 1991. 343–8. Print.

Sterne, Jonathan. "The mp3 as Cultural Artifact." *New Media & Society* 8.5 (2006): 825–42. Print.

Virilio, Paul. *Ground Zero.* Trans. Chris Turner. London: Verso, 2002. Print.

Chapter 3
Technostalgia and the Resurgence of Cassette Culture

Craig Eley

Figure 3.1   The Picador, Iowa City, Iowa, 2008. Photo courtesy of Mark Palmberg

Before I heard that cassette tapes were coming back into style, I saw it—painted larger than life on a building in downtown Iowa City. It was the fall of 2007, and the rock club in town had recently changed owners. The new staff had designed a mural around a pre-existing narrow window on the building's façade, including a custom curtain that gave the appearance of a tape spool (Figure 3.1). A striking addition to the building's otherwise fortress-like exterior, this painted display of tape affection seemed, at first glance, a logical expression of the romanticization of cassette tapes that had become, in Simon Reynolds' words, a defining characteristic of music fandom in the first decade of the 2000s. This trend has been displayed variously in literary works like Nick Hornby's 1995 novel *High Fidelity* (and its 2000 film adaptation), Thurston Moore's 2004 art book *Mix Tape: The Art of Cassette Culture*, and Rob Sheffield's 2007 memoir *Love is a Mix Tape*. Hardly confined to popular literary remembrances, however, this trend also crossed over into methods of music distribution, as a growing number of independent musicians and labels in the second part of the 2000s returned to cassettes as a way to record and circulate their music. This return to form, so to speak, was especially true within the "noise" music scene, which, as Marc Masters points out, had evolved over the decade to encompass a range of styles including "abstract improvisation, ecstatic free jazz, lo-fi pop, outsider avant-rock, minimalist drone, power electronics, and more." In 2009, critic Cici Moss identified 101 distinct cassette record labels, and by 2010 the tape resurgence was being covered in mainstream outlets such as *The Guardian* and *The Los Angeles Times*.

Like tapes themselves, the popular discourse surrounding this "new cassette culture" has two sides, even though both attempt to locate the significance of today's tape culture in the 1980s. On one hand, proponents of today's noise music scene trace its lineage to the underground cassette scene of the 1980s, when a loosely connected network of experimental musicians circulated home-recorded cassettes through the mail as an alternative to the mainstream music industry's distribution methods. Developing out of the do-it-yourself (DIY) attitude that originated in 1970s punk culture, 80s cassette culture has been widely celebrated as a similarly oppositional subculture that introduced a new generation to DIY aesthetics (Spencer 226, 343–8). While there is some truth here, which I will discuss in more detail later, this origin story allows contemporary participants to feel as if they are part of "an organic underground movement" independent of the mainstream music industry's hype machines (Hogan). Additionally, because of the continued low cost of making cassettes, advocates insist that tapes create a more participatory experience between musician and listener. According to Britt Brown, founder of Not Not Fun records, "Tape fits in with a belief system of how intimate music is made" (quoted in Brown).

On the flip side, critics have implicitly or, in some cases, explicitly noted that participants in today's cassette culture would likely be more familiar with the near-ubiquitous mass-produced cassettes in the late 1980s than with the small-batch tapes of the early 80s underground—a fact reinforced by musicians within the scene. For instance, Nathan Williams, whose contemporary low fidelity noise band performs under the name Wavves, finds comfort in tape culture: "It's what I was around growing up ya know, so it sticks with you … it's almost comforting in a way" (quoted in Richard). Rather than a coherent belief system about intimacy or anti-corporate opposition, today's cassette culture can be read as obsessed with lost youth and sentimentality. *Los Angeles Times* writer August Brown has noted that tapes often "evoke high school mixes from nascent crushes and trips to the beach soundtracked by sun-bleached tunes recorded off the radio." However, not all critics have responded enthusiastically to this resurgence. Writing for the web magazine *PopMatters*, Calum Marsh characterizes the cassette revival as "a confused, regressive cultural misstep" that ignores the "democratic dissemination" of digital music solely to promote a sensibility of "cool."

Though writers on both sides of this debate are quick to write off cassette culture as flimsily nostalgic, doing so not only ignores the history of the period that they are seemingly nostalgic for but also eliminates the possibility for new meanings of cassettes to exist today. As Marsh correctly notes, as influential as the underground cassette movement in the 1980s might be to tape lovers today, that original scene had little to do with tapes per se—they were simply the cheapest distribution method available at the time. Recalling that period, Robin James says that "the spirit" of the scene had "nothing to do with the cassette medium" (quoted in Campau). Additionally, a recent examination by Bas Jansen of writings about mix tapes led him to conclude that the nostalgia that people feel for their old tapes is not triggered directly by the objects themselves, but rather by the stories associated with those objects, including the acts of making and giving them to others (44). Yet, overwhelmingly, it is the cassette itself—its materiality—that people in today's noise music scene mark as its most important characteristic. As Chris Jahnle, founder of the LA-based Kill/Hurt tape label, claims, "Cassettes sound terrible anyway, so why not have something that sounds terrible that you can hold?" (quoted in Brown).

Because of its position in-between the valorization of the vinyl record and the mainstream acceptance of the music download, the cassette's sudden reemergence within this particular subculture suggests a dissatisfaction that extends beyond critiques of the music industry and issues of fidelity into the realm of politics. But to excavate the significance of the cassette resurgence, we must address and ultimately move beyond a discourse that fixes its meaning solely in relation to the 1980s—be that meaning nostalgic or retro. Not to do so would be to ignore the ways in which technologies are socially constructed, a process that is always "both ongoing and multiple" (Altman 21). Instead, we might understand the resurgence of the cassette tape among noise musicians under the more specific term "technostalgia," a fascination with vintage technologies. As it applies to music and musicians, technostalgia suggests a "movement toward both new sounds and new interactions, whether aural, social, or physical, made concrete through combinations of the past and present" (Pinch and Reinecke 166).

This was the real meaning of Iowa City's cassette mural, as I eventually discovered. The tape on the front of The Picador was more than mere decoration or throwback icon; rather, it was a symbol of the impact that physical cassettes were having on the local music scene. At shows around town, it seemed that everyone had started a noise band and was swapping tapes, including people on the very periphery of the scene, like myself. The local cassette-only record label, Night People, was being celebrated for its catalog of experimental, psychedelic, and noise rock in national blogs and magazines such as *Rose Quartz*, *Foxy Digitalis*, *Impose*, and *Signal to Noise*. Thanks to this growing network of bands, promoters, friends, and fans, Iowa City was developing into a Midwest hub for touring experimental musicians of all varieties, many stacking their merchandise tables with their latest cassette releases.

It is in the physicality of the cassette—both in its form and in the relationships it fosters—that allows it to simultaneously serve as a site for creating new connections between people as well as a place for resisting mainstream music industry practices and dominant political ideologies. Cassettes also, it should be noted, create their own set of problems. Even as cassettes have increased in visibility, showing up as icons on T-shirts and belt buckles and even iPod cases, today's functioning musical tapes remain almost wholly out of reach beyond a relatively small group of musicians and collectors. Always produced in limited runs, often sold hand-to-hand and rarely digitized, the tape avoids widespread distribution through either legal or illegal channels. Therefore, as a part of DIY culture, cassette tapes ultimately "form relationships not intended by capitalism" (Holtzman, Hughes, and Van Meter 45).

To attend to the physicality of cassettes is also to attend to the energy that has reconfigured their magnetism. The sounds on today's noise tapes reflect a very particular kind of discontent, drawing their influences from the music popular during two distinct Cold War moments: 50s and 60s garage and girl group, and mid-80s electronics. By looking at and listening to a selection of tapes from popular cassette artists like Wavves, Vivian Girls, and Dirty Beaches, we might hear that, for some musicians, resistance has less to do with music and lyrics and more to do with form and function.

Cultural theorist Alexi Monroe calls the redeployment of technologies outside of their original contexts a "sleeper agent," something that can cause technologies "to activate at some point in the future when they themselves are rediscovered and/or re-invented, destabilizing their own time and potentially releasing a further set of unintended consequences in another 2 to 3 decades" (quoted in Bailey). Strikingly, the redeployment of cassette technology, as a means of cultural and political destabilization, was one of the main tactics of Osama bin Laden following the events of September 11. Of course, in the Middle East, and in many developing nations, the cassette has remained the dominant form of audio circulation (including music as well as political and religious speeches), and its political implications for the cultures there have been well documented (Abu-Lughod).

But for participants in today's noise music cassette culture—a mainly young, white, middle-class, and Western demographic—the release of bin Laden's tapes and the invasion of Iraq in 2003 can be understood as the sleeper agents for today's tape revival; those events signaled changes in the meaning of those technologies at those moments. As Mark Greif has noted in his essay on changes to so-called hipster style, the larger cultural mood swing in the United States from "mourning to patriotic aggression and violence" made previous subcultural markers like trucker hats and "wife beater" shirts seem less subversive. What he defines as the "White Hipster" was replaced by the "Hipster Primitive," a "subculture" that is more amenable to women and whose points of reference include "animals, wilderness … a fascination with early-eighties computer electronics" and, of course, cassette tapes. Scathingly critical of hipsters as lacking any politics beyond what he calls "rebel consumerism," Greif sees the Hipster Primitive as one who steals from more subversive groups like "anarchist, free, vegan, punk, and even anti-capitalist communities."

Greif's gripes aside, the noise music cassette scene is one that is legitimately subversive. By lauding the cassette tape above other media, the scene's participants challenge the narrative of Western superiority—technologic and cultural—over the "backwards" cultures of the Middle East. An outspoken example can be found in Alan Bishop, who runs Sublime Frequencies, a label that releases collages of music collected from other countries, much of it via cassette tapes. Writing for *The New York Times*, Douglas Wolk argues that Bishop "sees in his projects a victory over cultural hegemony." Thus, even though Greif, among others, laments the lack of politics he sees among "hipsters," we should acknowledge that their return to "primitive" technologies like the cassette tape forges—perhaps briefly, perhaps only symbolically—connections between the West and its so-called "enemies," rather than bolstering a separation between the two.

Of course, the idea that magnetic tape embodies a form of radicalism is not a particularly novel one. From the tape collage experiments of Pierre Schaeffer and John Cage to the more recent work of William Basinski and Philip Jeck, tape has been widely celebrated for its importance in avant-garde composition (Hegarty). But with its widespread adoption in the late 1970s and early 1980s, the cassette tape also allowed everyday people to reshape cultural production and to challenge traditional corporate models of music recording and distribution. Experimental and amateur musicians used cassettes to record and release their own material, and music fans likewise used them to create compilati. .s and share songs with their friends via mixtapes. Eventually, however, the latter practice resulted in the now-infamous "Home Taping is Killing Music" campaign, launched by the British Phonographic Industry against consumers who were, allegedly, practicing copyright infringement. While the campaign was highly criticized by both fans and artists at the time (the classic example being Bow Wow Wow's pro-home-taping anthem "C:30 C:60 C:90 Go!"), the labels have used similar strategies in today's copyright wars over digital file distribution (McLeod 278–96). Where the cassette once served as the most inexpensive way to circulate music, that function has gone digital: first to the CD-R, and now to the mp3, which any label executive will tell you is literally killing music via peer-to-peer file distribution. Today's cassette culture, by eschewing contemporary media forms for more esoteric ones, is building on the older cassette culture tradition of rejecting dominant industry formats.[1] However, contemporary cassette distributors aim not so much to make

---

[1]   It is because of these older traditions and historical context that I have chosen to focus on the cassette, though it is certainly not the oldest or most outmoded technology out there. I have anecdotally heard of a band who released an mp3 of their single on a 3.5" floppy disc, and bands have experimented with the 8-track format since the 1980s.

music cheap and widely available as much as they do to make it physical, and, ultimately, collectible.

Traditionally, aspiring rock bands saw the cassette tape as a low-quality jumping-off point on the way to bigger money and higher fidelity. Its most common usage was for demo tapes—cheaply produced recordings that bands assembled with the hopes of scoring record contracts, professional studio time, and, eventually, a vinyl LP with their name on the cover. Then, as now, such a scenario was unlikely, and many bands hoping for major label success invested vast quantities of their own time and money into releasing their own records. John Foster, founder of the Lost Music Network and editor of their *OP* magazine, tried his best to discourage this practice: "A word of advice to bands contemplating pressing a 45 [rpm record] … don't do it unless you have a large local following, are planning on touring a lot, or are prepared to lose all your money with little to show for it" ("Optional Reading").

With Foster at the helm, *OP* became one of the most important players in 1980s cassette culture. Founded in Olympia, Washington in 1978, the magazine was imagined as a way "to educate others about musics not widely known" by "sharing contacts, information, and ideas"—roles it took quite seriously (Foster, "Message"). With a design aesthetic and general attitude that owed much to the punk collage, the magazine featured an extensive listing of zines, radio stations, labels and distributors of all types of music, in addition to more traditional music news, interviews, and reviews. Foster recalled that in the early days of the magazine "an independent cassette-only release was an anomaly" ("OP"). However, due to artist dissatisfaction with industry practices and the emergence of relatively inexpensive home recording equipment, that anomaly soon became the norm. By the summer of 1981, the magazine had an entire column devoted to cassette releases, called "Castanets." Each column included brief, mostly descriptive reviews of tapes, as well as the prices and mailing addresses where fans could order them.

OP magazine and the "Castanets" column not only established the term "cassette culture" but also cemented two deeply related principles that were critical to its development, success, and continued deployment today: the facilitation of subcultural interactions not restricted to specific local geographies, and the establishment of an alternative economy for the circulation of music.[2] While *OP* was based in Olympia and prominently featured labels and musicians from the Pacific Northwest, its function as a clearinghouse allowed it to connect a wide variety of people from around the world. Today, of course, that function is performed not by postal mail but by the Internet. Shawn Reed, who runs Night People, has noted, it is through digital technologies that cassettes can "flourish" and reach a wider audience (quoted in Hogan).

---

[2]   Though the term "cassette culture" is a generally accepted one that, at least contemporarily, conjures a primarily white male demographic in noise music circles, tapes have played a major role in hip-hop culture and in many "jam band" communities as well.

Reaching that audience involves the process of creation, and, as tends to be the case in DIY circles, that process emphasizes handmade production, which has always been the most affordable means by which amateur artists can work. Though contemporary cassette culture operates in a different economic paradigm than that of the 1980s, there is still an emphasis on handmade goods and uniqueness. Nevertheless, the value for such goods in the marketplace has increased exponentially. While cassettes are still certainly cheap to record and make, the motivation behind their use for contemporary bands and labels cannot be understood as purely financial, especially for distribution, which, as mentioned earlier, is only limited by access to the Internet. Timothy D. Taylor notes that that the revival of old technologies in the digital era "in part registers a new ambivalence and anxiety over today's digital technology" (96). He continues, "At the same time, these resurrections mark a disillusionment with technology, for they are often manifest as a kind of nostalgia for past versions of the future, a future that never arrived" (96).

The technological "ambivalence and anxiety" of the current cassette culture is centered around the Internet, which, ironically enough, is viewed as a failure as both a music delivery model and as a mode for personal expression. While in the 1990s, a kind of post-everything utopianism dominated discourses about "cyberspace," the realities surrounding issues like governance and technology soon painted a more realistic picture (Lessig 3). In the twentieth century, this utopianism, at least in the context of musical distribution, has transformed into a kind of fatigue resulting from the seemingly limitless supply of music via legal channels like iTunes and *Amazon.com*, as well illegal ones like BitTorrent networks. Tape label owner Alex Davis laments the isolationism that this kind of distribution fosters: "The further and further I got away from the experience of listening to full albums, going to the record store, and sharing what I found with friends, the more I realized I was becoming a pretentious fuck with a full iPod, not someone cherishing a collection of albums I was in love with" (quoted in Hogan). Here, Davis' critique of his own "pretension" (which certainly extends well beyond himself) is not linked to esoteric knowledge or even the act of collecting— things we might normally associate with musical pretention—but rather to what he imagines as the insular, solitary practice of reading about music, downloading it, and loading it onto a device.

In essence, Davis is critiquing the online music blog culture that places a premium on "new" music, demanding a near-daily devotion to—or contention with—the latest buzz band. This critique is consistent with cassette culture's more broad criticism of the Internet's core failure: an inability to generate more intimate interactions between musicians as fans. Mark Sniper, who runs tape label Captured Tracks and performs under the name Blank Dogs, has taken issue with fractured web communities: "I'm not opposed to tracks on the Internet. [My] entire discography is on iTunes, for example. [But with my] blog, it just became a situation where people were not getting the point of it. You really can't do anything these days without getting attacked for it" (quoted in Mules).

The response to these twin failures—turning people on to new music, interacting more closely with fans—was to begin trafficking in cassettes, a technology that Shawn Reed has called "old and outdated, intentionally obscure and marginal, almost pointless in some way" (quoted in Hogan). Steve Rosborough of the label Moon Glyph uses almost identical language, when he notes that many people "chose the format for its lack of modernity and as an attempt to be willfully obscure" (quoted in Hogan). For Rosborough, this turn away from modernity is ultimately a rejection of "mass digitization and the loss of the physical format" (quoted in Hogan). As straightforward as this rejection might seem, it is not until contemporary consumers actually begin looking for cassettes that the extent of their subversiveness becomes clear: they are nearly impossible to obtain.

Certainly, cassettes' limited availability has a great deal to do with their status as handmade DIY artifacts. In simple terms, tapes sell out quickly, rendering them instant collector's items. Some tape labels even celebrate this scarcity. For instance, the UK label The Tapeworm proudly displays on their website that for each cassette release, no more than 250 copies will be made (for example, see "TTW#02"). Other tape labels have done the same: Fuck It Tapes have released a total of sixty-six cassettes, only two of which remain in print. ("Fuck it Tapes"). The label Night People has distributed 100 tape releases, of which twenty-one remain available ("Night-People"). And these labels certainly are not unaware of the black market this lopsided supply-and-demand creates. As of this writing, one (out of a total of forty) blue cassette release of the album *Blissed Out* by the Dum Dum Girls was selling on eBay for upwards of $50—not only a ridiculous mark-up on an item that probably cost less than a dollar to produce but also a steep cost of entry for any outsider to the scene. Like a toy that never leaves its box, the ostensible function of this cassette—to create a sense of intimacy and to distribute music to a community of fans—is evacuated in the name of collectability.

This distribution model, while significantly ironic, ultimately reinforces the rejection of contemporary music industry practices that lie at the heart of cassette culture. According to cultural critic Will Straw, "To collect the obscure and formerly unhip is to 'refuse the mainstream,' or to exhibit a 'a transgressive anti-conventionalism'" (quoted in Taylor 101). While cassettes might reject Internet distribution and the digitizing of music, they do so at the expense of availability. Whatever cassette culture might be, it is certainly not democratizing. The dominant narratives of both American foreign policy and music technologies are about "access" to "freedoms," whether that means democracy or digital downloads. In positioning themselves and their music away from these tropes, noise musicians mobilize the physicality of cassettes in a way that is often opposite of earlier cassette culture. Rather than facilitate access, they facilitate a kind of fetishism.

The politics of technology aside, it would be easy to claim that cassette culture itself is not political. For one, many participants in the scene either refuse to acknowledge any political implications in their decision to put out their music on tape, or they claim ignorance as to why they put out a tape in the first place. Nathan Williams of Wavves epitomizes that self-conscious ignorance about recording to tape. When asked why he chose that particular medium for releasing his debut (on Fuck It Tapes), he responded, "Maybe the same thing that attracts me to music and culture from the 80s and 90s … It's such a different medium, it's so muddy sounding, but it's almost comforting in a way. And then I let some drunk dude tattoo a cassette on my arm at my friend's house when I was 16 so that was that" (quoted in Richard).

Regardless of motivation, Williams' music exemplifies the technostalgic impulse: the use the past to make sense of the present. The debut album's opener "Intro Goth" is a 100-second synthesizer solo containing layers of vintage-80s Casio sounds looping around each other. Then, with little warning, a wall of electric guitars interrupts the flow to initiate the track "Losers Yeah," a garage-rock-meets-surf-rock-meets-punk-rock anthem (complete with "Woo-oohs" and a guitar solo). The chorus, barely audible through all the distortion, asserts, "I know I am a loser." The album is peppered with these kind of era-bending musical styles, including big, 60s-sounding drums and girl-group backing vocals. Nevertheless, for all of the melody and energy, there is a sadness that permeates the record, a stoner loneliness that makes lines about being a "loser" resonate much deeper than Beck's mid-90s ironic claims.

While it is generally acknowledged that the musical styles and production aesthetics of much of today's noise and lo-fi pop scene often have as much to do with the 1950s and 60s as they do with the 80s, it's almost never mentioned that the music echoes many of the same Cold War anxieties present in those times. Exemplary in this regard is East Vancouver's Dirty Beaches, who draw on rockabilly to create haunting, cinematic scenes that seem both to reinforce and undermine the aggression and self-assurance of so many traditional rockabilly songs. Similarly, Super Furry Animals' frontman Gruff Rhys situates the physicality of the cassette as a kind of indestructible shelter against the looming—and ultimately flattening—presence of the Internet: "Cassettes and vinyl are the analogue cockroaches to the nuclear Armageddon that is digital formats" (quoted in Hogan).

Brooklyn, NY's Vivian Girls, who share a label with Wavves, also suggest that past technologies construct an aesthetic that brings the past and the present into communion with each other:

> We definitely have a recording aesthetic, we don't want our records to sound like the 90's. I think the best records were made in the 50's and 60's and all those recordings were made live or on one mic usually. So I feel that we're trying to get closer to that type of recording sensibility than we have been. For instance our first record was recorded digitally, our second record was recorded on a 16 track tape machine, but I think for the third record we're going to try to stay exclusively with 8 tracks and 4 tracks of either cassette tapes or reel-to-reel, and try to get away from multi-tracking as much as possible. (quoted in Ramone)

This decision to eschew digital recording and to strive for the fewest number of tracks—in combination with their band's already fuzzy, distorted guitar tones—

inevitably results in a "unpolished," "lo-fi," and occasionally harsh, sound. But while some bands use noise in a deliberately aggressive way, the "noise" music of the cassette culture scene is not meant not to isolate, but rather to bring people together. When the band Woods (who run the label Vivian Girls is on) were asked about the "lo-fi" aesthetic of many of their recordings, they defined it not via aesthetics but via personal relationships: "I think the problem with 'lo-fi' is that people take it as a genre term, or to come up with a name for a 'scene.' It's not so much a 'scene' as it is a lot of people making music near one another" (quoted in Craine).

When The Tapeworm Collective launched their cassette label in 2008, they deliberately positioned their work outside of commercial music culture, their website proudly proclaiming, "No barcodes. The cassette will never die! Long live the cassette!" ("The Tapeworm"). In an interview with *Wire* magazine, an anonymous spokesman for the collective said that their fascination with the cassette stemmed from its "non-digital awkwardness; the clunk; the effort required of the listener, an enforcement of A versus B" (quoted in Young). As they articulate, and as I have argued, the physicality of the cassette is its most important characteristic as a subversive response to mainstream music culture. However, just as an overdub does not always fully erase what came before it, the connections that cassettes have to their past still resonate, and they fuel the contemporary cassette's power as both a scarce—and collectible!—material object as well as a powerful point of connection for those inside the culture.

Ultimately, the physicality of cassettes makes any "enforcement of A versus B," impossible, since those things are united by the tape itself—they are, literally, two sides of the same tape. The physicality of cassettes and the music on them represent a new kind of protest music in a post-9/11 world. That tape labels are predicated on masculinist practices of collection and the desire for limited editions is undeniable. Moreover, the ability to acquire a physical copy of a cassette that has gone on to be critically celebrated—physically or economically— is often limited to people with inside access or deep pockets. But by sonically bathing their music in an aesthetic of uncertainty, distance, longing, and mechanization that characterized moments of the Cold War, tape artists use technology and technostalgia to express their ambivalence toward dominant music culture practices as well as global politics. In an increasingly digitized culture, the physical becomes political.

Works Cited

Abu-Lughod, Lila. "Bedouins, Cassettes and Technologies of Public Culture." *Middle East Report*, 159.4 (1990): 7–11. Print.

Altman, Rick. *Silent Film Sound*. New York: Columbia UP, 2004. Print.

Bailey, Thomas Bey William. "Interrogating Tech-Nostalgia (An Exchange with Alexi Monroe)." *Vague Terrain*, Oct. 11, 2010. Web. Oct. 12, 2010.

Brown, August. "A Sonic Rewind." *Los Angeles Times*, Aug. 1, 2010. Web. Oct. 1, 2010.

Campau, Don. "Robin James Interview." *CassetteCulture*. Mar. 7, 2006. Web. Sept. 30, 2010.

Craine, Paul. "Woods Wants No Part of Your Lo-Fi 'Scene.'" *The Onion AV Club*. Aug. 20, 2009. Web. Oct. 15, 2010.

Foster, John. "A Message from Lost Music Network Coordinator John Foster." *OP*. L Issue (1983): 3. Print.

——. "Optional Reading." *OP*. F Issue (1983): 1. Print.

——. "OP, 'Castanets,' & the Cassette Revolution." *Cassette Mythos*. Ed. Robin James. Brooklyn, NY: Autonomedia, 1992. 52. Print.

"Fuck it Tapes." Woodsist.com. *Woodsist Records*, n.d. Web. Jan. 18, 2011.

Greif, Mark. "What Was the Hipster?" *New York*. Oct. 24, 2010. Web. July 11, 2011.

Hegarty, Paul. "The Hallucinatory Life of Tape." *Culture Machine* 9 (2007). Web. Feb. 26, 2011.

Hogan, Marc. "This is Not a Mixtape." *Pitchfork*. Feb. 22, 2010. Web. Feb. 22, 2010.

Holtzman, Ben, Craig Hughes, and Kevin Van Meter. "Do It Yourself … and the Movement Beyond Capitalism." *Constituent Imagination: Militant Investigations / Collective Theorization*. Ed. Stevphen Shukaitis and David Graeber. Oakland, CA: AK Press, 2007. Print.

Hornby, Nick. *High Fidelity*. New York: Riverhead Books, 1995. Print.

Jansen, Bas. "Tape Cassettes and Former Selves." *Sound Souvenirs: Audio Technologies, Memory and Cultural Practices*. Ed. Karin Bijsterveld and José van Dijck. Amsterdam: Amsterdam UP, 2009. 43–54. Print.

Lessig, Lawrence. "The Laws of Cyberspace." *Readings in Cyberethics*. Ed. Richard Spinello and Herman T. Tavani. 2nd edn, Sudbury, MA: Jones and Bartlett, 2004. Print.

Marsh, Calum. "Reconsidering the Revival of Cassette Tape Culture." *PopMatters*. Dec. 4, 2009. Web. Jan. 30, 2010.

Masters, Marc. "The Decade in Noise." *Pitchfork*, Sept. 14, 2009. Web. October 1, 2010.

McLeod, Kembrew. *Freedom of Expression: Overzealous Copyright Bozos and Other Enemies of Creativity*. New York: Doubleday, 2005. Print.

Moore, Thurston (ed.) *Mix Tape: The Art of Cassette Culture*. New York: Universal Publishers, 2004. Print.

Moss, Cici. "101 Cassette Labels." *Rhizome*. New Museum of Contemporary Art, Aug. 19, 2009. Web. Oct. 4, 2010.

Mules, Adrian. "TLOBF Interview // Blank Dogs." *The Line of Best Fit*, Sept. 14, 2010. Web. Oct. 5, 2010.

"Night-People." Raccoo-oo-oon.org. *Night-People Records*, n.d. Web. Oct. 10, 2010.

Pinch, Trevor and David Reinecke. "Technostalgia: How Old Gear Lives On in New Music." *Sound Souvenirs: Audio Technologies, Memory and Cultural Practices*. Ed. Karin Bijsterveld and José van Dijck. Amsterdam: Amsterdam UP, 2009. 152–66. Print.

Ramone, Cassie. "Interview with Vivian Girls." *Letter to Jane*. 2010. Web. Oct. 10, 2010.

Reynolds, Simon. "The 1980s Revival that Lasted an Entire Decade." *The Guardian*, Jan. 22, 2010. Web. Sept. 30, 2010.

Richard. "Interview: Wavves." *Rose Quartz*, Nov. 18, 2008. Web. Oct. 8, 2010.

Sheffield, Rob. *Love is a Mix Tape: Life and Loss, One Song at a Time*. New York: Three Rivers Press, 2007. Print.

Spencer, Amy. *Diy: The Rise of Lo-Fi Culture*. London: Marion Boyars, 2005. Print.

"The Tapeworm." *Tapeworm.org.uk*. Tapeworm, n.d. Web. Oct. 8, 2010.

Taylor, Timothy D. *Strange Sounds: Music, Technology & Culture*. New York: Routledge, 2001. Print.

"TTW#02—Jean Baudrillard—Le Xerox et l'Infini." *Tapeworm.org.uk*. Tapeworm, n.d. Web. Oct. 8, 2010.

Wolk, Douglas. "Heard on the Streets (of the Axis of Evil)." *New York Times*. Nov. 20, 2005. *Academic OneFile*. Web. July 11, 2011.

Young, Rob. "Unofficial Channels: Tapeworm." *Tapeworm.org.uk*. Tapeworm, n.d. Web. Oct. 8, 2010.

PART II
Hail to the Thief:
Post-9/11 Experimental Music

Chapter 4

Why Protest Albums Can't Teach Dissent: The Emergent Complexity of Post-9/11 Protest

Conrad Amenta

By the middle of the twentieth century, nearly all control of the production, distribution, marketing, and sales of recorded music in America belonged to a small number of corporate entities. It was in their interests that music was organized into genres: sustainable commodities subject to economic forecasting, traceable as they penetrated demographics of age, class, and ethnicity, and with their own body of legitimized (and legitimizing) historical articles. Until recently, the touchstones of the protest genre remained Depression-era folk, such as Aunt Molly Jackson, labor-rights-era Woody Guthrie, Vietnam War-era Bob Dylan and his "The Times They Are A-Changin'" (1964), Civil Rights-era soul such as Marvin Gaye's *What's Going On* (1971), and funk such as Sly and the Family Stone's *There's a Riot Goin' On* (1971). Similarly, the wellspring of rock and roll and punk music, to which we so often refer when speaking about subversion and rebellion, carried on protest's narrative tradition of blue-collar catharsis and accentuated otherness. As those owning the rights to protest sought to maximize its traction with the American counterculture, historical articles and the cultural atmosphere from which their authors drew came to be used interchangeably as not only evocative but also mutually representative of one another. Protest music was not simply a message from a subculture, but yet its albums were treated as units of it, as if to purchase *The Freewheelin' Bob Dylan* (1963) was to possess some portion of Dylan's principles—political urgency conflated with the act of consumption. To this stratification of culture into markets one could then attribute hierarchy and determine which unit of culture was "most seminal," which is to say most representative of a cultural atmosphere. Those who consider themselves among what historian Thomas Frank calls the "Culture Trust" expend much time and energy examining the permutations of this hierarchy, and the impact its occasional reordering has on society. The twentieth-century music listener was consigned to this limited array of cultural products, and the assurance of their lasting relevance.

Whether or not we should question the assumption that an iconic article can signify culture should be at the forefront of our minds when acknowledging that America in the 2000s—increasingly embroiled in wars abroad and divided at home by contentious domestic politics—saw no resurgence in the sales of protest music, much less the emergence of a revised but allusive variation. Surveying *Billboard*'s Top 200 list of bestselling albums during the 2000s revealed no surfeit of popular (or populist) music easily cross-referenced to a "big tent," impetus to rebellion (though, according to Tim Lemke of *The Washington Times*, in the days following the terrorist attacks there was a clear uptrend in the sales of music with strategically patriotic themes). Protest music remains commercially stagnant. Is this so because musicians and their audiences are unaffected or unengaged? Are we to assume that no such big tent exists, or did the size, number, location, and clustering of tents change while we were watching the charts? I posit that it is our reliance on a compromised referent, an entrenched, corporate account of the popular protest movement that prevents us from seeing mass expressions of politicized dissatisfaction and the sites of strategic non-participation. Today's popular movement is the vast migration of consumers from traditional systems of material accumulation to socially networked emergent systems of organized complexity: the blogs, subcultural websites, peer-to-peer networks, and the necessary impermanence of their multiform variations.

Systems based on emergent organized complexity emphasize the tracking and grouping individual preferences, which allows for true ratification by public alignment with and reciprocal interpretation of subject matter. These systems are evident in the lattice of online networks across which source material and its iterations are disseminated. Inside these systems, commercial products are complicated beyond the baseline affiliations of their market demographics, potentially capturing fleeting and iterative resonance via social mechanisms. The interactions and interpretations these systems enable and perpetuate are both more appropriate representations of a culture's complex contemporary mood than a static article and a public, living record of a social history. Where narrative historical accounts, such as those we attribute to expository genres of music like protest, seek to embody a period of time, social history, as embodied by emergent complexity, favors the interplay of small events over the long term. These interactions build on what Fernand Braudel terms the *longue durée*, or the evolution of historical structures rather than the enclosed examination of events. It is to Braudel's concept that we should turn to help us understand what emergent systems mean in a historical context, and where these systems are located, and to properly measure post-9/11 American protest where it naturally occurs.

The kind of protest that is occurring now is both an explicit and unconscious eco-systemic event: the mass abandonment of structures that allow for limited interactions. The line between the politics of content consumption and use of medium has blurred; to use a medium is now to participate indelibly in the formation of content. These are the increasingly evident social ramifications of a powerful new media, a return to the fundamental play of media on the creation of information itself. Marshall McLuhan's work, now decades old, still offers insight into the dynamism with which political thought is imbued when the speed and complexity of communication is increased. He points out that "as the speed of information increases, the tendency is for politics to move away from representation and delegation of constituents toward immediate involvement of the entire community in the central acts of decision" (204). He goes on to state that "this mosaic form has become a dominant aspect of human association; for the mosaic form means ... participation in process" (210, ellipses added). Socially networked systems accelerate the dynamic described by McLuhan, and the natural interplay between small events that form the meshwork of history. Braudel's organization of time is systematized, and the mosaic, social form of history is made traceable and concrete. Just as in the last century the organization of music into track-listings was based on the capacities of the dominant media of the time—the radio, the 45, the long-playing record, the compact disc, all transmitting their content in unalterable forms—so too are socially networked systems placing new emphasis on access to content and participation in content creation at the expense of centralized ownership. An array of sincere and ironic renditions of pop hits appear on *YouTube* and *Facebook*, and the effect of their appearance is twofold: they communicate that the authorship of song material is no longer the exclusive purview of the artist or their label, and that the medium of music consumption is no longer the static and unsatisfying form of material accumulation. With each new interpretation of material, the underlying notion of the content's sanctity, and thus its tendency to ossify, is diminished. The standard that recorded music takes is under constant determination, but one can be assured that the periods of dominance enjoyed by each form—and thus the locus of control over content in the context of that form—will become shorter so long as there exist platforms that are founded on the principle of unimpeded access to content and content creation tools.

Distinguishing trends in these systems is not unlike an analysis of coded behavior in subcultures; the detection of patterns that are immersed in apparent chaos and are often imperceptible to those outside of the collective behavior that produces them. Steven Johnson also points out that "the technologies behind the Internet ... have been brilliantly engineered to handle dramatic increases in scale, but they are indifferent, if not downright hostile, to the task of creating higher-level order" (118–19, ellipses added). Thus the purpose of this essay is not to capture or explain new or uncategorized forms of fluid protest, but to suggest that the methods with which we measure information trends such as protest and its dialects should include an interdisciplinary perspective, due primarily to the rapidity and complexity with which information is communicated via the force of new reciprocal media. It is as important now to turn to shifts in statistical research, such as the kinds of bottom-up quantitative analyses and web metrics that comprise the study of emergent systems of organized complexity, as it is to examine the cultural studies and strategic readings on which the humanities and social sciences have relied in the past, and which have the potential to entrench our reliance on cultural artifacts. Events develop after as many as millions of local interactions; their antecedents are the multiform body of reactions, of the resonance and dissonance, of reciprocal communication itself.

For example, the emergence of the file-sharing network *Napster* may not have been a higher-level catalyst for a larger dissatisfaction with the music industry, but the result of a localized set of interactions that grew to a sea change, as consumers, already alienated by industry practices and pricing but relegated to traditional means of material accumulation, were prepared to abandon a system in which they no longer had faith. As agents in an emergent system of organized complexity naturally develop behaviors that engender the continued survival of the whole, so too did post-9/11 consumers' series of migrations from a system that systematically closed down spaces for expression (which need not have been explicitly political so much as discussions of the monetary value of music) contribute to the formulation of a new majority outside what had been perceived as the mainstream—a macro-political response given form and exponential mass by socially networked media. For Johnson, our focus should be on the shift in how systems come to meet the requirements of its users: "It's about altering a system's behavior in response to [changing] patterns in ways that make the system more successful at whatever goal it's pursuing. The system need not be conscious to be capable of that kind of learning, just as your immune system need not be conscious to learn how to protect you from the chicken pox" (104).

The cure for the pox is the mass exodus from systems of music consumerism, where trends are artificially inseminated, to systems in which memes are socially conceived: ratification through numerous local interactions rather than the simulacra of a unilateral myth. Contemporary protest is marked by absence and abandonment. The movement has already reached what is called, in the parlance of emergent complex systems, its statistically robust "climax stage," the point at which it must be acknowledged as a macro-social trend. For example, *Facebook* reports having 500 million users, each creating 90 pieces of content a month and connected to 80 community pages, groups, and events ("Press Page"). Though the music industry may not have produced an allusive variant of the protest genre to correspond to post-9/11 agitation, the degree of this much broader form of information consumption is also evident in the crumbling edifice of the troubled music industry itself, its key messages drowned out by cacophonous discussion.

But before taking a perspective of systems and structures, one that explains our social networks and emerging dialects, one should first understand why transgressive products—rock albums released in the 1960s, for example—continue to be relied upon as iconic representations of protest while no longer sufficient to help us understand "how" to protest. Vital to the flawed correlation between albums and cultural resonance is an ongoing scripting of protest music—specifically music stored on tactile media, distributed via retail sales, and stylistically and lyrically rooted in their periods of production—as the sole authentic medium for marginalized voices. These articles are legitimized by a tactically deployed nostalgia, and are encoded with a highly narrativized, retroactive continuity. The key logical fault of relying upon this dynamic between article and culture is that, in locating contemporary protest in a historical spectrum of work lauded for the sensibility it supposedly imposed on American political reality, the genre now provides a sense of instant resolution, invoking a nostalgia-infused historical change, real or imagined, in place of a fresh interrogation, leading one to conclude that the lack of a similar contemporary movement indicates a lack of engagement. Protest has become what Jean Baudrillard might call a "simulacrum," a commercial simulation that has come to replace its referent. As a simulacrum, protest music comes to constitute parameters for politicized dissatisfaction, narrowing normalized spaces for dissent rather than allowing them to feed an output of locally specific expressions. Protest's legitimized historical articles contain both the problem and the solution to the agitated impulse, a package for the restless demographics, and are frozen in a compromised state rather than fluid in the emergence of new structures wherein individuals construct meaning. Thomas Frank invokes social critic Camille Paglia to demonstrate this all too simplistic narrative of protest, which suggests that "rebellion is one-half of an all-too convenient and fictive formula, against a supposedly static oppressor, whose great opponents are, of course, liberated figures like 'the beatniks,' Bob Dylan, and the Beatles. Culture is, quite simply, a binary battle between the repressive Apollonian order of capitalism and the Dionysian impulses of the counterculture" (quoted in Frank 35). Baudrillard goes further, rendering the problem as macro-social. He posits simulacra as cyclically self-legitimizing, entrenched collaborations between audience, author, and media, and he suggests that simulacra "are the ones that interrogate us, and we are summoned to answer them, and the answer is included in the question. Thus all the messages in the media function in a similar fashion: neither information nor communication, but referendum, perpetual test, circular response, verification of the code" (75). Protest music today, be it contemporary or canonical, acts as a panacea, a balm of stylistic and lyrical catharsis that has difficulty calling into question the materialism upon which it depends for its dissemination. Thus, our legacy of rebellion can be seen as having no referent at all, compromised and never having been accommodating enough for complex and fluid cultural movements.

Depictions of the counterculture have become as conflicted and disposable as the concept of "cool" itself—that exclusivity and novelty upon which the marketing of revolution has so often relied—because commercialism long ago learned to make novelty an ineffable part of its appeal. John Leland, in his history of "hip," suggests, "There is no difference between commercialized hip and the real thing ... Even at its most pure, hip is just a cog in an expansionist economy, conjured to create the radical consumers that the market needs to sell ever-newer stuff. Its fetish for novelty trains us to embrace obsolescence and constant turnover" (284, ellipses added). A protest album cannot represent and teach agitation that is continuously changing, just as an album with subcultural capital cannot represent the culture it seeks to distill, because lifestyle brands long ago suggested these notions as a reason to buy up the excess that the industry was creating, and imposed stability, sluggishness, and myth on the dialogue. The terms "rebellion" or "revolutionary" were hollowed-out and lightened, conflated seamlessly with the principles of an omnipresent lifestyle commercialism that consists "of a sort of Nietzschean antinomianism, an automatic questioning of the rules, a rejection of whatever social prescriptions we've happened to inherit"; or, put simply, "Just Do It is the whole of the law" (Frank 32). Those belonging to the Baby Boomer generation of the 1960s, commonly portrayed as a catalyst of cultural upheaval—less Moloch than media personality making appeals to anti-establishment ideologies—yielded the great corporate entities of capitalism in the latter half of the twentieth century. "As existential rebellion has become a more or less official style of Information Age capitalism," Frank explains: "It has become difficult to understand the countercultural idea as anything more than the self-justifying ideology of the new bourgeoisie that has arisen since the 1960s, the cultural means by which this group has proven itself ever so much better skilled than its slow-moving, security-minded forebears at adapting to the accelerated, always-changing consumerism of today" (34–5). It is not that protest's historical articles, and the establishment against which they pushed, were once and now-complicated truths; they are in fact the essence of our simulacra, whose very historical validity can be called into question because of the corporate lens through which they are viewed.

Thus, agitation has withered on the margins of our traditional systems of material accumulation. Even if protest were still encoded in the works of a Guthrie or Dylan, whose personalities, biographical narratives, and attendant myths are now embedded in the sale of the article, in seeking legitimization by comparison to a historical article, one pre-empts the ability of a work to respond to or capture the contemporary essence of mimetic information. The occurrence of a social response is subsumed into the systematization of belief; are simulacra affixed with myth: narrativized, encoded, concrete, and cumulatively (and often unconsciously) reified. Protest music leverages the weight of mythology in its push for commercial traction, and in so doing snuffs out non-synergistic accounts. "[We] can discern … two mechanisms through which a body of dogma has always made itself believed," Michel de Certeau explains. He goes on to say:

> On the one hand, the claim to be *speaking in the name of a reality* which, assumed to be inaccessible, is the principle of both what is believed (a totalization) and the act of believing (something that is always unavailable, unverifiable, lacking); and on the other, the ability of a discourse authorized by a 'reality' to distribute itself in the form of *elements that organize practices*, that is, of "articles of faith" These two traditional resources are found today in the system that combines the narrativity of the media—an establishment of the real—with the discourse of products to be consumed—a distribution of this reality in the form of "articles" that are to be believed and bought. (185, emphasis added)

The protest genre is essentially constituted by the articles of faith to which de Certeau alludes, the discourse of "legitimized" products which organizes the practice of protest by providing the language, and more importantly the rigidly controlled medium, via which we understand how to express politicized dissatisfaction. Protest is an entrenched and unresponsive dialect which speaks for, or rather in place of, reality, not so much unreal as *anti*-real, frozen in the past, a coda of dilemmas packaged with their resolutions, and rendered by a strategically employed nostalgia as distant, disconnected narratives. But where protest music has become inadequate and unsatisfying, it may be useful to imagine where a critical dissatisfaction forms. While de Certeau describes the degree to which the article of faith has come to constitute the justification and of belief, he also points out that "this instrument that 'creates opinion' is manipulable by those that have it at their disposition," and that "it is legitimate to inquire into the opportunities it offers for changing 'belief' into 'mistrust' into 'suspicion,' and indeed into denunciation, as well as into the opportunity for citizens to manipulate politically what serves as a circular and objectless credibility for political life itself" (189).

This is the subtext of a narrative about an unmotivated counterculture: the perpetual asphyxiation of the cultural by omnipresent sponsorial entities has driven contemporary expressions to accommodatingly pliable mediums, a migration to systems currently attaining the statistical robustness at which they make themselves known paradigmatically and without the legitimization of a historical referent. Corporately owned information-management and communications platforms in the twenty-first century, such as *Google*, *Facebook*, *MySpace*, and *Napster*, along with the community of independent music blogs and websites offering original content, such as *Daytrotter*, *Pitchfork*, and *Blogoteque*, are iterations of a largely free information exchange whose perpetuity and ease-of-access accelerate the change demanded of underlying systems, such as copyright law, material accumulation, or personal privacy. They are the venue, and sometimes the substance, of America's subcultural meshwork.

In Steven Johnson's exploration of socially networked online platforms as both manifestations and perpetuations of emergent systems of organized complexity, he describes the behavior evident in these systems as "higher-level patterns arising out of parallel complex interactions between local agents," replete with socially defined parameters that only emerge when the statistical sample becomes large enough (19). Socially networked systems are Braudel's *longue durée* given contemporary form, capturing social trends as they emerge over time. These two notions privilege social history over narrative simulacra, and suggest we should look for the historical action (in this case, instances of resistance) in the migration between systems within, away from, and returning to traditions. For the goal, Braudel asserts, should be "to define a hierarchy of forces, of currents, of particular movements, and then tackle them as an entire constellation. At each moment of [historical] research, one has to distinguish between long-lasting movements and short bursts, the latter detected from the moment they originate, the former over the course of a distant time" (125). In this context, what we might view as a scarcity of protest in the music industry is in fact an over-reliance on a short-term manner of measuring social resonance (retail sales by genre, and in a relatively short period of time (such as the decade following 9/11), while all around us the way music is created, listened to, owned, and valued is changing. What drives that change has formed over a much longer period of time than that rendered by the *Billboard* Top 200 or attenuation to market cycles.

As Leland informs us, subcultural histories are rife with accounts of paradigmatic and technological shifts:

> Uptown, a Jamaican man named Clive Campbell called himself Kool DJ Herc and pulled apart records nobody wanted, isolating the "break beats," or strong percussive sections, and repeating them on two turntables. Downtown, pseudonymous musicians like Dee Dee Ramone or Stiv Bators pulled apart old pop forms that had lost their savor, hammering them to their own equivalent of the break beat … Hip in the age of DIY came with a strain of guerilla capitalism. (298, ellipses added)

Social networks, though corporately owned, extend the do-it-yourself aesthetic from entertainment to the discourse and medium surrounding entertainment, rendering the iterative social construct the subject of an information transaction predicated on cultural, rather than monetary, capital. What we see in the emerging patterns of information across these platforms is the brusque dismissal of the establishment/rebellion dichotomy, a de-sanctification of historical articles in our strata of allegiances.

Predicated on dynamic reciprocation, appropriation, and a creative interpretation of information, emergent systems ripple with dissatisfaction and strategic non-participation. Post-9/11 dialectics may be informed by awareness and acknowledgment, an understanding that to be a consumer is to inhabit an active and politicized state, or it may occur unconsciously—almost defensively—arising out of a general inability to effectively communicate, or to communicate in an appealing or fashionable way, in pre-empted, compromised systems of production and distribution. These scenarios may too exist simultaneously, but are both defined by a self-organizing principle of destratification and restratification, the deconstruction and constitution of both information and the systems through which it passes. The brands of emergent systems are themselves impermanent events in Braudel's *longue durée*, but they, by their very nature, allow for the statistical tracking of social histories as they emerge, and are driven by adaptation and transparency. It is true that organized complexity is simply another way of organizing units of time, a non-objective way of conceiving of the social unconscious, but this speaks to a suspicion that one's actions take place in an overarching stratum of history. The individual commits to public record their affinities and choices, and then engages in dialogue, thereby assuming an active role where once variations on passive consumption were all that were offered. The metrics are built into the very foundation of the system itself, allowing for a statistical description of language usage, content generation and sharing, and demographics. In this way, emergent systems of organized complexity make explicit unconsciously developed memes. They are the contemporary manifestation of Braudel's ideal, allowing those concerned with measuring history to "get past superficial observation in order to reach the zone of unconscious or barely conscious elements, and then to reduce that reality to tiny elements, minute identical sections, whose relations can be precisely analyzed" (135). The article, such as the album, in isolation is self-legitimizing and disconnected. Emergent complexity, by contrast, places emphasis on the perpetual reconstitution of elements of the social, and then the linking and tracking of reconstituted elements. The temporary ascendancy of an icon like Bob Dylan is rendered less important than the social trends and themes connoting a preference for someone like Bob Dylan at that time, and the conditions which may give rise to another like him.

The fluidity that these systems enable—their composition of absorbing and absorbed information—means that variations on protest have difficulty coalescing into something that might be recognized and/or legitimized by established or more stable commercial norms. However, what the protest taking place in these systems lacks in traceability, it makes up for in pure mass. Linkages between units of information—made on minuscule, peer-to-peer levels but across a staggering array of transactions—develop into meta-coverage. Their exposure, which itself begins to mutate and become a part of the information, expands exponentially, and each variation on the original message incorporates local concerns into the communal whole. Social networking sites—which rely not only upon statistics-based learning software that links pieces of information, but also on the feedback loop that is generated when others perpetuate and interpret that link—respond to the original message and modify its information, creating a space for commentary. Effectively, what these systems allow for is the socialization, and thus cumulative legitimization, of information in lieu of a corporate entity's explicit authorship or endorsement. One aligns oneself with a piece of information on *Facebook* not because *Facebook* is sponsoring it, but because one's friends are. The platform is designed in such a way as to capitalize on the impulse to comment on, approve of, modify, or link pieces of information, and to make visible each of these actions in what amounts to a declaration of affinity. Similarly, ease of access to and use of blogging tools such as *Blogger*, *WordPress*, and *tumblr*, and their integration with social networks, allow content to be shared seamlessly across platforms, and enable blogs to emerge and link with one another in what may constitute a contemporary variation on the community. Music blogging has become vast and complexly interwoven, where the taste-making capital of sites such as *Pitchfork* and *Said the Gramophone* combine with the collating power of aggregators such as *The Hype Machine* to form seemingly ubiquitous access to dynamic, culturally resonant music. Codification is established and destroyed in the arc of listening patterns developing via millions of communications transactions involving content sharing and modification. Johnson elaborates on how the system works when he says: "Generically, you can describe those rules as a mix of positive and negative feedback pushing the system toward a particular state based on the activities of the participants" (159). The key difference between today's agitation and that of the 1950s and 1960s is that socially networked systems have exponentially accelerated the constitution, adoption, and destruction of the subcultural to the point where capitalization by corporate entities—production and marketing for the purposes of mass dissemination—cannot keep up with the meshwork of interpretations and alignments implied by this mix of feedback.

I posit that social networks, powered by a socially significant emergent complexity, allow for a kind of unification that is not possible in the retail sale of Protest music, and which facilitates one's ability to express politicized dissatisfaction. A social network enables and encourages users, via the conduit of their preferences for and modulations and interpretations of content, to form groups and clusters of groups. They are so encouraged because these clusters feed and refine the networks' fundamental algorithms, driving the system toward an economy of accommodation. They observe fractious, unpredictable embellishment as not only an aspect but also a pillar of the system itself. What was once a demographic—understood in inflexible terms, subject to slow reconstitution and consisting of individuals that may not have been involved in the definition of its parameters—has become an enmeshed series of peripatetic local interactions whose mosaic whole comprises staggering substance. Individuals in the network, grouped by their preferences, are more actively invested in the definition, and direction, of messages emitted by that group. To make decisions in a social network can be politically motivated and contextually, locally defined, or it may be an unconscious, but active identification of preferences, becoming a form of socialization that in turn contributes to the statistical robustness of the messages produced by each shifting cluster of groups: big tent resonance from a landscape of small tents. Nonetheless, the accommodation is natural; as Johnson points out, "The needs of most progressive movements are uniquely suited to adaptive, self-organizing systems: both have a keen ear for collective wisdom; both are naturally hostile to excessive concentrations of power; and both are friendly to change" (224). Or, to quote McLuhan again: "All media are active metaphors in their power to translate experience into new forms" (57). Social networks are no exception.

One convenient contrast, which illustrates the dynamic of user feedback, occurred between Radiohead's 2003 album *Hail to the Thief* and their 2007 release, *In Rainbows*. The lyrics of the former album are fatalistic and cynical—invoking, for example, Orwellian paranoia in the opening song, "2+2=5"—which can be interpreted as dissatisfied in the explicitly lyrical fashion of the protest genre. Released on Capitol Records via retail distribution channels and on tactile storage media, *Hail to the Thief* is a classic case of top-down dictation from commercial artist to a forecasted demographic. Its follow-up album, *In Rainbows*, contains less overtly political lyrical content, but was initially delivered to consumers via an independent online distribution service featuring consumer-determined pricing. If one undertakes to compare *Hail to the Thief* and *In Rainbows* in terms of their political motivation, countercultural resonance, and the willingness of the band at the time of each album's release to challenge the status quo, to what degree should the albums' respective media influence our findings?

I suggest that *In Rainbows* represents a more broadly contemporary agitation than *Hail to the Thief*, though to rely on the script provided by protest music one would invariably find the inverse. Where protest music relies on a top-down approach to establishing countercultural credibility—the artist who articulates a broader dissatisfaction, the record label that capitalizes on that artist's potential resonance, the marketing firm that introduces the artist to buyers and propagates the artist's resonance—*In Rainbows* relies primarily on feedback loops among potential and existing consumers to legitimize both the brand and the information in play, discussions that were themselves part of a greater feedback loop about the migration to alternative distribution channels for the dissemination of content. *In Rainbows* was absorbed into the feedback loop, which contributed to its volume. Radiohead, once considered a band of the "alternative" music trend in the 1990s, now presented their listener base with something that was, however temporarily, truly an alternative, both of and enhancing the sociohistorical arc of migration to an accelerated form of communication, one event and site of interactions in the meshwork that is a newly dominant paradigm.

One facet of the feedback loop was *In Rainbows'* consumer-determined pricing scheme, which *Pitchfork*'s Matthew Solarski went so far as to describe as "a moral question" (Maki). This aperture in the previously inflexible sales structure provides both space to discuss, and valuable insight into, the perceived value of music and the participatory nature of consumerism: the transformation of the commercial action into a discussion about that action, or an unconscious migration to more accommodating mediums that implied the users' feelings about music's relative monetary worth.

In Rainbows was reported to have sold 1.2 million copies in its first week of release, at an average selling price of £4, easily outpacing the first week sales of the band's previous three albums (Manjoo). These figures originated from sources connected to the band itself, and were not recognized by Billboard, vitally complicating the albums' traditionally understood legitimacy and cultural resonance. *Hail to the Thief*, the final Radiohead album released via Capitol Records, sold 300,000 copies in its first week of release, and one assumes with a significantly smaller proportion of per-album revenues directed to the band members. These numbers, which may simply indicate a natural advantage presented by alternative music distribution channels to those artists with the resources to develop and implement them (or a preference for *In Rainbows'* songs to those on the band's previous album), may also illustrate a shift in discussion from a strictly lyrical exposition of agitation to individual control over production and distribution itself. The relative success of *In Rainbows* in comparison to its predecessors surely points to the existing popularity of the band, but also to the self-legitimizing nature of online distribution, the "floating-price" model, and non-participation in tactile systems of information management and control.

The assumption that the very nature of these systems meets the demands of progressive and politically active individuals, however idealistic, may speak to the anxiety that produces a paradigmatic overhaul in the first place. The notion that new media is simply a defensive measure, made necessary by the culture's conscious or unconscious desire to privilege rather than marginalize the minority opinion, is an appealing one. If that concept proves to be the case, the impetus to non-participation in systems of material accumulation may very well be the primary cause of the economic deflation of the music industry. Thus the potential for a naturally occurring mass exodus—not just from the music industry, but from the Culture Trust at large—is enormous. The unilateral myths of narrative history are yielding to a complex manifestation of a social one, a history in which the countercultural may be accelerated to a point of widespread, perpetual discourse.

Works Cited

Baudrillard, Jean. *Simulacra and Simulation*. Trans. Sheila Faria Glaser. Ann Arbor: U of Michigan P, 1994. Print.

Braudel, Fernand. "History and the Social Sciences: The *Longue Durée.*" Trans. Arthur Goldhammer. *Histories: French Constructions of the Past*. Ed. Lynn Hunt and Jacques Revel. New York: The New Press, 1995. 115–46. Print.

de Certeau, Michel. *The Practice of Everyday Life*. Trans. Steven Rendall. Berkeley and Los Angeles: U of California P, 1984. Print.

Frank, Thomas. "Why Johnny Can't Dissent." *Commodify Your Dissent: Salvos from* The Baffler. New York: W. W. Norton, 1997. 31–46. Print.

Johnson, Steven. *Emergence: The Connected Lives of Ants, Brains, Cities, and Software*. New York: Scribner, 2001. Print.

Leland, John. *Hip: The History*. New York: Harper Perennial, 2004. Print.

Lemke, Tim. "Patriotic Music Sales Eases Industry Slump." *The Washington Times*. Sept. 26, 2001. Web. Nov. 9, 2010.

Maki. "Radiohead's *In Rainbows*: A Look at Anti-Marketing in the Music Industry." *DoshDosh*. Oct. 2, 2007. Web. Sept. 15, 2010.

Manjoo, Farhad. "A Blockbuster for Radiohead's *In Rainbows*?" *Salon*. Oct. 11, 2007. Web. Sept. 15, 2010.

McLuhan, Marshall. *Understanding Media: The Extensions of Man*. Cambridge, MA: MIT 1994. Print.

"Press Page." *Facebook*. 2011. Web. Jan. 14, 2011.

Chapter 5
On a Maddening Loop: Post-9/11 Rubble Music

Isaac Vayo

In the aftermath of 9/11, rubble abounded, be it that of the World Trade Center and the Pentagon, or of the shattered myth of US invulnerability. That rubble was swiftly cleared and its fragments forcibly coalesced into a pseudo-unity in the face of purported threat. Music was not immune to that process, and an examination of the song "Fly Me to New York" by the tape-collage artists Cassetteboy reveals how that forced coalescence fails in its attempts to enact a public amnesia, instead producing a rubble music that underlines US guilt via an alternate coalescence. This forced coalescence, this jointure, is imperfect, the fissures serving only to highlight the uneven reassembly of pseudo-unity. Based around samples from Frank Sinatra songs, and also featuring excerpts from songs by The Smiths and a number of hip-hop artists, "Fly Me to New York" narrates the events of 9/11 from the perspective of one of the pilot-hijackers and, in its reconstitution of disparate fragments, is the best example of the rubble music arising from 9/11. The choice of Sinatra as a centerpiece is not accidental, and it reflects his noteworthy place within American popular song, making his work an ideal jumping-off point for the reflexive critique of US guilt in relation to 9/11. This critique is typical of rubble music, a music reconstituted from the shattered fragments of a national psyche in the wake of a traumatic event, from the elements of the past and the passed/pasted nation, composed of the decomposed, newly mortalized state, soldered together crudely, the cracks and accompanying caulk speaking and occupying volumes. Such a rubble music acts reflexively, establishing a new perspective of self-critique from materials of old that were deficient on that account, rearticulating an inarticulate past into a more erudite present and future, one professed by the confessor, the artist owning up to and reflexively apportioning guilt.

Begin the Big Up: The Song (of) Itself

I begin my analysis of Cassetteboy's "Fly Me to New York" by first briefly introducing the artist and song (with further attention to follow), then turning to the song's engagement with sampling, and finally unpacking the ramifications of its citational tendencies in relation to an articulation of rubble music. The song was produced by the British tape-collage artists Cassetteboy (Steve Warlin and Michael

Bollen), featuring DJ Rubbish, and appears on their 2002 debut album *The Parker Tapes*. A brief glance at a handful of the Frank Sinatra samples demonstrates the way in which "Fly Me to New York" functions as a footnoted, citational text, an amateur recontextualization of professionally produced recordings that yields greater critical insight when the sources of the samples are traced and analyzed. For instance, the latter half of the line "I've got a razor in my pocket" is drawn from the Dean Martin song "Money Burns a Hole in My Pocket" (often sung with Sinatra in Rat Pack performances), which also features a reference to the Texas oil industry, paralleling George W. Bush's past and present relations with Big Oil and their influence on the decision to invade Iraq. Similarly, the sampled line "you think you've flown before" is part of "The Best is Yet to Come," specifically the phrase "you think you've flown before, but you've never left the ground." "Fly Me to New York" also contains an indirect reference to flight training, paralleling the preparation of pilot-hijackers Mohamed Atta, Marwan al-Shehhi, Ziad Jarrah, and Hani Hanjour (or Nawaf al-Hazmi) at US flight schools.

Furthermore, the first half of the line "I'm mental, and I'm flying the plane" comes from "I Won't Dance," and is part of a verse addressing the singer-narrator's burning passion (so fiery as to overwhelm even asbestos) for a woman dancing the Continental. This verse recalls the airline as point of vulnerability (Continental being another carrier in the US), and the inferno that overwhelmed the fireproofing of the World Trade Center towers, as well as concerns over the potentially harmful collapse-plume that lingered over lower Manhattan. Additionally, the second half of the line "let's fly into buildings, let's turn to ashes" cites the line "watching my dreams turn to ashes" from Sinatra's "What Now, My Love?" The song also contains a verse addressing the tumult of a crumbling relationship, aptly describing the topsy-turvy feelings in the wake of the towers' collapse. Finally, the middle portion of the line "and now my skin is melting away" comes from "I've Got You Under My Skin," referencing the hijackers' presence within the US before the attacks and within the national psyche thereafter. Another verse states the singer-narrator's determination to pursue his quarry despite warnings of imminent failure, drawing attention to the hijackers' suicidal devotion, the unheeded warnings before 9/11, and the difficulties of waging a "War on Terror."

Other samples are drawn from "Fly Me to the Moon," "Theme from *New York, New York*," "Come Fly With Me," "Leaving On a Jet Plane," and "My Way," illustrating Cassetteboy's mining of Sinatra's broad catalogue and use of songs both immediately recognizable and slightly obscure. A closer examination of the methodology of "Fly Me to New York" in relation to citationality will demonstrate the manner in which Cassetteboy call upon that citationality to facilitate their autoreflexive critique of US culpability for 9/11, with the deliberate choice of Frank Sinatra serving as a foundational masterstroke.

Mash Notes: Resembling the Rubbles

Cassetteboy's ability to citationally renarrate 9/11 through a recontextualization of fragments gives "Fly Me to New York" a significant critical bite, one which, at an abstract level, methodologically resembles the machinations of al Qaeda while maintaining sufficient distance for a renarrativization that gives form to a new rubble music—a production of the future composed of the present and past. Simply put, Cassetteboy's methodology resembles that of al Qaeda in terms of their online presence. Jon Nelson emphasizes this point in his blog entry on *Some Assembly Required: Tape Manipulations, Digital Deconstructions and Turntable Creations*. Nelson notes that "[f]or the longest time, this was a group so underground that although their work had been well received, no one knew who the heck these guys actually were. That is to say, their online presence has been shrouded in mystery and misinformation." Out of context—de- and then recontextualized—citationalized into a discussion of al Qaeda, Nelson's statement holds true, reflecting the commonalities between Cassetteboy's efforts to create anonymously, to act notoriously, and al Qaeda's likeminded desire to operate under the literal and figurative radar and to bring glory to the *jihadist* movement, both retaining an anonymity that refers in an amateur fashion, an evasion of celebrity that accordingly evades professionalism.

Beyond the methodological parallels evident in Cassetteboy's tightly managed online presence, additional similarities to al Qaeda can be located at the level of target selection, where a desire to confront the seemingly inappropriate in a not so appropriate manner finds precedent in the band's back catalogue, a lineage that manifests itself once more in "Fly Me to New York." The first appearance of this methodological striking at the symbolic heart of a nation dates back to fall 1997 and the death of Princess Diana, an event which spurred Cassetteboy to create the song "Di and Dodi Do Die," composed from edited samples drawn from televised and radio broadcast tributes to the fallen princess. Rather than taking that tragic event as cause for a moment of national mourning, Cassetteboy instead decided to act, with little mind to the relative sanctity of the situation: "Sod her lads, this is great material." In so doing, Cassetteboy set a precedent for swooping in upon moments of national misery, however misplaced or overblown, to gather raw materials for their productions, taking the pulse of the country as a portion of its pulse ebbs, and allowing the blood spilled across media outlets to pool into a fluid renarrativization at the hands of the sampler. That this pattern should repeat itself in the case of 9/11, an event of greater magnitude, albeit different national referentiality, is no surprise.

Much as al Qaeda strikes at soft targets, not so much looking to inflict damage upon the literal defenses of a country, including military outposts and government officials, but rather the figurative defenselessness of a country, as underlined by civilian attacks upon symbolic locations, so too do Cassetteboy in placing Princess Diana and 9/11 within their sights. There are few softer targets than a nation in mourning, a nation that has placed certain topics off-limits during a period of post-trauma, a nation content to lick its wounds and to lap up narratives of victimhood and valor, and Cassetteboy do not miss their mark, trimming away the pretense around each event and exposing what lies (are) beneath. The Middle Eastern meets Western mash-up present in the death ride of Egyptian department-store and hotel heir Dodi Al-Fayed and Diana Spencer is met with another Occident on Orient pseudo-accident upon 9/11, a similar targeting of the soft (the besieged celebrity wishing only to fade from the limelight, the pseudo-innocent superpower doing its best to be an able steward to the world). It is not the harder targets that are to the liking of al Qaeda and Cassetteboy, but rather the fish in a barrel, the auto-sacred (whether of wheel or wing) whose offensive re-rendering serves to highlight the offenses that incur that rendering.

Off (the) Fence: Picking Nits and Sides

Cassetteboy's methodology for constructing "Fly Me to New York" is premised on offense, an offense that jars via its recontextualization of the grave (9/11) into the humorous (a satirical pastiche), the maudlin romantic (Frank Sinatra) into the Muslim ecstatic (the unnamed pilot-hijacker narrator), a citationality that provokes reflection on the centrality of Sinatra to narratives of US nationalism and, more specifically, metropolitan splendor vis-à-vis New York City. Chris Dahlen's "The Pop Culture of 9/11" focuses on this methodology in its discussion of the song within the frame of *The 9/11 Commission Report: Final Report of the National Commission on Terrorist Attacks Upon the United States*, with Dahlen asserting that "[w]hether out of bad taste, an attempt at political insight, or because they wanted to take us down a notch, Cassetteboy spliced together a mockery of the disaster at the World Trade Center." Dahlen provides a shorthand listing of the spectrum of motivations ascribed to Cassetteboy, neatly tracing a trajectory of affect from the rupture of bad taste, the lingering metallic flavor of charred buildings and rung bells, to the trenchant insight (and its implied notch-taking, alongside the bedpost/belt notch of the successfully penetrative hijacker) contained within the song's manipulation of its chosen samples, a discarding of the tenets of professionalism and its dictates concerning taste in favor of an amateur, unflinching incisiveness.

Elsewhere, in his review of *The Parker Tapes*, Dahlen describes Cassetteboy's methodology in more direct terms: "The guys break things up with dozens of music clips and remixes, from hip-hop to pop, making for a kind of post-modern vaudeville, and they construct each voice track with attention to rhythm and flow" ("Get That"). Song and dance men of a sort, Cassetteboy provide the choreography of the plot, following the pilot-hijacker through his daily rounds, bringing an airiness to the narrative that simultaneously lets the air out of the US's bombastic sense of immaculate victimhood.

The decision to base "Fly Me to New York" around Frank Sinatra samples, principally those drawn from the songs "Fly Me to the Moon" and "Theme from *New York, New York*," stands as the first and perhaps most affecting transgressive step taken by Cassetteboy, a step that proves particularly jarring to the US psyche. Given his rise to prominence in the run-up to, during, and shortly after World War II, Sinatra is inseparably linked to ideas of American nationalism, victory, and postwar affluence, making his fragmentation into sampled lyrics and reconstitution into a hijacker narrator especially affecting. Dahlen reinforces this point by stating that "nothing is as profane as when they [Cassetteboy] retell the events of the day from the hijackers' point of view, by splicing together clips from New York icon Frank Sinatra" ("Pop"). This claim demonstrates the unusual sanctity accorded to Sinatra (especially given his relatively seedy past with alleged ties to organized-crime figures) and his iconic status at both the New York City and, by proxy, national levels. The description of Cassetteboy's manipulation of Sinatra, a cracking open of his often hackneyed lyrics as profanity, also ties his import closely to the linguistic level through the common linkages to profane speech and deviation from sacred/biblical tenets and their rooting in the primacy of the Word. Sinatra himself is almost secondary in Dahlen's indictment, as the main complaint pertains to the voice given to the pilot-hijacker's point of view, not the voice taken from Sinatra, pulled from his throat to pull shapes in the choreographed space outlined by Cassetteboy.

Dahlen gives further credence to the profanity of Sinatra's (mis)use by Cassetteboy in an installment of his recurring column "Get That Out of Your Mouth" on *Pitchfork* entitled "Negativland and Cassetteboy Steal Music," which redoubles Sinatra's untouchable status as suggested by his potential mob ties (though he is less an Eliot Ness figure than an Al Capone in this case). Discussing *The Parker Tapes* in relation to the issue of sample clearance (the act of gaining permission to use a sample from the sampled artist), Dahlen observes that "[t]hey [Cassetteboy] didn't get the rights to any of the material and in some cases, no amount of money would have worked—like when they mix lines from Frank Sinatra's greatest hits into a mockery of the tragedy at the World Trade Center" ("Cassetteboy"). Aside from its upholding of intellectual property rights such that all samples must be cleared with the artists in question, a process that greatly limits the potential for citationality and does much to increase the survival rate for accepted narratives, Dahlen's statement reflects the unthinkable disservice done to Sinatra's music and his legacy by "Fly Me to New York," a disrespecting of his elevated ranking by the rank amateurs in Cassetteboy. What Dahlen fails to recognize is the degree to which Sinatra's particular vision, one of a bootstrap America in which the child of Italian immigrants can scale the heights of fame and celebrity through sheer talent and charisma, is premised on the very sort of exclusionary mythology that so infuriates the ideologues behind 9/11. Such opportunities are not available to everyone or accorded to just anyone, be they members of racial, gendered, or economic underclasses in the US or religious (Muslim fundamentalist) or national (non-global north/western European/ predominately white) undesirables around the world, and Cassetteboy's de- and reconstruction—and de- and recontextualization—of the Sinatran fragments points to the crucial flaws at the heart of the American-dream mythos.

Subject to the cut in the act of sampling, Sinatra is also subjected to the perils of poor taste in his citational implementation in "Fly Me to New York," a bitter pill swallowed with a chaser of bile as brought about by the destabilization of his narrative. In good taste, "Fly Me to the Moon" would have been excluded from airplay in the weeks after 9/11, much like the songs and artists included in the 2001 Clear Channel memorandum issued after the event (of which "Theme from *New York, New York*" was one) (Wishnia). Instead, those two songs form the backbone of a scathing critique of US culpability for 9/11, an effort indirectly saluted by Dahlen: "I just have to hand it to Cassetteboy that not only is the piece disturbingly brutal, but their decision to build it around samples from Frank 'New York, New York' Sinatra is the final nail in the coffin of good taste" ("Get That"). If "Fly Me to New York" is indeed the final nail in a nation-sized coffin, one wonders what other spikes found their way into the woodwork (perhaps Toby Keith's "Courtesy of the Red, White and Blue [The Angry American]" and its ever so delicate expression of wounded aggression or, perhaps, the "War on Terror"?).

If nothing is indeed sacred, or if nothing remains sacred for all that long, then that conclusion can only be the result of a probing, a calculated sounding of the event that looks for its flaws, detects its deficiencies as an efficient way of constructing counternarrativities, a seemingly offensive act that reveals both the offenses that motivate the pseudo-victimization of the event and the doubly offensive response that follows. Dahlen identifies Cassetteboy's particular sonography, a fluid-facilitated ultrasounding of the event that generates scarce conclusions and more numerous questions: "Cassetteboy found our weak spot—that we consider 9/11 untouchable … In the US, 9/11 is sacred. To much of the world, it isn't. Are we ready to criticize, or even satirize it? If we censor ourselves, how can we even talk about it?" ("Pop"). This demonstrates the proclivity to accepted narrativity that follows the event, a national blinkering (or rather deafening) in the wake of the shock, a hearing loss that results in a ringing, the call to rally round the flag that can only flag over time, as well as drawing attention to the national distantiation that may grant the Brits in Cassetteboy a different, less sentimental/romantic/Sinatran perspective than that held in the US (though "Di and Dodi Do Die" suggests otherwise). Therefore, seeming offense is less offensive to nebulous criteria like taste than to the according of sacred-cow status, calling instead for a knives-out scenario where the aural cut serves to sever the aura around the event, while also speaking its own language.

That "Fly Me to New York" may be considered offensive is an unavoidable conclusion, at least if one is willing to accept the terms of discourse essential to typical analyses of taste; that said, its purported offense is more aptly filed under "offensive, going on the," a card played also by the US in its actions prior to and in the wake of the event. In his or her review of *The Parker Tapes*, *Everything2* discussion board participant Hazelnut asserts that "Fly Me to New York" "is supremely offensive and thus a must have," placing the offense and the offensive at the heart of Cassetteboy's methodology and the value of its work. Likewise, it is the offensive –gone on, taken to, and exercised against the Muslim world – that characterizes the US pre- and post-event.[1] At least when Cassetteboy makes/takes offense, it is only the class of 1997/98 (Di dying in August of the former, Sinatra in May of the latter) who die, or who are already dead, if slightly turned in their graves; the same is not true for the US make and take, underlining the centrality of offense to its methodology.

Cassetteboy's choice to resort to offense, to resort to the samples it draws from Sinatra and elsewhere, permits an evasion of accepted narrativity, such that the anthracite humor of "Fly Me to New York," a black coal-escence (or coal essence), may be aptly construed as being a protest song within the new genre of rubble music.[2] In his entry on the song, included as part of *The Stylus Magazine*'s "Non-Definitive Guide to the Pop Protest Song" (2003), Todd Burns states, "With the aid of sampling technology, Cassetteboy does something here that nearly no artist has been able to do with a guitar and voice in the past year—convey the terror, the hurt, the disorientation caused by the September 11th attacks—and disconnect the jingoistic sentiments that commonly go along with them." The focus on sampling technology reinforces the neo-narrative potentiality contained within the sampler, while also conveying the depth of emotion that may be captured through the seemingly simple recombinant recontextualization of samples. Burns finds Cassetteboy to be exceptional, though not for their supposed offensiveness (exceptionalism being more fittingly assigned to the US pre- and post-event due to its mythic victimhood narrativity); rather, its exceptionality is rooted in the act of disconnection that results from the connection of samples.

Placing a song like "Fly Me to New York" within the pantheon of protest songs, alongside such venerable institutions as Bob Dylan (whose "Masters of War" and "Blowin' in the Wind" make the *Stylus* list), Bruce Springsteen ("Born in the USA"), and Creedence Clearwater Revival ("Fortunate Son"), seems nearly impossible: how could a song that openly mocks a national tragedy by editing the voice of a national treasure register as anything other than a crass utterance of the "too soon" maxim at best, a treasonous act of amateurs only possible in the extra-national space of Britain at worst? This difficulty may be resolved by looking at the narrative positionality of each of the songwriters in question, an exteriority that places the narrator in clear opposition to accepted narrativities, instead offering a distanced perspective much like that found in "Fly Me to New York." As Dylan

---

[1]   A number of offenses may be noted here: the desertion of Afghan proxy forces after the expulsion of the Soviets from Afghanistan in the 1980s, the exclusion of *mujahid* volunteers and the continued stationing of US troops near the holy sites of Mecca and Medina in Saudi Arabia, the perpetual favoring of the Israeli side of the Israel-Palestine conflict, or the invasion of two nations and subsequent problematic detentions in Afghanistan, Iraq, CIA black sites, and Guantanamo Bay.

[2]   The choice of *anthracite* for this comparison reflects the relevance of one of its other names, "blind coal," a deviation from the visual that resonates with the primacy of sound as opposed to the blinkered mono-narrativity of the accepted US victimhood narrative that surrounds 9/11.

provides meditations on the turbulence coming from the burgeoning civil rights and anti-war movements prior to and during Vietnam, as CCR casts a critical eye on the prospect of serving there, as Springsteen ventriloquizes an amalgamated vet to portray the actual experience of those who served upon their return, so too do Cassetteboy step outside of the event by stepping into it, claiming the unoccupied shoes of the pilot-hijacker, left empty in the course of the devotional act/event, and filling those shoes by narrating a critical reading of the event. Sampling's necessary decontextualization of the citation (though not a complete divorce, with the sample subjected to shared custody by its originary progenitor and its recontextualizing projector) creates an auto-externality, an auto-critical positionality that grants a new perspective as a matter of course, though it matters, of course, who renders that new narrative.

Rock and Role: Cementing Rubble Music

The citational act of recontextualization/reassembly/renarrativization is necessarily premised on the presence of fragments, be they the samples extracted from various originary loci or the crumbled remains of the collapsed World Trade Center towers, a rumble that emerges from the rubble into a rubble music, a spectral speech rising from the ashes, redoubling the phoenix of the ignored memo to memorialize the event, though not in accordance with accepted narrativity.[3] This rubble music critiques reflexively, reconstituting the shattered fragments of a national psyche in the wake of a traumatic event, in this case 9/11, and filling the void of anti-critique with an ante-critique. Such a music locates the detritus of past conceptualizations, those thrown off in the violence of the event, devising new arrangements bent on not so much a reconstruction, but a re-construction, a new constitution, a sidelong amble that diverges from the arrangements of origin, filling the ruptures and fissures with a new mortar, lobbed o'er the ramparts with a mind to shattering previous conceptions, and providing a critical construction that demonstrates the contrary, the dissonant, which has existed all along.

A listing for *The Parker Tapes* on retail music website *Forced Exposure*, one of the few locations that stocks the album, references the site of that speech at the World Trade Center site, "under the wreckage of the twin towers" ("Browse").

---

[3]   The Phoenix Memo is a memorandum sent by FBI agent Kenneth Williams on July 10, 2001 advising further investigation of students at civil aviation schools in the US after behavior at area schools aroused suspicion. The memo's stated purpose was "to advise the Bureau and New York of the possibility of a coordinated effort by USAMA BIN LADEN (UBL) to send students to the United States to attend civil aviation universities and colleges" (Williams). Williams' recommendation was ignored, though the oversight was noted in *The 9/11 Commission Report: Final Report of the National Commission on Terrorist Attacks Upon the United States*, as well as in a whistleblower action by FBI agent Colleen Rowley.

One can imagine a shattered hijacker, the Sinatran narrator whose desire to "turn to ashes," whose "skin is melting away," realized in the carnage of its creation where it comes to rest, returning via the recording to haunt you down among the wreckage. In this case, it is the fragments that speak, the reassembled samples and their ventriloquist, the fragmented pilot-hijacker, flecks of flesh formatting magnetic flecks on the tape, shifting the deeply American Sinatran *bon mot* into its own bon voyage, a leaving never to return that can only return, again and again, in the spectral hijacker voice.

Sinatra's aforementioned linkage to ideas of American nationalism, victory, and postwar affluence is additionally evidenced by his status as recipient of the Presidential Medal of Freedom from Ronald Reagan in 1985 and a Congressional Gold Medal in 1997, honors which underline his centrality to American identity and the significant import of his voice to the critical weight of the rubble music. Such a rubble music establishes a new perspective of self-critique from materials of old that were somewhat deficient on that account, fracturing Sinatran platitudes into their nationally referential components, then recombining them into the narrative of the Sinatran unconscious—everything you always wanted to know about the neo-cons but were afraid to ask Frank.[4] The spectral voice is itself fragmentary, speaking through a tattered voice box, its dispatches patchy at best as they filter through the tons of rubble above, requiring an assembly to signify, an assembled audience to resonate.

The Vinyl Curtain

In extending into the past and future via a separation from temporal limitations, citational sampling, as practiced by Cassetteboy in "Fly Me to New York," expands sound as well, broadening the scope of recognized speech more specifically and aural data more generally, and thereby widening the discursive space to include a music of the spheres, an inaudible audibility present in the rubble and its own music. Speaking of the benefits of certain recording techniques in his *More Brilliant than the Sun: Adventures in Sonic Fiction*, Kodwo Eshun reminds us that "[c]lose-miking expands the field of hearing. Perception blows up and in the ruins, the listener goes travelling, climbs the desolate rubble of headphone consciousness" (112). This field expansion is present in the case of rubble music as well.

As an aural event, 9/11 shorts the circuits, exceeds the limits of perception in a patent failure of imagination, forcing the listener to seek other locales, other auralities where it may find a suitable narrativity that will enable it to reconcile the event, settling finally on the still-settling fragments of the collapsed World Trade Center towers, in the rubble that gives up the spectral voice after giving up its own

---

[4] This neo-narrative is therefore a more relevant version of Slavoj Žižek's *Everything You Always Wanted to Know About Lacan (But Were Afraid to Ask Hitchcock)*, a shift from the psychoanalytic/filmic pairing to a more psychotic/phlegmatic one.

structural integrity. Headphone consciousness, the exclusionary privileging of the aural above other senses, narrows this search, letting the spectral hijacker's voice ring true as it sounds the disintegration, the citationality of sampling manufacturing a structurally sound neo-narrativity whose ribs may be visible in the retained fissures, but who promises to have a longer lifespan than the aluminum cladding of the departed towers. "Fly Me to New York" therefore speaks through the rubble, for the rubble, after its commission but during the mission, making the spectral hijacker voice and its hijacker always already present through the present-tense narrativity.

Works Cited

"Browse by Artist: CASSETTEBOY." *Forced Exposure*. Web. June 1, 2009.

Burns, Todd. "The Pop Protest Song: The *Stylus Magazine* Non-Definitive Guide." *Stylus Magazine*. Oct. 31, 2007. Web. June 1, 2009.

Cassetteboy. "Di and Dodi Do Die." *MySpace*. Aug. 29, 2007. Web. June 1, 2009.

——. "Fly Me to New York." *The Parker Tapes*. Barry's Bootlegs, 2002. CD.

Dahlen, Chris. "Cassetteboy: *The Parker Tapes*." *Pitchfork*. Dec. 5, 2002. Web. June 1, 2009.

——. "Get That Out of Your Mouth #15: Negativland and Cassetteboy Steal Music." *Pitchfork*. June 23, 2005. Web. June 1, 2009.

——. "The Pop Culture of 9/11." *Pitchfork*. Mar. 28, 2005. Web. June 1, 2009.

Eshun, Kodwo. *More Brilliant Than the Sun: Adventures in Sonic Fiction*. London: Quartet Books, 1998. Print.

Hazelnut. "Cassetteboy." *Everything2*. May 13, 2006. Web. June 1, 2009.

Nelson, John. "Cassetteboy." *Some Assembly Required: Tape Manipulations, Digital Deconstructions and Turntable Creations*. Nov. 15, 2008. Web. June 1, 2009.

Sinatra, Frank. *The Complete Reprise Studio Recordings*. Warner Brothers, 1995. CD.

Williams, Kenneth. "The Phoenix Memo." *The Memory Hole*. July 25, 2003. Web. June 10, 2009.

Wishnia, Steven. "Bad Transmission: Clear Channel's Hit List." *Lip Magazine*. Oct. 24, 2001. Web. June 9, 2009.

Žižek, Slavoj. *Everything You Always Wanted to Know About Lacan (But Were Afraid to Ask Hitchcock)*. 2nd ed. New York: Verso, 2010. Print.

Chapter 6
Terrorism and the Politics of Improvisation[1]
Rob Wallace

High-strung, like a violin string, [the oppressed] weep and moan for life, so relentless, so cruel, so terribly inhuman. In a desperate moment the string breaks. Untuned ears hear nothing but discord. But those who feel the agonized cry understand its harmony; they hear in it the fulfillment of the most compelling moment of human nature.

Emma Goldman "The Psychology of Political Violence"

Beyond the world of improvised music-making in jazz and other genres, the term "improvised" has been used frequently since 2001 in a surprising place: in reference to Improvised Explosive Devices, or IEDs. If improvisation is not solely the domain of jazz musicians or other artists and can just as easily be used in discourse about violence, how are these two realms of improvisational practice related beyond the level of semantics? The following chapter meditates on that question, and investigates why the term improvised—rather than "homemade" or "amateur," for example—has been used in a military context. Ultimately, I argue that the appearance of the word "improvisation" in descriptions of the events of 9/11 and after is only the most recent variation on an underlying theme. Improvisation—largely due to its connection with African American cultural practices such as jazz—has historically been perceived in the West as a suspicious activity.

Improvisation at Ground Zero

A few days after September 11, 2001, German composer Karlheinz Stockhausen infamously declared that the terrorists who destroyed the World Trade Center had created "the greatest work of art that is possible in the whole cosmos"—something that Stockhausen denied he (and, by implication, anyone else) could do with

---

[1]   The seeds of this project were presented as a paper at the 2009 Improvisation, Community, and Social Practice (ICASP) conference in Montreal, "Lex Non Scripta, Ars Non Scripta." A video of the entire panel is available at www.improvcommunity.ca/research/panel-conflict-justice-and-improvisation. This chapter is in some ways a companion to my piece "Kick out the Jazz!" from the forthcoming volume, co-edited by myself and Ajay Heble, entitled *People Get Ready: The Future of Jazz is Now!* (Duke University Press).

his music (quoted in Lentricchia and McAuliffe 6).[2] Many commentators have explored what Stockhausen might have meant by his statements. Frank Lentricchia and Jody McAuliffe, for example, link Stockhausen's seemingly ridiculous claim to a long succession of artists who have viewed the creative process as a site of potential revolution and even violence (5–17). Stockhausen thus follows in a lineage of musicians who have placed a mystical and transformative power at the heart of their musical practice.

Stockhausen, along with mid-twentieth-century (white) composers such as Earl Browne and, arguably, John Cage (despite his own pejorative statements on improvisation), bucked the long-standing trend in Western art music by opening some of his pieces up to improvisation. He admired and was admired by many musicians outside the world of European art music, including Miles Davis and Sun Ra, whom he once noted was capable of "first-class avant-garde experimental music that you can't put in any box. It was incredibly asymmetric!" (quoted in Toop 27). Anthony Pay, a clarinetist who worked extensively with Stockhausen, has noted that the composer would "say to us that perhaps we should try and prepare ourselves for each performance by thinking of something that we hadn't ever done before. That after each performance we could prepare ourselves in a mental way for the next performance by thinking of something new" (quoted in Bailey 73). But the men who destroyed the World Trade Center only had a chance for one unique and completely novel performance; Stockhausen seemed particularly impressed that such "artists" could "practice like crazy for ten years, totally fanatically for a concert, and then die" (quoted in Lentricchia and McAuliffe 6).

The September 11th terrorist attacks provoked confusion precisely because they were, from a conventional viewpoint, improvisational. Rather than the efforts of an expensive, well-armed military, the spectacle of violence on 9/11 was caused by a handful of men using utility knives and fanaticism to make airplanes into missiles. It soon became clear that the attacks, "improvisational" or not, were obviously the result of careful planning, not to mention financial expense. Yet to an audient like Stockhausen, not accustomed to experiencing the "asymmetric" music of Sun Ra or the guerilla tactics of al Qaeda, such a horrifying improvisation seemed all the more mysterious and unique. This is assuredly not to say that Sun Ra's music is the same as, or is motivated by the same impulses as, terrorism—or, for that matter, that terrorism is art (a common misconception of Stockhausen's statements). Rather, improvisation, whether it comes in the form of terrorism or music, seems to have the potential to surprise and shock. In music, this effect can lead to aesthetic pleasure, whereas in an act of terror it can lead to unprecedented forms of killing.

The authors of the US Government's official public record of the September 11th attacks also explicitly saw improvisation on 9/11, but from a very different

---

2   I quote here from the English translation of Stockhausen's comments which music critic Anthony Tommasini used to excoriate Stockhausen. The original German version of Stockhausen's interview is accessible at www.stockhausen.org/hamburg.pdf.

perspective. The first chapter of *The 9/11 Commission Report* includes a section subtitled "Improvising a Homeland Defense," wherein we learn that "the defense of US airspace on 9/11 was not conducted in accord with pre-existing training and protocols. It was improvised by civilians who had never handled a hijacked aircraft that attempted to disappear" (31, emphasis added). And while the civilians in question are not explicitly blamed for their ignorance in dealing with the hijackers, the connotation of "improvisation" here contrasts with the spirit of artistic innovation that Stockhausen saw in the terrorist attacks. The response to the hijackings, we discover, was a failure at multiple levels, therefore necessitating improvisation as a last course of action rather than a creative and appealing approach to saving lives. The terrorists "broke the rules," so to speak, whereas government and civilian officials responding to the attacks tried to stick to rules which were not designed to facilitate improvisation. These officials, claims the 9/11 Commission Report, "struggled, under difficult circumstances, to improvise a homeland defense against an unprecedented challenge they had never before encountered and had never trained to meet" (45). Such ambivalent views of improvisation are, as we shall see, commonplace throughout the history of the term's use.

Fear of a Jazz Planet

The word "improvisation," like "jazz," has had a dubious history. Like—and because of its connections to—jazz, improvisation has been alternately lauded and damned for its supposedly unplanned and thus irrational, unscientific, primitive, and suspiciously "ethnic" origins. As Daniel Fischlin and Ajay Heble have documented, some of the earliest dictionary definitions of improvisation link the word to a form of "ethnic othering in which the consistent association between improvisatory discourse and Latin/Mediterranean cultures are implicitly opposed to Anglo-Saxon culture" (16). For example, peeking into the Oxford English Dictionary we find an early usage of improvisation cited in the phrase "Poor Tuscan-like improvisation"—perhaps a reference to the itinerant Italian improvisatore who, as Philip Pastras has noted, functioned as a foil to the craftsmanship of "respectable" poets throughout the eighteenth and nineteenth centuries (Pastras 9; Wallace 9–11).

Yet improvisation, in music or in any other aspect of life, is not necessarily a positive or negative action. It is simply something we do every day; we practice improvisation as we live. Every situation that we encounter, no matter how familiar it may appear, is a new experience that we learn to adapt to. Improvised music such as jazz merely foregrounds the practice of improvising, making it a principle aesthetic element. The connection between ethics and morality in terms of musical improvisation, however, becomes more relevant in relation to the history of improvised music in the Americas. More than an aesthetic preference, improvisation was often a necessity.

The African Americans who developed the musical forms of jazz and other music drawing on improvisational practice used the only options they had been given. Denied access to legal and political agency, music, poetry, story-telling, and other creative pursuits became for slaves a primary means of spiritual and political survival, in addition to the benefit of entertainment and enjoyment provided by art. The music traditions stemming from slavery are thus more than entertainment—more than art. But this artistic surplus was not the same as a Romantic transcendence of culture. Slave artists and their descendents in the segregated Americas were not Shelley's "unacknowledged legislators." They weren't even acknowledged as people for much of their history in the West, and thus they had to create modes of legislation outside of the rationality that the Western Enlightenment provided, creating what Paul Gilroy in *The Black Atlantic* dubs a "counter-culture to modernity" (16).

Nevertheless, the connections between Romantic transcendence and power envisioned in artistic practice remain tied to (mis)understandings of jazz and other improvised music. And hence Stockhausen missed the point—if he was looking for art that changed the world, he needed look and hear no further than the deep wellspring of music originating in African American culture and now proliferating around the globe. The suffering of slavery—the psychological and physical violence of capitalism transmuted into music like jazz or blues. Such transformations should give us pause when we discount the "real-life effect" that art can have on the world. That one of the legacies of slavery could be a cultural matrix so powerful that it would influence almost every society in the world is surely a testament to the social power of art. Artistic endeavors that undeniably helped slaves survive, or at the very least allowed them to feel more human than their masters would warrant, inevitably will be attractive to anyone who wants art to matter in the world.

Thus it follows that jazz history is rife with musicians and critics alike stressing an explicitly political value in the music, for good or ill. The creators of jazz, primarily African Americans from the southern United States, were themselves held responsible for the positive and negative effects that the improvised art form was thought to embody. When the effects were perceived as negative, the line between racism and music censorship blurred, and the resistance to explicitly improvised art became a part of the denial of human rights for a significant group of American citizens. Even white musicians, such as the Original Dixieland Jazz Band's Nick LaRocca, were proclaiming the potentially chaotic effects of jazz just as it was beginning to gain mainstream exposure. In a 1919 interview, LaRocca declared that "jazz ... is a revolution ... I even go as far to confess we are musical anarchists" (quoted in Parsonage 135). At a time when actual anarchists were committing acts of violence, LaRocca's hyperbole would nevertheless have sounded provocative. In 1920, for example, just after the Original Dixieland Jazz Band first toured outside North America with their "revolutionary" music, an Italian anarchist named Mario Buda bombed Wall Street in what one military-industrial complex company calls the "first major improvised explosive device incident in the USA." Thus, at the start of the Jazz Age, almost a hundred years before the 9/11 attacks, anarchic terror erupted in lower Manhattan.

Whether jazz was actually "anarchic" or not, the perceived threat of African American equality via artistic creation was met by more than just fear of or annoyance at the latest dance craze: lynching, legally sanctioned segregation, and psychological, physical, and political oppression, among other horrors. Such antipathy is echoed more recently in the Tea Party's fear of a black president. Improvised, provisional music and improvised, provisional politics: "community organizing," or the anarchic, minority proletariat taking control? Jazz improvisation, then, was as potentially anarchic as a bomb in the crowd. United against the ruling whites, dark hordes of improvising musicians and their fans might turn into an actual army, improvising politics and violence to bring about a real revolution.

Jazz or Jihad?

Sayyid Qutb, one of the most influential twentieth-century theorists of the Wahhabi Islam advocated by al Qaeda and other Islamist terrorist sects, was himself no fan of jazz. In an account of his visit to the United States in the late 1940s, Qutb claimed that jazz was "a type of music invented by Blacks to please their primitive tendencies and desire for noise" (quoted in Gray 24). While Qutb critiqued American culture from the perspective of a devout Muslim following a strict interpretation of the Qu'ran, his dismissal of jazz as a primitive impulse of African Americans was not far from the already long-standing hostility facing jazz and jazz musicians in the United States.

Ironically, the same racialized and racist rhetoric that has surrounded jazz throughout its history can also be found in the discourse responding to terrorism, which curiously leads us back to Improvised Explosive Devices. If the Arab-Egyptian Qutb heard jazz from the same perspective as many racist Anglo-Saxons, the mainly white and Western empires of the twentieth century often approached their enemies with similar race-and-culture-based fear. Here the worlds of improvised music and Improvised Explosive Devices collide against the backdrop of both real and imagined threats to civilization—real in the form of undeniable carnage that often kills indiscriminately; imagined in that the history of discrimination promoted implicitly and explicitly by those faced with IEDs (Western armies, for example) labels the improvised and provisional as a primitive throwback that must be destroyed. If the bombs are dangerous, then the bomb-making people and their cultures, broadly conceived, are dangerous, too.

Like the improvised music of the Americas, the history of Improvised Explosive Devices reveals a metaphorical and real battlefield of complex and contradictory racial and ethnic struggle. And, like "jazz," it is difficult to find the precise origins of the IED acronym, but it certainly predates the present conflicts in Iraq and Afghanistan. As of this writing, I have not found any precise date of origin or a specific person responsible for creating the term. Eydie Herrera,

Executive Assistant to the Center for Asymmetric Warfare Naval Postgraduate School, informed me that "the term was used as early as the 1945 when a Captain Metress was killed while dismantling a Japanese IED. However, there is no mention of where the term came from ... It could have possibl[y] come from the UK based on the British Bomb Disposal experience." Ms. Herrera's suspicions are confirmed by at least one source which I will discuss later, Lt.-Col. James Styles' account of British Explosive Ordnance Disposal (EOD) teams, dating back to the late-1940s. Regardless of who coined the term, it almost certainly originated from the perspective of a formal, organized military, facing a surprisingly adaptable opponent.

The US military and NATO definition given here occurs in print at least as early as 1988, and states that IEDs are "those devices placed or fabricated in an improvised manner incorporating destructive, lethal, noxious, pyrotechnic, or incendiary chemicals, designed to destroy, disfigure, incapacitate, distract or harass. They may incorporate military stores, but are normally devised from nonmilitary components" (Joint Chiefs of Staff 178). The kinds of IEDs commonly used in Iraq and Afghanistan are either roadside bombs detonated remotely or by timers, or car bombs acting as modern incarnations of what Mike Davis calls "Buda's Wagon" (the horse-drawn cart that anarchist Mario Buda used back in 1920 to blow up Wall Street). A particularly confusing and terrifying feature of modern IEDs is that they can both be detonated by innocuous objects (cell phones, for example), and they can themselves take the form of innocuous objects.

Still a principle ingredient of bombs, plastic explosives (PE) are almost limitless in their malleability; the bomb becomes a creative object. From World War II accounts of resistance fighters accidentally eating the explosives, "mistaking it for chocolate in the dark," to more recent devices made from cassette decks and cell phones, improvised bombs display a high degree of ingenuity and adaptability (Foot 56). Chris Soghoian notes that German saboteurs in World War II actually did make "chocolate-bar bombs" to intentionally fool victims. He also catalogues two kinds of IEDs—improvised explosive devices and improvised electronic devices, which have been the subject of controversy recently due to US Homeland Security's crackdown on all items deemed "suspicious." These have included, among other objects, home-made electronic musical instruments. In the shadow of 9/11, it seems that creativity in the form of any homemade electronic gadgets is a potential threat. All IEDs are bad IEDs.

Anarchist theorist Mikhail Bakunin once stated that "the passion for destruction is also a creative passion," and it is this mixture of creation and destruction that draws both admiration and fear from those facing IEDs of the destructive variety (quoted in Gray 21). Irish historian A. R. Oppenheimer's recent book tracing the Irish Republican Army's use of explosives notes that "the IRA's 'engineers' achieved the highest level of ingenuity and inventiveness with their IEDs ... To this day, the IRA remains the world's most advanced builders of IEDs and its talent in making bombs has sadly influenced other terrorist groups" (8). One of the British EOD operatives assigned to deal with the IRA's "creative destruction" was Lieutenant

Colonel James Styles, whose career as an EOD expert began during the Burmese insurgency of the 1940s and 50s. His gripping memoir, *Bombs Have No Pity: My War Against Terrorism*, provides an insider account on an earlier era of IED-driven fear. Behind his steely determination and bravery in the face of terrorism, however, Styles sometimes resorts to rhetoric aligning his Irish adversaries with the uncivilized, treacherous stereotype that has plagued Irish-English relations for centuries. In a passage where he describes a failed bomb attack, for example, Styles wonders: "Did they pick the unconnected pipe deliberately as a warning of their potential? Or was it Murphy's Law in operation, the 'Mick factor'?" (83). The Irish terrorist—and by extension, all "Micks"—remains essentialized and essentially unknowable; a paradox of cunning and stupidity caused by ethnic inferiority. Oppenheimer's account of the IRA's bombing campaigns notes that:

> In a television news bulletin in July 2006 on the ongoing and increasingly bloody insurgency in Iraq, the term 'IED'—Improvised Explosive Device—was said to be a new one that we would all have to get used to. The IED is hardly new, having been introduced in the Second World War to describe devices used by anti-Nazi resistance groups, and then gaining regular coinage in the late 1960s and early 1970s when the Provisional IRA bombing campaign took off in earnest. Indeed, so closely connected with the IRA campaign were IEDs that you could be forgiven for calling them Irish Explosive Devices. (7–8)

As Oppenheimer points out in this passage, "IED" permeated the global English-speaking vernacular in the early twenty-first century, but the term itself dates back to at least the mid-twentieth century, at a time when IEDs were connected in the English public's imagination with an ethnically distinct adversary—the Irish. Improvisation linked to jazz by this point had already been closely monitored as a potential threat from African Americans—a black magic blown up from trumpets and drums. And, for at almost half a century, "improvisation" linked with bombs has denoted the threat of a dark terrorist.

Improvising against Improvisation

Like every community, the military has developed its own terminology to describe the world and to allow its insiders to communicate with one another in shorthand. We might even conclude that the standard shortening of Improvised Explosive Device to IED takes out the potential negative associations of the word "improvised" since we don't actually hear or see the word. Yet it is significant that the original formulation uses "improvisation" and not "homemade" or "non-military," "non-standard": HED or HMED would be convenient acronyms, for example. So why "improvised"? One recent blogger, whose blog title derives from the Talking Heads song "Life During Wartime," notes that there should be "[n]o mincing words about it. A bomb is a bomb whether here or there. Calling it an

IED masks its meaning, much as collateral damage does for civilian deaths. No, we aren't being bombed to pieces in Iraq. Yes, there are some IED casualties. Doesn't that sound better? (Citizen X). The military euphemism thus belies at least three interrelated ideas: IED takes the bang out of the bomb and turns the always changing, dangerous devices into a technical problem; IED makes the actual bloody events less real and, again, more technical and academic; but, perhaps most importantly, IED bears the definition of improvisation, which dominant cultures have typically used to describe their enemies, who coincidentally or not usually happen to be ethnically distinct—whether they be the blacks in the United States, the Irish in the United Kingdom, or Arabs and South Asians throughout the Middle East and Afghanistan.

Thus, even the actions of "friendlies," the laudable improvisers, so to speak, become uncanny and perplexing. Journalist Peter Maass, detailing the attempts by the US military to retrain Iraqi army units, notes:

> The American way of combat is heavily planned, with satellite maps, G.P.S. coordinates and reconnaissance drones. The Iraqi way is improvisational, relying less on honed skills and high-tech than gut instinct and (literally) bare knuckles. It is the Americans who are learning to adapt. In briefings that American soldiers receive, a quotation from T.E. Lawrence is sometimes included: "Better the Arabs do it tolerably than that you do it perfectly." (46)

The resultant struggle is learning to tolerate what has been intolerable, letting go of perfection in favor of potential failure, risk, or death. There is even a common US military slogan: "adapt, improvise, overcome."[3] US soldiers have had to constantly follow the slogan during the recent wars, especially when faced with Donald Rumsfeld's initial philosophy of "going to war with the army you have" (rather than equipping them and training them properly)— "doing it tolerably" when your own government won't.

And thus, the paradox of contemporary combat: how does an army trying to follow rules improvise against an enemy who can constantly change the rules? Or, as an article on the struggle against IEDs in Iraq puts it:

> How do you defeat a foe who can destroy million-dollar machines with devices that can be built off the Internet for about the cost of a pizza ... America is still the world's greatest superpower, and the US military's capacity to take out a moving vehicle piloted from half the world away should still provoke a little shock and awe. But the IED—cheap, easy to make and adapt, and deadly—has in its own way proved equally powerful. (Thomas and Barry 28)

---

3   The myriad ways in which soldiers have followed this motto is detailed by Iraq war Veteran and author Paul Rieckhoff in *Chasing Ghosts*.

The United States government has claimed that it is promoting democracy in Iraq and Afghanistan. Mainstream jazz critics and musicians have claimed that jazz is a kind of American democracy in musical form (in fact, the US government had already made this latter claim during the Cold War). America's simultaneous desire for and fear of improvisation, borne out on the bandstand and the battlefield, demonstrates that incorporating improvisation into the democratic process is a challenge at the heart of the American psyche yet to be accomplished.

Conclusion: Sonic Warfare

Musicians are often just as ready to say that their music has no political meaning or force as they are to boast of its revolutionary powers. An important reason for such ambivalence is that musicians usually don't want any one person—even themselves, at a particular moment in time that they might later come to regret— to place a strict interpretation on their sounds. But claiming that there is political significance to a piece of music, even political force and agency, is different from claiming that there is a direct correlation between what happens when performing or listening to music and what people do during "actual" political organizing (and what people do as a result of listening to or performing music). Music is always more than just sound, yet we sometimes forget the very physical nature of sound itself. If music cannot create some kind of universal response in humans, then it can nevertheless have a physical effect on people. Sound is vibration, and humans have historically regarded music as a mystical area of vibration, harnessing the various culturally specific traits of musical systems to the inherent physical properties of sound. Making and listening to music is a physical act. Music very literally makes things happen—it causes vibrations in the air which travel around and into our bodies. And, as composer R. Murray Schafer quips, our "sense of hearing cannot be closed off at will. There are no earlids" (Schafer 11).

During the creation of be-bop in the 1940s, jazz drummers developed a fluency on the bass drum that departed from the standard "four-on-the-floor" pattern— that is, constant quarter notes in $\frac{4}{4}$ time—so common to swing music. While they maintained steady time, they also began to punctuate the tempo with loud, vigorous accents on the bass drum, a technique that became known as "dropping bombs" (see Berliner 326–7). At the height of World War II, drummers began to command greater esteem as they bombed their way into the heart of the melodic and harmonic activity of the band. Percussionist and author James Blades even suggests that the instruments which would take millennia to develop into the modern drumset were themselves weapons, if not bombs. "Percussion—the act of striking," writes Blades, "was an art in which primitive man was well skilled. He survived in every sense by the dexterity of his blow; from which it is fair to assume that the first instruments to augment the hand clap and stamp of the foot may have been the implements or weapons upon which he relied for food or survival" (35).

But sound itself is also a real weapon. As debates surrounding torture administered by the US military and intelligence agencies have increased in the decade since 2001, accounts of the use of music in interrogation and battlefield settings have been widely circulated. In 2007, for example, The Society for Ethnomusicology issued a statement against the use of music as torture.[4] However, sonic warfare as a theory and practice goes beyond playing Metallica at high volume (something which many people, Iraqis included, find enjoyable). As Colonel John B. Alexander notes in his book *Future War*: "The best known use of acoustic weapons dates to the time of Joshua and the battle for the seemingly impenetrable walled city of Jericho … The cause of the structural failure of the stone walls has long been debated. [One] interpretation suggests that the acoustic vibrations set up by the rams' horns actually weakened the internal structure of the walls" (95). Alexander goes on to describe how this biblical incident is merely one of many examples of acoustic warfare. He cites the use of loud rock music by the military as more of a "poorly designed psychological [operation]" than a true acoustic weapon (96). More interesting and potentially effective, he claims, are "three levels of acoustic frequencies that might be applied as weapons: infrasound, audible sound, and ultrasound" (97). Of these three frequency ranges, the infrasound, or low-level frequencies, seems to have the most promise as a weapon in Alexander's analysis: "At low frequencies, it is possible to cause internal vibrations that generate a number of effects, depending on the frequency and power levels employed. The effects cannot be overcome through hearing protection, personal perseverance, or being impervious to pain" (98). While Alexander disputes some wilder, more violent effects claimed by previous acoustic warfare research (the subtitle of *Future War*, after all, states that non-lethal weapons are the book's subject), the implications of sonic weapons are chilling to anyone who believes in the positive power of sound.

To my knowledge, jazz has never been used as a sonic weapon or music of torture by the US (or any other) military. However, at least one jazz musician has been arrested as a terrorist—a relatively unknown bassist named Tarik Shah. Interestingly, despite his connection with musicians like Pharaoh Sanders who are associated with arguably the most politicized era of jazz—the "avant-garde" or "New Thing", beginning in the mid-1960s—Shah has not explicitly claimed that his music is political; in fact, he has stated that being a jazz musician was the perfect cover for his goals as a *jihadi*. Shah never committed any violent act; he was arrested and convicted for conspiring to give "material support and resources" to al Qaeda.[5] As a practicing Muslim, Shah follows in a long tradition of black jazz musicians who converted to Islam, took Muslim names, and/or were influenced by Islamic philosophy and theology, including Randy Weston, Art Blakey, and

---

[4]   This statement can be found online at the following website:http://webdb.iu.edu/ sem/scripts/aboutus /aboutsem/positionstatements/position_statement_torture.cfm.

[5]   For more on the controversial nature of Shah's comments as well as the government's case against him, see Feuer, as well as jazz critic Howard Mandel's coverage of the case.

Dizzy Gillespie, for example. But putting the ideas of Islamic fundamentalism into practice, for Shah at least, seems to be fundamentally antithetical to the improvised music which sustained so many musicians throughout the twentieth century. Perhaps Sayyid Qutb was correct in suspecting that jazz and *jihadis* don't mix well.

Improvising in politics, music, and war is potentially dangerous, albeit in different ways. As improvising musician Bob Ostertag argues, "When organizing clandestine resistance to a brutal regime, the consequences of making mistakes are life-and-death matters. In music, the consequences of making mistakes are nonexistent" (63). At worst, then, improvising poorly in music can lead to relatively inconsequential embarrassment or boredom. But the particular discipline of improvisation can also be the foundation of a meaningful experience for both listener and performer.

And here, in closing, we might return to Stockhausen, and to the city of 9/11's Ground Zero. Stockhausen once noted that:

> Anyone living today … is confronted daily with the hurtling together of all races, all religions, all philosophies, all ways of life … New York, the prime blueprint for a world society, is without question an indispensable experience for the contemporary artist. Ideas one might have about possible integration, about a coherent unification, or about possible syntheses of the influences issuing from all parts of the globe, all these must be tested against living experience if they are to lay claim to any truth. (quoted in Woerner 139)

Ironically, Stockhausen, writing here over thirty years before the 9/11 attacks, portrays the city most associated with those attacks as a prime space for improvisation—in life and in art, a city where, as William James remarked in 1907, near the beginnings of jazz, "the great pulses and bounds of progress … give a kind of drumming background of life" (quoted in Douglas 118). Guns or butter? Perhaps the choice is actually between bombs and drums, learning to improvise against violence, rather than with violence. Art would be meaningless if it did not move us—and music moves us, quite literally, whether it is "political" or not. We can let it explode randomly, like a bomb in the crowd, or we can try to understand its contours as we feel it moving through bodies and history.

Works Cited

The 9/11 Commission Report: Final Report of the National Commission on Terrorist Attacks Upon the United States. New York: W. W. Norton and Co., 2004. Print.

Alexander, Colonel John B. *Future War: Non-Lethal Weapons in Twenty-First-Century Warfare*. New York: St. Martin's Press, 1999. Print.

Bailey, Derek. *Improvisation: Its Nature and Practice in Music*. New York: Da Capo, 1992. Print.

Berliner, Paul F. *Thinking in Jazz: The Infinite Art of Improvisation*. Chicago, IL: University of Chicago, 1994. Print.

Blades, James. *Percussion Instruments and Their History*. New York: Frederick A. Praeger Publishers, 1970. Print.

Citizen X. "Improvised Explosive Device." *Life During War: Ordinary Life In Extraordinary Times*, Aug. 12, 2008. Web. Oct. 14, 2010.

Davis, Mike. *Buda's Wagon: A Brief History of the Car Bomb*. New York: Verso, 2007. Print.

Douglas, Ann. *Terrible Honesty: Mongrel Manhattan in the 1920s*. New York: Picador, 1995. Print.

Feuer, Alan. "Bronx Man Pleads Guilty in Terror Case." *New York Times*. April 5, 2007. Web. Oct. 15, 2010.

Fischlin, Daniel and Ajay Heble, eds. *The Other Side of Nowhere: Jazz, Improvisation, and Communities in Dialogue*. Middletown, CT: Wesleyan UP, 2004. Print.

Foot, M. R. D. *SOE In France: An Account of the Work of the British Special Operations Executive in France, 1940–1944*. London: Her Majesty's Stationery Office, 1966. Print.

Gilroy, Paul. *The Black Atlantic: Modernity and Double Consciousness*. Cambridge, MA: Harvard UP, 1993. Print.

Goldman, Emma. "The Psychology of Political Violenc." *Anarchism and Other Essays*. New York: Mother Earth, 2010. 85–114. Print.

Gray, John. *Al Qaeda and What It Means to Be Modern*. New York: The New Press, 2003. Print.

Herrera, Eydie. Message to the author. Nov. 17, 2009. E-mail.

Joint Chiefs of Staff of the United States Armed Forces. *The Official Dictionary of Military Terms*. Cambridge, MA: Hemisphere Publishing Corporation, 1988. Print.

Lentricchia, Frank, and Jody McAuliffe. *Crimes of Art and Terror*. Chicago: University of Chicago, 2003. Print.

Maass, Peter. "The Way of the Commandos." *The New York Times Magazine*. May 1, 2005. Web. Oct. 14, 2010.

Mandel, Howard. "Tarik Shah Update." *All About Jazz*. Jan. 8, 2006. Web. Jul. 7, 2011.

Oppenheimer, A.R. *IRA, the Bombs and the Bullets: A History of Deadly Ingenuity.* Portland, OR: Irish Academic Press, 2009. Print.

Ostertag, Bob. *Creative Life: Music Politics People and Machines.* Urbana, IL: U of Illinois, 2009. Print.

Parsonage, Catherine. *The Evolution of Jazz in Britain, 1880–1935.* Aldershot, Ashgate, 2005. Print.

Pastras, Philip James. *A Clear Field: The Idea of Improvisation in Modern Poetry.* Dissertation, Graduate School of New Brunswick, Rutgers, State University of New Jersey, 1981. Print.

Rieckhoff, Paul. *Chasing Ghosts: A Soldier's Fight for America from Baghdad to Washington.* New York: NAL Caliber, 2006. Print.

Schafer, R. Murray. *The Soundscape: Our Sonic Environment and the Tuning of the Word.* Rochester, NY: Destiny Books, 1977. Print.

Soghoian, Chris. "Homeland Stupidity: Security Policies that Place the Public at Risk." *CNET News.* Sept. 25, 2007. Web. Oct. 14, 2010.

Styles, Lieutenant Colonel George G. C., as told to Bob Perrin. *Bombs Have No Pity: My War Against Terrorism.* London: William Luscombe, 1975. Print.

Thomas, Evan and John Barry. "A New Way of War." *Newsweek.* Aug. 20–27, 2007: 28–30. Print.

Toop, David. *Ocean of Sound: Aether Talk, Ambient Sound and Imaginary Worlds.* London: Serpent's Tail, 1995. Print.

Wallace, Rob. *Improvisation and the Making of American Literary Modernism.* New York: Continuum, 2010. Print.

Woerner, Karl Heinrich. *Stockhausen: Life and Work.* Trans. Bill Hopkins. Berkeley: U of California P, 1973. Print.

Chapter 7

Nine Inch Nails' *Year Zero* and the Biopolitics of Media Convergence

Katheryn Wright

After the events of September 11, 2001, popular music provided a forum where artists like Nine Inch Nails' Trent Reznor could speak out against changes in American domestic and foreign policy that, arguably, curtailed civil liberties in the name of homeland security. The USA PATRIOT Act, enacted in October 2001, followed by the 2003 invasion of Iraq, represented a renewed domestic interest in securing the United States by any means possible. The PATRIOT Act increased the power of the federal government to search and detain citizens and immigrants indefinitely, under the auspices of protecting American freedom, while the invasion of Iraq was conducted to pre-empt an attack from the country's mythical weapons of mass destruction. This national and political emphasis on homeland security is a contemporary example of biopolitics at work, where biological life as "we" know it is "protected" at all costs. Any (extremist) threat against that life is rendered worthy of eradication by any and all means necessary as a means to preserve the American way of life.

Released in 2007, the concept album *Year Zero* by the industrial rock group Nine Inch Nails (NIN) critically engages with the biopolitics of control. The album presents a dystopia where the United States is enveloped in a perpetual war, wherein religious extremism and environmental degradation justify State control over all aspects of social life. *Year Zero*, however, is more than an album. It is a narrative world that can be pieced together from a variety of constituent parts, including tracks from the album itself, an online alternate reality game, and a variety of fan contributions spread out across the landscape of the World Wide Web. This multimedia world, what I am calling The Year Zero Experience, offers a compelling example of media convergence at work, and it is especially unique given how the music industry has been uprooted by changing social expectations regarding online music distribution. *Year Zero* is an important contribution to the study of post-9/11 popular music because it represents an intersection of the politics of media convergence with the biopolitics of control. More narrowly, Reznor's critique of post-9/11 America includes the power struggle over how popular music should be managed, and about how media should be produced and consumed in the twenty-first century.

Control and Convergence

The concepts of "control" and "convergence" come from two distinct research trajectories in poststructural theory and critical media studies respectively. First, Michel Foucault examines the implications of control in the chapter "Right of Death and Power over Life" from the first volume of *The History of Sexuality*. Here, he outlines two basic forms of "power over life": disciplinary power and biopower. Disciplinary power focuses on the body "as a machine: its disciplining, the optimization of its capabilities, the extortion of its forces," while, he argues, biopower focuses on "the species ... the body imbued with the mechanics of life ... effected through an entire series of interventions and regulatory controls" (Foucault 139). Biopolitics extends the power of the State from control over bodies within a population to control over bodies *as a population*. Biopower nurtures biological bodies so that they can maximize their productive capacities as a collective.

In his short essay "Postscript on the Societies of Control," Gilles Deleuze describes a dystopic vision of contemporary society that pushes Foucault's reading of biopower to its extreme: a system of domination determined by the nature of code. Deleuze explains, "In the societies of control ... what is important is no longer either a signature or a number, but a code: the code is the *password* ... The numerical language of control is made of codes that mark access to information, or reject it" (5). In other words, all aspects of society, from the law to education, filter through the coded logic of control that aims to remake bodies into productive machines which serve at the will of the corporation(s). *Year Zero* offers a dystopic vision of such a world, one where its citizens have become mechanized and are bound to the service of the panoptic State.

In a statement about the album, Reznor explains that *Year Zero* presents "a world [that] has reached the breaking point—politically, spiritually and ecologically" ("Year Zero"). The historical frame of reference for the formation of this dystopia is post-9/11 America where, ironically, the fundamentalist logic that justified the terrorist attacks in New York and Washington, DC was met by a brand of American fundamentalism required of all of its citizens in the aftermath. Popular slogans like "Support the Troops" or "Freedom isn't Free" were transformed into chants of exclusion for those voices who spoke against both the PATRIOT Act and the Iraq War, or later, those critiquing the Bush administration's stance on torture, the no-bid government contracts to corporations like Halliburton, or the policies of discrimination against suspected terrorists that justified the erosion of civil liberties in the United States.[1] This "America" was a reaction to 9/11. Citizens were asked

---

[1]   Live performances of certain selections from *Year Zero* make explicit connections to the Bush administration. For the *Lights in the Sky* tour during the election cycle of 2008, a large screen behind the band slowly morphed a headshot of George Bush into the Republican presidential candidate John McCain during the performance of "Capital G," visually connecting Bush's present America to the future a McCain presidency would offer for the audience.

to surrender legal rights in the name of security and freedom for themselves and others, submitting to the kind of regulatory controls that Foucault describes. To put it another way, America's citizens, a particularly ill-defined group in the wake of post-9/11 jingoism, were asked to submit to a coded nationalism and remake themselves in the image of corporate America. Attempts to construct alternative discourses as resistance to these security measures meant the denial of access to— or total exclusion from—society through arrest on suspicion of terrorist activities.

The second research trajectory that informs *Year Zero* is that of convergence culture. From a broader perspective, the term *convergence* refers to the changing relationship between the production and consumption of media—including print, radio, cinema, television, and, of course, popular music. Two factors driving this transformation involve, from a production standpoint, the concentration and horizontal integration of media ownership and the impact of digitization on cultural practices associated with media consumption.[2] Henry Jenkins, one of the foremost researchers of this trend, argues that "convergence ... is both a top-down corporate-driven process and a bottom-up consumer-driven process" (18). In the era of convergence, audiences consume and create content online, molding that content to their own desires. These cultural practices contribute to the creative evolution of the media text; the material boundaries of the book, movie, or television series begin to fade. A story "so large it cannot be contained within a single medium," like *The Matrix*, unfolds across multiple platforms as a film trilogy, web comic, and computer game spurred by fans' collective commitment to learning more about the world (Jenkins 93). The synergistic marketing strategies of *American Idol*, perhaps a more mainstream example, also illustrate a transmedia story. *AI* (an uncanny abbreviation, indeed) is simultaneously a musical performance, reality television show, web series, and movie franchise. Transmedia storytelling positions the media text as an open system, one that is always evolving through its interactions with consumers who collectively participate in the production and consumption of the narrative using relatively inexpensive digital technologies. This evolution facilitates cultural practices and media literacies dependent on active participation and group collaboration. For Jenkins, these practices anticipate "digital democracy," offering a "changed sense of community, a greater sense of participation, less dependence on official expertise and a greater trust in collaborative problem solving" (208–9).

The move toward media convergence represents a seismic shift in the production and consumption of popular media. Arguably, the reverberations of this shift caused more panic in the music industry than they did anywhere else. In July 2001, only two months before the terrorist attacks on the United States, the legal battle between A&M Records and the file-sharing service Napster ended when the website was found to be in violation of the Digital Millennium Copyright Act. The rise, and eventual demise, of Napster represented a turning point for a music industry that had flourished in the late 1990s due to corporate consolidation,

---

[2]   A process cemented by the Telecommunications Act of 1996.

which ultimately led to higher-priced tickets and CDs, and limited radio access for independent acts. After the demise of Napster, decentralized peer-to-peer file sharing platforms, like BitTorrent, enabled fans to download music directly to their home computers, eschewing middle-men corporate record stores—and, by extension, labels—in the process. The response from the Recording Industry Association of America was adversarial, resulting in lawsuits filed against music fans for illegally downloading music from these file-sharing sites. Though these suits were intended as a means to exert control over consumers and to protect the sacred product, the music industry's antagonism toward file sharing ultimately highlighted its inability to adapt to the digital world.

However, despite this top-down resistance, many musicians went rogue, employing their own digital hardware and the vast expanses of the Internet, particularly on websites like *MySpace*, to organize a kind of virtual grass roots movement to distribute music on their own terms. This movement, no matter how fragmented and decentered it might have been, ultimately gained enough force to collide—converge—with old media models of music distribution. It is the energy of these movements that NIN harnessed when creating The Year Zero Experience and, as I will argue, ultimately improved, as the band concluded their touring career by giving their music away entirely for free.

Shortly after the release of *Year Zero*, Reznor came into conflict with Interscope Records, NIN's record label. Reznor felt the label was charging too much for the album in Australia, where it was retailing for approximately thirty US dollars. As a result, he encouraged the band's fans to "steal his album" during a Nine Inch Nails concert (Van Buskirk). To do so, fans would have to download mp3 tracks online. In the well-publicized split between Interscope and NIN that followed, the label, quite obviously, expressed anger at Reznor's subversion. This exchange added an intriguing twist to the ongoing debate about the merits of online file sharing, NIN being in clear conflict with the profit-earning motives of their record company and, it would seem, with their own need to earn a living from their work.

Sadly, attempts to control digital music distribution, like the ones displayed by Interscope Records, continued to miss the mark when it came to recognizing how the emergence of new cultural practices associated with media convergence changed not only the way popular music is distributed but also the form that music takes—what an album actually is, in other words. As with other popular media, the material boundaries of the album have been challenged by convergence culture, particularly at a time when fans' practices like remixing and sampling make them participants in the (de)construction of album formats. Without Interscope's consent, and prior to his split from the label, Reznor unofficially released remixable tracks from *Year Zero* online. "Survivalism" was first made available in the form of high-quality multitrack audio files that fans could download and remix a month prior to *Year Zero*'s official release. In the following months, additional files circulated through BitTorrent and other peer-to-peer file sharing modules. In addition, Reznor independently financed and developed, with the help of the production company 42 Entertainment, a scavenger hunt and alternate reality game (ARG) as a means to expand *Year Zero*'s sonic and thematic reach. As the game's proverbial puppetmaster, Reznor initiated a virtual scavenger hunt in which participants could piece together a series of hidden messages, links, images, audio cues, cryptic websites, and discussion forums. It is here, in this maze of digital information, that The Year Zero Experience converges.

Intersections: Past, Presence, and Potential

As much as *Year Zero* is a product of convergence culture, it also represents the precise moment, to use Jenkins phraseology, when old and new media collide. The physical CD was released via traditional corporate distribution models, complete with paratextual elements like cover art and liner notes. These elements, much like the title or preface of a literary work, frame the music contained on the album. For example, the foldout of *Year Zero* features images of a suit-clad arm holding a Bible to the left and a muscular arm holding a machine gun to the right. This image portends the themes of the lyrics to *Year Zero*'s tracks "God Given" and "Capital G." Additionally, and perhaps most strikingly, the album's cover art depicts the blurred image of a large figure as seen through a windshield, the streets of a small town lined with military vehicles in the background. Though serving as a prefatory note for the album contained within the sleeve, this image also harkens back to a mystery that began with the viral release of the promotional trailer for *Year Zero*. In the video, camera footage shot from the window of a moving vehicle captures the same giant shadowy figure emerging from a desolate desert landscape. After capturing the image, the screen degrades to black. Players of the ARG ultimately discovered the meaning of this figure: it is named The Presence, and it is a mass hallucination caused by the introduction of the drug Parepin into the American water supply.

Ultimately, it is the vast collection of websites discovered only through playing the ARG that tell the back-story of *Year Zero*. What players uncover is the state of a world unraveling into chaos: biological weapons, nuclear warfare, restrictions on free speech, terrorist attacks on cultural institutions, impeachment of the first female president, the end of free elections, the use of Parepin, the establishment of a "Coalition for Peace" between governments and multinational corporations, and a new world order marked by the introduction of a calendar that renames the year 2022, year zero BA (Born Again). These fragmented contextual details explode the material boundaries of the album, recasting *Year Zero* as a transmedia narrative. As such, it asks listeners to explore what else an album can do by participating in the construction of a narrative world through the ARG, along with the narrative presented on the physical CD. Reznor is emphatic that the two are absolutely linked: "What you are now starting to experience IS 'year zero.' It's not some kind of gimmick to get you to buy a record—it IS the art form … and we're just getting started. Hope you enjoy the ride" ("Year Zero").

What makes *Year Zero* so compelling beyond its transmedia components are the political implications of its structure in the context of the Bush administration's post-9/11 America—arguably a society of control. To highlight these implications, I have structured my analysis of The Year Zero Experience with the temporal markers of *The Past*, *The Presence*, and *The Potential*, all three of which loosely correspond with the three acts of the concept album and ARG. The Past discusses two major topics: the fictional historical events that contextualize The Year Zero Experience, culminating with the dissolution of the American government, and the "old" pre-convergence distribution models of the music industry. The Presence, a play on the figure of "The Presence," explores the moment of transition in both Reznor's society of control and the changing form of the album. The Potential, ultimately, speculates about what could be, a revolution formed through the promise of active participation and group collaboration. My core thesis is that The Year Zero Experience sketches out the emergence of a new kind of subjectivity that, for Reznor, is the only way to combat the society of control that he sees looming in the future post-9/11 American cultural landscape.

The Past

A large part of the ARG, and the first act of the album, outlines a historical trajectory that reinvents America as a society of control, presumably a process that had already begun by the date of the album's release (April 17, 2007 worldwide). Two months prior to the release of the album, in February 2007, a Nine Inch Nails shirt went on sale in Lisbon, Portugal, the text of which contained a cluster of highlighted letters that spelled the declaration, "I am trying to believe." Savvy fans who searched the sentence online were led to the website http://iamtryingtobelieve.com. This site contained pictures of newspaper clippings which introduced visitors to the fictional drug Parepin, an immunity booster and anti-depressant added to the US water supply in order to pre-emptively control the effects of bioterrorism. Those fans who scoured the Internet following the discovery of this site, essentially, began playing the ARG, which had no initial rules or foreseeable resolution.[3] Moreover, the game crossed boundaries between old physical media and new virtual ones, as the album's track list, publicity flyers, a succession of chain email messages, posts on discussion boards, eerie voicemail messages, the physical CD's liner notes, billboards, and USB flash drives planted secretly in NIN concert venues (to name just a few components of the game) all led to the discovery of a seemingly endless amount of hyperlinks and web pages. Even as the game, at least for the foreseeable future, has reached its end, the NINWiki archive includes a future history of *Year Zero*, suggesting that, as Fox Mulder might say, the truth is still out there.

The term *Year Zero* refers to the establishment of a new international calendar by the United States with the support of the Coalition of Peace, a collection of

---

[3]   See Rose for a detailed timeline of the alternate reality game.

multinational corporations and governments. The dates prior to year zero are negative, so the year 2011 would be represented as -11. This notation is a kind of countdown to the reestablishment of a new world order by the United States. This countdown begins on the date 10/17/-15 (2007), which is fictionalized as the date on which President George W. Bush signed the Military Commissions Act, an act suspending *habeas corpus*, essentially allowing for the unlawful detention of prisoners (the actual Military Commissions Act of 2006 denies enemy combatants this right). In Reznor's dystopia, the government has the ability to hold anybody it deems an enemy to the State. After a terrorist attack on the Academy Awards using the toxic chemical ricin on 02/22/-13 (2009), the United States drops nuclear bombs on Iran and North Korea. Like with the Iraq War, no evidence of a connection between these countries and the attack is ever established in the game. Eventually, Muslim nations band together to fight the United States, and the Emergency Measures Act restricts free speech. The end of free elections, a bioterrorist attack on Seattle that might be staged, and a country, Belize, devastated by a hurricane becoming a refuge for American citizens in -02 (2020) all lead to the re-creation of the United States as an international military postindustrial complex where a separation between Church and State no longer exists.

The ARG reconstructs the timeline leading to the establishment of Year Zero, exposing how what Brian Massumi calls the "logic of preemption" has taken hold of American culture (par. 15). This logic assumes that the mere possibility of a terrorist attack justifies preemptive security measures and/or military force in the name of preserving the bodies—their physical beings as opposed to the abstract collection of constitutional rights that define American citizenship—of American citizens. When the logic of pre-emption dominates political discourse, the renegotiation of civil liberties and human rights like *habeas corpus* and free speech becomes less important than preserving biological bodies that can be remade into productive citizens that serve the will of the State—the Coalition of Peace in Reznor's world. To pre-emptively craft American citizens means to provide models of correct behavior that must be followed so that the entire population can be safe from impending threats. The future security of the whole rests in the capacity to control the behavior of individuated bodies.

Rather than providing listeners with specific historical details, like the ARG provides its players, the first act of *Year Zero*, the album, deals specifically with individual choices that collectively enable the logic of pre-emption to take root. Tracks like "The Beginning of the End" and "Survivalism" ask: How could this have happened? What makes Americans so willing to submit to the networks of control that can overtake their lives? The lyrics of "The Beginning of the End" explain that "you'll be left behind" if you don't fall in line with policies and practices enacted by the American government intended to pre-emptively secure the population. Eliding any specifics, Reznor focuses on the passivity of the average citizen who enables the growth of the government's control over the population through a general passiveness to what is taking place. Inaction makes "you" (the citizen) unable to, as the lyrics of the song explain, recognize yourself.

This theme of inaction mimics the passive consumption models of old media, like the cinema and television, and even the standard music album, where audiences are spectators as opposed to active participants in the production process.

Year Zero's first single, "Survivalism," echoes this message. The song's heavy, rhythmic beat mimics a marching mass held together through, as the lyrics explain, the need to take more and more. "Mother nature" is there to service this rampant consumerism and conspicuous consumption that leads to environmental degradation and political upheaval. While the ARG tracks historical artifacts, the first act of the album focuses on the transformation of the American citizen. Interestingly, the more general nature of the lyrics enables listeners without knowledge of the ARG to make connections not with the fictional dystopia Reznor constructs, but with the Bush administration's post-9/11 policies. As the Year Zero timeline, beginning with the signing of the Military Commissions Act, reminds us, this path is not as far off as it may first appear.

While the content of The Year Zero Experience speaks to the dangers of the concentration of power in the hands of a few, its form as a transmedia text extends this critique to include the corporations that produce and distribute popular music. Much like Reznor's reading of the American government, record companies have historically controlled and exploited artists as much as they enable artistic creation. From the perspective of the listener, they remain subject to the "one to one" distribution model—a compact disc sold to each listener—that made record companies so much money in the mid to late 1990s. This model reflects the biopolitical power structure that enables Year Zero to take shape, where one power source (the government) has the capacity to control individuated bodies at the biological level, bypassing the messiness of human rights and civil liberties. As such, Interscope Records, and the larger corporate infrastructure of which it is a part, are not so different from Reznor's dystopia. This dual-edged critique is also reflected in Reznor's political commitment to the flexible licensing of creative content, which was directly in conflict with the contractual agreement between NIN and Interscope Records.

The Presence

While a significant portion of the ARG, along with the album's first act, traces the past events of a future narrative that strategically relates to the "present-day" political turmoil of America in 2007, *Year Zero*'s second act situates the present as a transitional moment. Within The Year Zero Experience, artists, citizens, and governments stand at a threshold. In February 2007, a USB flash drive was found in Lisbon, at the same concert where the highlighted shirt was unveiled, which contained the mp3 file of the album track "My Violent Heart" and a URL hidden in the drive's ID3 tags that revealed the website http://anotherversionofthetruth.com. This website contains a brightly colored political poster of a red farmhouse nestled in a green field, the archetypal windmill prominently displayed near the center of the screen. Flowing translucently across this image is an American flag framing the paradoxical text, "A New Beginning: Zero Tolerance, Zero Fear—America is Born Again." At the bottom of the screen resides a message proclaiming the site's sponsor: the fictional US Bureau of Morality. At the time of the USB's discovery, and for several years after *Year Zero*'s release, the farm image would transform when the site visitor would track the mouse across the screen (this transformation no longer took place as of this chapter's composition). When the mouse cursor was moved across the screen, the image wiped away to reveal the same location but now in black-and-white and resembling a war zone complete with a wire fence, smoke, and, sadly, a dilapidated windmill. The image was framed by an ominous message that read, "The Beginning of the End: Zero Hope, Zero Chance—Another Version of the Truth." In this space, government propaganda quite literally transitioned into a call for revolution through user interaction. If the user clicked the phrase "Another Version of the Truth," a hyperlink would lead to a message board with posts from the year 0000, which contained threads like "Cops Murder Muslim Kid" and "Missing in Action," both of which are vague enough to seem real, even if they are fictionalized in the context of the ARG. That seeming reality is where Reznor's political work takes hold, as the information in these forums encourages players to question the motives of the American government and the culture of fear it had been promoting post-9/11.

Similarly, the second act of the album presents a choice: either submit to or question institutions of power. In a society of control characterized by masked loyalties and shifting perspectives, this choice is anything but easy. The speaker of "Me, I'm Not" cannot believe what he has become, asking, "Can we stop?" while "Capital G" assumes the perspective of Americans who seem to abandon their own morality in the name of, basically, what amounts to global domination. These tracks capture the fraught internal dialogue of subjects who struggle—often in fear—with the networks of power that seek to control every bodily movement in an effort to secure the safety of the population.

The track "God Given" finds the struggles of these subjects reaching their collective climax. Here, the speaker faithfully believes that he is one of the "chosen ones." However, this faith is momentarily broken, as the speaker begins to question the validity of his beliefs. Although the song returns to an (ironic?) statement of faith, it also concludes with a nearly incomprehensible wall of sound, the chaos of the transition—echoing, arguably, the chaos captured on http://anotherversionofthetruth.com. For Reznor, the present is always illegible, fuzzy, and potentially terrifying.

It is not surprising, then, that The Year Zero Experience is personified by that shadowy hand-like figure The Presence adorning *Year Zero*'s cover art. The origins and significance of this figure are the central mysteries in the ARG. (The Year Zero timeline ends with the appearance of The Presence over the US Capitol on 2/10/0000.) As the textual fragments on the website http://iamtryingtobelieve.com speculate, The Presence is generated by the introduction of the drug Parepin into the water supply. Because water consumption cannot be controlled, the amount of drugs that enter into someone's system cannot be regulated. In keeping with the second act's theme of inquiry, the "official" documents archived on this site are littered with marginal comments that question these claims. Two black-and-white photographs depict The Presence with a subtitle that reads, "'The Presence'— Legitimate Phenomenon or Parepin-Induced Mass Psychosis?" This knowledge, which is available only through participation in the ARG, clarifies the meaning of selected tracks from the album. For instance, "The Warning" references a "sign" coming down from the sky to warn the greedy that their time to control the population is coming to an end. Ironically, one of the side-effects of Parepin is recognition of the mechanisms of control.

Therefore, The Presence also symbolizes transition. It represents a tool of control turning back on itself, reawakening a population that, in the past, gave into (willingly or not) to overarching biopower that promised both security and freedom while simultaneously negating civil liberties and human rights. This moment of transition is marked with masked national loyalties, shifting political perspectives, and chaotic cultural modulations, all of which are paralleled in Reznor's use of new digital media, at the levels of production and consumption, to broaden the scope of his—and his audience's—cultural vision.

The Potential

Year Zero's final act offers the means through which Reznor's fictionalized society of control can be interrupted. In simple terms, this act outlines the beginnings of a revolution. The track aptly named "The Great Destroyer" assumes the perspective of a subject with "limitless potential" to interrupt the society of control. Similarly, the hopeful "In This Twilight" promises something better beyond the dystopic reality of the present tense. Perhaps most dramatically, the album's final track, "Zero-Sum," directly addresses the audience and chastises them for allowing the current dystopia to emerge. The audience is shamed for being "just zeroes and ones" rather than asserting their own powerful presence in the past. Ultimately, "Zero-Sum" points to us, "real world" citizens that have allowed the dystopia of post-9/11 America to sediment itself in our collective consciousness. In Reznor's mind, our silence has rendered us as digital code to be manipulated by the mechanisms of control. Here, Reznor recalls Deleuze, arguing that, in a society of control, "code" determines accessibility, while the collective "we" has been reduced to a statistical data set. As a result, it is fitting that the physical CD on which *Year Zero*'s music is coded is a heat-sensitive thermo-chrome disc that reveals a message of ones and zeros, along with copyright information, when it is held for roughly five minutes. Quite literally, data exists beneath the surface of the album. And this data, in all of its multimedia forms, is what opens up The Year Zero Experience, an experience that involves audience participation—not passivity—and which suggests that such participation is the key to avoiding control in all its forms.

It is fitting, therefore, that the ARG relied so heavily on user collaboration. In it, the narrative is interactive, configuring players as archeologists who uncover digital fragments of a future world already past. As such, the intersection between the form and content of The Year Zero Experience speaks to the emergence of a new subjectivity through collaboration and a collective call to action. While the ARG was openly available for anyone who had access to play along, it was also geared toward a specialized demographic consisting of people who could decode messages by cleaning up static; use a spectrometer; maneuver through a great deal of physical and digital information; and, most importantly, effectively collaborate with others in an online environment. This form of collaboration points to a subjectivity based on collective agency rather than individual autonomy, which has historically been the stuff of countercultural activism. Even though these players would work together, the game did not encourage them to submit to the will of the "mass" or to participate in some empty groupthink exercise. Instead, success in the game demanded that participants learn to collaborate with strangers across national boundaries and under the radar of institutional power, not the least of which was that exerted by Interscope Records.

The engaged collective is what The Year Zero Experience inevitably creates. Rather than standing as a finished product, the physical album stands as merely a part of a larger narrative—one that allows fans the freedom to create their own stories, realities, and political statements. The Year Zero Experience's political potential rests in its capacity to bring participants together in a shared constitution other than through the networks of control that define the biopolitical population. Here, players are more than statistical output. Rather, they are collaborators in a productive, artistic process that provides the revolutionary answer to control in all its forms.

Postscript: After 0000

If Reznor's dystopic yarn concludes with The Presence looming over the US Capitol, the seat of American government and a building in which we can surely hear *capital* echoing throughout its halls, then it is fitting that he concluded Nine Inch Nails' recording career (for now) by offering the band's final album, 2008's *The Slip*, for free online. For a songwriter who lamented monolithic control and power in virtually every song that he wrote, there could not be a more perfect ending to his career (again, for now). In the end, he gave it away.

Works Cited

Deleuze, Gilles, et al. "Postscript on the Societies of Control." *October* 59 (1992): 3–7. Print.

Foucault, Michel. *The History of Sexuality, Volume One: An Introduction.* Trans. Robert Hurley. New York: Vintage Books, 1990. Print.

Jenkins, Henry. *Convergence Culture: Where Old and New Media Collide.* New York: New York UP, 2006. Print.

Massumi, Brian. "Potential Politics and the Primacy of Preemption." *Theory and Event* 10.2 (2007): n.p. *Project Muse.* Web. Dec. 1, 2010.

Nine Inch Nails. *Year Zero.* Interscope, 2007. CD.

Rose's, Frank. "Secret Websites, Coded Messages: The New World of Immersive Games." *Wired.* 20 Dec. 20, 2007. Web. April 3, 2010

Van Buskirk, Eliot. "Trent Reznor Escapes His Label's Clutches." *Listening Post. Wired.* Oct. 8, 2007. Web. April 3, 2010.

"Year Zero." *NINWiki.* MediaWiki, Jan. 7, 2011. Web. Feb. 12, 2011.

PART III
What's Going On, Again?: Protest and Nostalgia

Casualties of War: Hip-Hop and the Old Racial Politics of the Post-9/11 Era

Aisha Staggers

I am a casualty of war—not a casualty of either war waging in the Middle East, but of a metaphorical war that has been waged against hip-hop on every political front since September 11, 2001. The reality is that, in the decade since 9/11, hip-hop has fought tirelessly for its very survival, as the genre has been the victim of endless pseudo-militarized censorship campaigns on mainstream radio airwaves. Similarly, battle-scarred hip-hop veterans remain absent in mainstream music media coverage—the missing men in the formation of contemporary pop culture.

Just as our nation has come to identify America in "pre-9/11" and "post-9/11" terms, I have come to define hip-hop in those same terms. I view these "pre" and "post" eras as distinct periods—the former a time in which hip-hop stood strong alongside of the towering canon of mainstream popular music, the latter a time in which hip-hop has crumbled and fragmented into a spectral plume of its former self. Indeed, it is worth noting that hip-hop largely came of age during a decade, the 1990s, that was bookended by wars in the Middle East: when rap legend Rakim sat down to write the lyrics to "Casualties of War," from the album *Don't Sweat the Technique* (1992), the United States had just ended its involvement in the Gulf War. Interestingly enough, the song prophesizes much of the social and political unrest that would occur in the years after 9/11, even though, obviously, no one could have foreseen the events of that day. Rakim writes of a call for a (George Herbert Walker) Bush "attack," and he also details the effects of post-traumatic stress disorder (PTSD) before it was widely applied to Gulf War—and Iraq War—veterans. Ultimately, Rakim attaches this trauma to potential terror on the homefront: "Every time a truck backfires I fire back / I look for shelter when a plane is over me / Remember Pearl Harbor? / New York could be over, G." Again, though about Desert Storm, "Casualties of War" is prescient in its description of a time of terror. Why, then, has this singular track, along with so many other hip-hop songs from the 1990s, slid into America's political—and musical—subconscious? This question is the central concern of this chapter.

At first glance, my appropriation of pre- and post-9/11 temporality as a means to contextualize hip-hop might appear unnecessary, because it would stand to reason that hip-hop would, by default, fall within the larger historical narrative of America. However, since hip-hop has been systematically excluded from the American mainstream, a move that parallels the social and political exclusion of

African Americans from the traditional "American Way of Life," these temporal markers are necessary for fully understanding the shifting significance of hip-hop culture since the early 1990s. These historical categories are also helpful for distinguishing two critical eras in hip-hop's development: a Golden Age of lyrical artistry and freedom, and a flashier Diamond Age driven by consumption of material wealth and unfettered capitalism.[1]

Though popular American discourse described 9/11 as an unreal event, it was, arguably, not inconceivable to many African Americans, whose reality is grounded in a history that is equally unimaginable. Given this unique historical perspective, African Americans could be disturbed by the events of 9/11 while also being more readily accepting of a new reality at the same time. Ironically, though, it seems that, in the years since 9/11, hip-hop has taken a sabbatical from addressing both the historic reality of African American culture as well as the reality of post-9/11 America. This thematic shift marks hip-hop's transformation in the post-9/11 era—a transformation that finds rappers constructing increasingly irrelevant rhymes that intend to desensitize contemporary African American youths to their own social, economic, political, and sexual strife. Hip-hop's narrations of egregiously carefree lifestyles ultimately invoke images of the past like Al Jolson and post-Civil War minstrel shows, rendering many current rappers akin to performers in blackface.

That said, a few artists have tried to breathe life back into hip-hop since 9/11, though with marginal success. In 2006 interviews supporting the release of his debut CD *Lupe Fiasco's Food & Liquor*, Lupe Fiasco addresses the Diamond Age, criticizing fans and artists for forgetting the social and political conditions in urban America. He abhors the fact that ignorance has gained such prevalence in hip-hop while poverty and crime continue to prevail in inner cities, wreaking terror on their inhabitants while, ostensibly, the nation is conducting a "War on Terror." By making such arguments, Fiasco is able to bridge together two seemingly opposing forces in hip-hop: entertainment and education. In doing so, Fiasco essentially redeploys the rap hybrid "edutainment," established by Golden Age rappers Boogie Down Productions. This style stands in stark contrast to the flimsiness of so much contemporary rap music. It is not surprising, then, that Fiasco has not reached the level of popular success of hip-hop artists like Lil Wayne or even The Black Eyed Peas. What is even more striking is that Fiasco is a Muslim (born Wasalu Muhammad Jaco), and his father was a member of the Chicago chapter of the Black Panther Party for Self-Defense. That such an outspoken and potentially "radical Muslim" cannot be heard in post-9/11 America is an eerie reminder of how close to home the witch-hunt for all threats "foreign and domestic" actually is (Frazier).

---

[1]   "The Golden Age of Hip-Hop" is a term used by hip-hop aficionados that roughly refers to the genre's ascendancy and peak as a popular cultural form, usually beginning with rap's first two breakthrough LPs in 1986 (Run-DMC's *Raising Hell* and the Beastie Boys' *Licensed to Ill*) and ending with the untimely and unsolved murders of Tupac Shakur in 1996 and The Notorious B.I.G. in 1997.

On a personal level, I cannot help but agree with Fiasco, and I find myself continually advocating for hip-hop to return to its roots. It appears that this sentiment is not unique to me, as many younger fans are arguing for the same thing as they approach their thirties and are, it seems, becoming disillusioned by the world in which they live. In her 2002 *New York Times* article "Hip-Hop Divides: Those Who Rap, Those Who Don't," Kalefa Sanneh claims that the desire to return to the euphoric Golden Age of hip-hop is most common among those who can remember when hip-hop was in its purest form during the 1980s and 1990s. This feeling of nostalgia is largely misunderstood in hip-hop's post-9/11 era because the assumption is that there cannot be anything wrong with music that is profitable. This assumption is flawed because, for those of us involved in hip-hop, it is not what we do, but rather, in the words of DMX, "who we be." Hip-hop is so deeply integrated into our beings that it may as well be a part of our DNA. That "being" part of us is consistently barraged with what amounts to musical Weapons of Mass Destruction—songs and artists that are so mass-produced and mass-distributed that their presence in the industry is damaging an already fragile musical structure, pulling the culture apart at its very foundation. This structural damage ultimately establishes a kind of DuBoisian double consciousness, wherein hip-hop culture is theoretically measured and valued by a business that looks upon it with "amused contempt and pity," and the souls of the folk in the culture are only allowed to view themselves through that perspective, one that is, as always, provided by those in power (11).

Therefore, to force this matter to its crisis, we need to ask how to reconcile hip-hop's conflicting realities. In the post-9/11 era, hip-hop has largely been commodified, transformed into a saleable product that, at one point, could help defer the looming post-9/11 recession. Though hip-hop had become progressively more marketable in the years leading up to 9/11, the final push that sucked the music into capitalism's all-encompassing vortex largely occurred after September 11, when most American political figures, President George W. Bush in particular, co-opted the attacks and encouraged Americans to stand up to the terrorists by investing in the economy and shopping with reckless abandon. In the pre-9/11 Golden Age, however, hip-hop's reality was largely concerned with "keeping it real." The majority of Golden Age rappers performed their music without spectacle—no pyrotechnic stunts, no tricks, and no money. For the most part, these artists were taking political and financial risks to speak the truth—to "keep it real." Even though this Golden Age had a spattering of commercially successful artists like The Fat Boys, MC Hammer, and DJ Jazzy Jeff and the Fresh Prince, their successes hinged on a fairly pronounced rejection of hip-hop and R&B fans as a means to gain approval from mainstream, mainly white, audiences. Their impact in the world of black music, in general, and hip-hop specifically, went largely unnoticed until hip-hop became solidly entrenched in American culture.

The fundamental shift in hip-hop from an openly political genre to an apolitical one in the years prior to the September 11th attacks was, ironically, a result of fear. For many MCs, that fear emerged from a recognition of their own mortality, particularly after the fatal shootings of Tupac Shakur in 1996 and The Notorious B.I.G. in 1997. At that time, the future of hip-hop as a distinct genre was largely uncertain; MCs began to explore other musical genres like hard rock, country, London dancehall, and alternative rock.[2] What compounded these tensions was another unforeseen fatal tragedy: the death of R&B singer Aaliyah, in a plane crash, on August 25, 2001. Aaliyah's death was not upsetting to the hip-hop community simply because she was a talented R&B artist or because she was only twenty-two at the time. Certainly, those things were true. Rather, it was the matter of *how* she died that bothered hip-hop artists and fans.

When Tupac and Biggie were murdered, the mainstream press largely justified their deaths with the adage that "if you live by the gun, you die by the gun." The same justification was deployed when Eazy-E died of complications related to AIDS in 1995. However, for many African Americans, the risk of dying in a plane crash has always seemed minimal. The music business has been shaken by fatal plane crashes in the past: John Denver in 1997; Ricky Nelson in 1985; members of Lynyrd Skynyrd in 1977; Patsy Cline in 1963; and perhaps most infamously, Buddy Holly, The Big Bopper, and Ritchie Valens in 1959. In the aftermath of Aaliyah's death, though, it was not just mainstream American musicians suffering these types of losses; R&B musicians had now lost fellow entertainers to plane crashes in the past as well.

While it is true that Otis Redding, along with four members of the Bar-Kays, died in a plane crash in 1967, many hip-hop fans were either in infancy or were not even born at that time, leaving them no first-hand recollections of Redding's demise. Therefore, the coverage of Aaliyah's death gained a particularly pronounced immediacy for her fans. In simple terms, her death seemed senseless, random. Indeed, the randomness of the crash has led to continuous speculation about whether or not the crash was avoidable. Still trying to make sense of that devastation, the hip-hop community, along with the rest of America, was shaken to the core just over two weeks later with a slew of devastating plane crashes. Hip-hop, already at an ideological crossroads, was left vulnerable and impressionable in the wake of 9/11—a target for both a corporate and political hijacking.

As America began to reclaim its soul in the aftermath of 9/11, hip-hop seemed to all but lose its own. Becoming less of a forum of socially conscious expression for young African Americans, and more of a novelty, the music did little to further the discussion of racial politics in America. This trend continued throughout the decade, which became all the more distressing as American politics finally saw the rise of an African American Presidential candidate in Barack Obama. It was believed that Obama's election would signify—and ultimately enact—sweeping change in the hip-hop community. During Obama's campaign, hip-hop artists, many of whom had been disillusioned with the political process, were taking to the airwaves, the Internet, and the streets to assist in getting Obama elected. These

---

2   A number of these ventures into other genres also occurred post-9/11, the most unlikely of pairings being Nelly and Tim McGraw in 2004 on their ballad "Over and Over."

artists mobilized a generation that was never welcome in the political process. For once, this generation believed in the optimism of the rallying cry, "Yes We Can." Rap icon Jay-Z possibly put it best: "The day Obama got elected, the gangsta became less relevant" (quoted in Redding). Indeed, it would seem that Obama's election would stand as the fulfillment of the collective thrust of Golden Age of political rap.

Regrettably, though, Obama's election did not inspire the grand, sweeping change for which many longed. While it is naïve to expect that the hip-hop industry would adopt stylistic flourishes and lyrics that would make it entirely unmarketable, it would seem that the election of a savvy, educated black leader would at least have inspired black musicians to interrogate racial divides that had been bolstered post-9/11 and the ratification of the USA PATRIOT Act. Given that the omnipresent pressure of that act is (still) squashing civil liberties, rappers, arguably, have far less freedom as artists now to express their dissatisfaction with the US than they have at any point in the past. Historically, and particularly in hip-hop's infancy in the early and mid-1980s, hip-hop artists could explicitly challenge key political figures because, quite simply, few people outside of the African American community listened to hip-hop. Moreover, even fewer political icons respected the genre.

That context stands in stark contrast to the contemporary one—a context in which hip-hop is popular among white suburban youths due in large part to the wide reach of MTV and other mainstream media outlets. In this era of media saturation, rap and hip-hop artists are outed when they express countercultural views. For proof, of course, we need not look any further than the outcry against Kanye West when he uttered his famous statement that "[:orge [W.] Bush doesn't care about black people" during NBC's *A Concert for Hurricane Relief* fundraiser, in the immediate aftermath of Hurricane Katrina, on September 2, 2005. Clearly, these musicians were no longer afforded the same privacy and protection they experienced in insular venues like underground clubs and house parties. The result, therefore, was that these artists—their rhymes and performances—have come under a form of scrutiny that has allowed savvy politicians to capitalize on the racial fears of middle-class white America—fears that the PATRIOT Act has only worked to enhance.

As is so often the case, this political scrutiny is largely misguided, no matter how much politicking might suggest otherwise. Jay-Z's influential album *The Blueprint* sold nearly half a million copies during the first week after its release. The album also entered the Billboard charts at #1, all in spite of the fact that *The Blueprint* was released on September 11, 2001, when virtually all business on the east coast was halted by 9:03 a.m. when United Airlines 175 flew into the South Tower of the World Trade Center. If nothing else, these sales figures illustrate hip-hop's broad appeal, suggesting that 9/11 has allowed mainstream Americans to relate to the sentiments of anger and hopelessness, as well as the fear of being attacked to which hip-hop speaks. On every September 11 *Billboard* Hot 100 chart week since that fateful day in 2001, a hip-hop song has occupied the number one spot every single year, not a patriotic one. Though Jay-Z eventually released *The Blueprint 3* during the week of September 11, 2009, a crass and seemingly explicitly commercial move, he has been open about directing portions of his overall profits to help families of fallen first responders. He also offers the children of these victims free access to his shows, and he regularly hosts parties and fundraisers on their behalf. He also wrote the song "Empire State of Mind," a testament to the post-9/11 resiliency of New York City. In plain terms, his philanthropic work as a famous rap artist and US citizen has been more effective than the very government that reserves the right to question his patriotism.

The expansive appeal of hip-hop also calls into question the narrative of American victimization that has been reiterated annually since the September 11 attacks. For the most part, the public face of the 9/11 victims is a white Christian one, a fact that the recent uproar about the Ground Zero Mosque has made clear.[3] Many people of color have quite understandably viewed this portrayal as a form of cultural whitewashing, as one 9/11 widow, Alissa Torres, has pointed out: "How did '9/11 victim' become sloppy shorthand for 'white Christian'? I wish someone would put out a list of all the ethnicities and religions and countries and economic levels of the victims. For all the talk of 'remembering 9/11,' I wonder if we've missed the patriotic message entirely" (quoted in Colmes).

Unfortunately, though, the literal destruction caused on that September 11 in 2001 simultaneously deconstructed the political import of hip-hop beyond rappers like Jay-Z. As has been well documented, prior to 9/11, hip-hop addressed the struggles of young African Americans in America's inner cities. The subjects of these narratives were not that familiar to white, middle-class America. For this reason, hip-hop artists were viewed as relative experts who could accurately describe and transcribe their own history in their own language. However, 9/11 was a day experienced by all of America; though its events occurred in specific geographic areas, the attacks were on an unspecified demographic. Therefore, hip-hop artists could not claim sole ownership of the pain associated with that day. Moreover, whatever pain they endured prior to 9/11—and have continued to endure since then—was not considered relevant to larger cultural narratives. Furthermore, and ironically enough, it was considered insensitive by many to dwell on individual struggles, even if those struggles involved daily threats from gang violence and police brutality, when the entire nation was allegedly under attack.

In this light, it is entirely fitting that one of the most popular rappers of the post-9/11 era has been Eminem, a white rapper from the suburbs of Detroit. According to *Billboard*'s Paul Grein, Eminem's *The Marshall Mathers LP* (2000) is the best-selling rap album of all time in the United States. Eminem's rise to fame, legitimized by repeated Grammy nominations and awards, is troubling not

---

[3]   There was a Muslim prayer room on the seventeenth floor in the South Tower of the World Trade Center—a fact that the outcries against building a mosque near Ground Zero entirely overlook.

so much because he is a white rapper, but rather because his work exudes the hyperbolic absurdity of so much contemporary rap music. Perpetually narrating a Freudian psychodrama with his mother; fantasizing in song about killing his ex-wife; endlessly describing drug use, in his lyrics and in interviews: all of these carnivalesque subjects define Eminem's career. Certainly, his songs are comic; but they are also tragic—both in their solipsism and in their failure to turn personal rage outward toward the equally tragic American political landscape. Though Eminem did record the 2004 single "Mosh" ostensibly as a protest song against George W. Bush, that one track represents a mere blip in an otherwise socially unconscious career. Not to mention that the song appropriated its title from a style of dance popular among white punk and hardcore fans—not from anything with its roots in hip-hop culture.

If music as a whole (and hip-hop in particular) is to survive this new era, we as consumers must persistently ask our composers for better material, hold them accountable when they don't deliver, and, if that is not enough, we must commit to writing, owning, and distributing the very music we desire. In the current Diamond Age of hip-hop, the entire genre will become irrelevant unless there is a massive restructuring in terms of business dealings, ownership, marketing, and sound. Essentially, it must revert back to the days when listeners, hip-hop enthusiasts, drove demand, not multinational conglomerates. Artists like The Roots, Common, Taleb Kweli, and Mos Def should have *their* stacks tapped for samples to bring a new authenticity to hip-hop. Artists need to become owners of the medium, the message, and most importantly, their masters of a new century. Only then will we see a new consciousness in hip-hop, a cultural awakening.

Just as change is inevitable, popularity is cyclical. The 1990s saw a resurrection of 1970s fashion and, similarly, the 1980s have made a comeback in the five years leading up to 2011. Musical expression is no different. Just as The Digable Planets brought forth a "Rebirth of Slick," and Method Man and Mary J. Blige revamped the Motown duet with "You're All I Need/I'll Be There For You," bringing Marvin Gaye and Tammi Terrell to a new generation, perhaps the Post-Post-9/11 and Post-Obama Era will see that which I loved return unscathed, and a new wave of MCs emerge and begin "Raising Hell" once again. It is possible, but in the meantime I remain hopeful and nostalgic. My nostalgia can be weathered through the songs stored on any number of electronic devices in my possession, it can feed my creativity as a writer of music and literature, and it has allowed me as a parent to expose my daughter to "my" music, the same way my parents exposed me to theirs. I don't think anyone can live without a bit of nostalgia; after all, it reminds us of where we've been, where we are going, and, if we aren't careful, where we could have been and where we still could end up. Musically, it is how I celebrate the life I live and the lives of those who have gone on, but have left an amazing catalog of art and sounds to last me a lifetime. With that said, there comes a time in the life span of any art form when becoming mainstream is a cause for celebration, the gaining of wider recognition, massive visibility, and reward for toiling in the fields of obscurity for so many years. Then there are times when the realization that not only is your art, you life's sweat and tears, owned by another, so is your soul. When that bomb is thrown, it will be "the best indication that the art is quickly losing its soul. Now is that time for hip-hop" (Kitwana).

Works Cited

Colmes, Alan. "9/11 Widow: 'How Did "9/11 Victim" Become Shorthand for "White Christian"'"? *Liberaland.* Sept. 8, 2010. Web. Feb. 1, 2011.

DMX. "Who We Be." *The Great Depression.* Ruff Ryders/Def Jam Records, 2001. CD.

DuBois, W. E. B. *The Souls of Black Folk.* New York: Bantam, 1989. Print.

Eric B. and Rakim. "Casualties of War." *Don't Sweat the Technique.* MCA Records, 1992. CD.

Frazier, Walter. "Lupe Fiasco Drops Label Beef to Focus on 'Lasers.'" *Billboard. com.* Dec. 30, 2010. Web. Feb. 1, 2011.

Grein, Paul. "Week Ending Jan. 30, 2011: Good News & Bad News." *Billboard. com.* Feb. 2, 2011. Web. Feb. 23, 2011.

Kitwana, Bakari. "The End: Once a Voice of the Voiceless, Hip-Hop Stands to Lose its Soul." *Newsday.* Feb. 16, 2003: A30. Print.

Redding, Jr., Robert "Rob." "Jay-Z says Obama Marks the Decline of the 'Gangsta.'" *Redding News Review.* Apr. 26, 2009. Web. Feb. 1, 2011.

Sanneh, Kalefa. "Hip-Hop Divides: Those Who Rap, Those Who Don't." *New York Times.* Dec. 22, 2002. Web. March 3, 2010.

Chapter 9

That Was Now, This Is Then: Recycling Sixties Style in Post-9/11 Music

Jeffrey Roessner

On their 1971 album *A Space In Time*, the blues-rock band Ten Years After released what would become their biggest hit, a song called "I'd Love to Change the World." Including lines such as "Tax the rich, feed the poor / till there are no rich no more" and the bluntly declarative "Them and us / stop the war," the song seems to take up the countercultural mantle of the sixties, protesting the Vietnam War, social inequality, and "world pollution"—that is, unless we pay close attention to the lyrics in the chorus. Opening with the line "I'd love to change the world" (a sentiment that could have come directly from The Beatles' "Revolution"), lead vocalist Alvin Lee continues, "But I don't know what to do / So I'll leave it up to you." In two brief phrases, the song puts ironic quotation marks around its brash lyrical posture, and abandons what initially seemed like staunch political commitment. Changing the world is a dream, after all, or at least a very difficult thing to achieve through a rock and roll song. Despite the fervent ideals supposedly bequeathed by the sixties counterculture, the singer remains uncertain "what to do." I suggest that, in its ambiguity, "I'd Love to Change the World" encapsulates a more accurate vision of the legacy of the sixties than many music critics and listeners want to admit.

Indeed, as Alvin Lee's song portends, the idealized politics of sixties music casts a long shadow over current debates about the effects of musical protest. The terrorist attacks on the World Trade Center and Pentagon in 2001 in particular renewed questions about the political responsibility of artists and the corporations that produce and distribute their music. Significantly, many critics have asked why rock music failed to serve as a more widely shared and effective means of protest after 9/11. Reebee Garofalo, for example, notes that the "dissent—and in particular the antiwar protest music—that helped provide the basis for the national debate on Vietnam was nowhere to be found on mainstream media during the invasions of Afghanistan and Iraq" (4). In such arguments, the premise quickly becomes clear: rock musicians did write and record songs of protest, but they were kept from effectively rallying dissenters because of both material constraints on the distribution of their music and fear of the costs of resistance. But a troubling, value-laden assumption lurks within this debate: the question really is why didn't recent music function more like that of the sixties, which galvanized the anti-war movement and served as a platform for the civil rights debate? In order to complicate this debate, I argue that the "resistance" in sixties rock was bound to its cultural moment, and that attempts to apply it to contemporary music ignore the complicated legacy of that decade's music. In short, post-9/11 rock music has been inaccurately read through the lens of an idealized vision of sixties politics—one that both distorts our understanding of the past and blinds us to the contemporary context reshaping the performance and reception of music.

Sing Out!

In limning the context of post-9/11 music, many theorists have focused on the significant issue of political protest. After all, artists reflecting a broad range of styles did produce songs with explicit political messages, especially as the "war on terror" began in earnest with the invasions of Afghanistan and Iraq. The initial anger and retaliatory sentiments of many musicians quickly gave way to bold lyrical assaults on the leadership of America and its militarism. In an essay for the Center for Political Song, Janis McNair offers a wide-ranging survey of protest songs delivered in the wake of the terrorist attacks, including Ani DiFranco's indictment of George Bush and his policies in "Self Evident" ("we hold these truths to be self-evident: #1: George W. Bush is not president / #2 America is not a true democracy"); The Dope Poet Society's "War of Terrorism," which identifies oil as the true cause for the conflict ("It's not a war on terrorism it's a war of terrorism ... America is killing for oil not for freedom"); and Steve Earle's "John Walker's Blues," written from the point of view of the young American John Walker Lindh, who joined Afghanistan's Taliban army. In the aftermath of the attacks, artists were clearly offering a provocative and ongoing protest of what they saw as the misjudgments, ineptitude, and hypocrisy of the US government.

However, despite the variety and volume of protest music during this period, it generally was not heard on American radio. As explanation for this troubling absence, music critics have typically described one major threat to free speech and its lingering effects. Garofalo, for example, highlights a provision in the 1996 Telecommunications Act that opened the door for fewer and fewer corporations to own an increasingly large share of the media market. He notes that, by the 1990s, "fewer than twenty" corporations controlled most of the radio markets in the country, and by the first decade of the new century Clear Channel had "acquired more than 1,200 stations in the United States" and "controlled 65 percent of the US concert business" (14). In a similar vein, describing Clear Channel's vast market share, Eric Klinenberg notes that the company's "various holdings reach roughly 154 million people, or 75% of the US population over the age of eighteen" (62). To media watchdog groups, the sheer size and staggering power of radio monopolies were cause enough for concern; however, the corporate response to voices of dissent proved even more disturbing. Most infamously, in the immediate wake of the terrorist attacks, Clear Channel circulated a list "containing more than 150 songs described as 'lyrically questionable'" and asked that "programmers use 'restraint' when selecting songs for airplay" (Nuzum 151). The list included everything from Metallica's "Seek and Destroy" and Carole King's "I Feel the Earth Move" to John Lennon's "Imagine" (Garofalo 15). The outrage at Clear Channel's list was magnified because the attempt to limit airplay was directed not only at songs with ominous overtones, such as Steve Miller's "Jet Airliner" and the Dave Matthews Bands' "Crash Into Me," but also at seemingly benign works, including Cat Stevens' "Peace Train" (Nuzum 151). Garofalo contends that "Clear Channel's practices could only be read as further reducing the diversity of voices in an era of already shrinking playlists" (16).

Eric Nuzum goes further, arguing that "while Clear Channel is quick to point out that there was no explicit censorship connected with the list, it is a perfect example of music censorship at its most implicit," and he thus worries about careening "down the slippery slope towards stifled free expression" (151). For critic Martin Scherzinger, Clear Channel's choices seem "motivated less by the content of the lyrics than by the religious beliefs, antiwar stances, or political persuasions of the musicians themselves" (96). So the "use restraint" list can be read as a form of intimidation directed more at the artists themselves than any particular song, with the effect of suppressing not only artistic expression of dissent, but also public debate of these issues.

Although Garofalo, Nuzum, and Scherzinger offer compelling arguments about the problem of corporate radio monopolies and the de facto censorship of music, each unconvincingly grants enormous power to the companies that produce and distribute music. Of course, it is troubling that Clear Channel owns so much of the airwaves, and that its policies dictate what a large portion of the public hears on a regular basis. Nonetheless, this perspective ignores the crucial question of audience and what it wants to hear. In short, how long does a company survive if it does not provide what a buying audience desires? We cannot simply argue that the radio stations make us like what we in other circumstances would loathe, any more than Kellogg could somehow force us to eat awful tasting breakfast cereal. In fact, even as he worries about the chilling effect of censorship, Nuzum himself notes that "anti-war music failed to ignite much interest among anti-war advocates at even the most grass-roots level" (154). He simply concedes that very few people, not even the anti-war demonstrators, wanted to hear protest music.

Moreover, granting corporate radio or the music industry itself so much power has become even more problematic given the way technology has changed the consumption of music, particularly since 2001. Post-9/11, many artists, including the Beastie Boys, R.E.M., and Green Day, offered their anti-war songs as free downloads online (McNair, Janis). So if a music-savvy and politically attuned younger generation wanted to hear protest music, it was literally there for the taking. To understand the politics of music after 9/11, then, we have to go beyond blaming corporations for quashing dissent. Instead, we need to interrogate the idealized view of sixties music that still holds sway for many critics, and explore how that vision in fact hinders our understanding of rock music produced in the wake of the 9/11 attacks.

Deliver Me from the Days of Old

Many cultural critics operate with an idealized notion of the politics of sixties music, as though the airwaves then were flooded with protest songs. They were not. If the argument is that media corporations stifled dissent after 9/11 because they did not promote protest music, then we should apply the same standard to the sixties. In doing so, what we quickly discover is that very few songs with explicit political lyrics charted in those heady days. If we compile the names of songs from the sixties with lyrics expressing resistance and protest, we arrive at a fairly short list. And if we trim that roster to songs that received substantial airplay, then we have, in fact, a minuscule list. It's true that Peter, Paul and Mary made the charts in 1963 with their cover of Bob Dylan's "Blowin' in the Wind," and that Barry McGuire had a #1 hit in 1965 with "Eve of Destruction." But when we look at a list of the most popular records in the sixties, protest music is virtually absent (Weinstein 5).

In fact, the bands and musicians that now stand as emblems for the sixties were strikingly apolitical in their lyrics. In the entire Beatles catalog, there is one song—one song!—that even comes close to taking an explicit political stance: "Revolution." And John Lennon was so ambivalent about its content that the two versions recorded by the band include slightly different lyrics: on the slower, *White Album* version, he sings "When you talk about destruction / don't you know that you can count me out ... in"; however, by the time the band recorded the faster, electric version, he had decided that wanted to be counted "out," a position that he reiterated throughout his life (Lennon 197). Ultimately, The Beatles' highly qualified endorsement of revolution led to excoriation from the New Left, who felt betrayed by their cultural heroes (Roessner 148–9). Other popular artists from the era exhibit a similar lack of political commitment: The Rolling Stones offer up "Street Fighting Man," for example, but little else.

If there is any basis for the vision of sixties music as steeped in protest, then, it is not in the chart hits of the decade, but in the folk protest tradition evident in Bob Dylan's early work. Drawing on the activist strain of his hero Woody Guthrie, Dylan served up a string of songs with overt political implications in the early sixties. Aside from "Blowin' in the Wind," he penned the anti-war anthems "Masters of War" and "A Hard Rain's A-Gonna Fall," and numerous tales of social and racial oppression along the lines of "The Lonesome Death of Hattie Carroll" and "Only a Pawn in Their Game"—the latter about the murder of civil rights activist Medgar Evers. However, although these songs admittedly helped solidify Dylan's folk-protest persona, they were generally not radio singles. And, more significantly, as early as 1964, Bob Dylan expressed the desire to eschew overtly political "finger-pointing songs," opting instead to pursue his poetic, French-symbolist-inspired brand of social commentary (Hentoff 65). And for every Dylan song of protest, of course, there were hundreds of hits performed by bands that had little interest in making a political statement. To take one prime example, The Beach Boys—or "America's band," as they eventually became known—

rarely ever came close to political engagement in their lyrics. Rather, with their dense harmonies, unusual instrumentation, and recording studio experiments, they represent the musical innovation that is as much associated with the sixties as any form of political rebellion.

So what accounts for the lingering notion that protest music saturated the airwaves and drove the debate surrounding the conflict in Vietnam? In his consideration of advertising culture in the sixties, *The Conquest of Cool*, Thomas Frank points toward an explanation of this potent narrative of rebellion. Specifically, Frank argues that we have been bequeathed a countercultural mythology in which the "unchanging and soulless machine" of capitalism is pitted against a youthful rebellion that represents a "joyous and even a glorious cultural flowering" (4–5). This narrative of sixties protest has become a seamless part of our popular culture, to the point that sixties iconography serves as an unquestioned sign of dissent. As Frank contends, "Commercial fantasies of rebellion, liberation, and outright 'revolution' against the stultifying demands of mass society are commonplace almost to the point of invisibility in advertising, movies, and television programming" (4). But for Frank, this is not a simple tale of co-optation, in which genuine rebellion is derailed by capitalists cynically using images of dissent to sell products. Rather, he argues that the "counterculture may be more accurately understood as a stage in the development of the American middle class" (29). In short, the values of the counterculture and of advertising/ capitalism were intertwined from the beginning, and it is a mistake to imagine them as polar opposites. As Peter Doggett argues, both The Beatles' "Revolution" and The Rolling Stones' "Street Fighting Man" were "the products of multi-national corporations, whose activities ranged from broadcasting to the manufacture of weapons" (220). He goes on to note that, by 1968, Columbia Records had begun its infamous "But the Man Can't Bust Our Music" campaign, as the company explicitly tried to identify itself with countercultural revolutionaries (220). Despite these inherent contradictions, however, the countercultural mythology persists in a seemingly endless media loop fueled, ironically, by the corporate advertising culture that was allegedly part of the problem.

Disseminated through commercial fantasies of resistance, the subversive aura of sixties rock is also supported by the highly charged political context of the era, which gave meaning to the music, rather than the other way around. Think of any documentary footage you can about Vietnam, the civil rights movement, or the assassination of John or Bobby Kennedy: these images almost immediately call to mind the soundtrack of sixties music that assuredly accompanies them. The images have been so closely linked to the music that listeners are led to ascribe a political charge to the music—even when it is utterly absent. Moreover, many contend that the lyrics of rock music in the sixties were beside the point: the politics resided in the sound of the music itself, which was brash, impudent and signaled a clear rejection of inherited values (Altschuler 107–108). The music was the aural equivalent of the famous dictum not to trust anyone over thirty: those were the adults who had driven the country to war in Vietnam, who had turned a blind eye to overt racism and sexism, and who treated the young with patronizing contempt. In short, the music provided a jolting, sonic shot across the bow, delivering the message that times had changed (Gitlin 41–2). From this point of view, the lyrics to The Beatles' "Revolution" may have been conflicted, but the distorted, slashing guitar intro accompanied by Lennon's shriek of primal rage delivered an unmistakable paean to revolt.

This argument about sonic rebellion has in fact been borne out by studies that suggest how wide the cultural rift between generations was in the sixties. It's worth reminding ourselves that most adults in the sixties did not like rock music or conceive of it as part of their culture: a study in 1966 indicated that a full 44 percent of adults positively disliked rock music, while a mere 4 percent identified it as their favorite genre (Taylor and Morin). So the feedback-laden guitar of Jimi Hendrix in his performance of "The Star Spangled Banner" at Woodstock, for example, was a politically charged sound wave with racial and countercultural overtones that could quite clearly be heard, both by young people who looked to him as heralding the future and by their disapproving parents.

But in the post-9/11 American soundscape, rock does not, prima facie, signify rebellion or a generational divide. As a recent Pew study makes clear, while rock was quite unpopular with adults in the sixties, currently a stunning 75 percent of those over age sixteen responded that they listen to rock often or sometimes; in fact, rock is the number one genre of music for every age category except those over the age of sixty-five (Taylor and Morin). So while boomers cranked the stereo in defiance of adult authority and hypocrisy, today's youth cannot easily deliver the same sonic message to their elders: "Don't trust anyone over sixty-five" hardly seems a radical sentiment. Moreover, as we have moved to inhabit a culture fully saturated with rock and the corporatized mythology of rebellion, the shift in musical taste has been accompanied by a corresponding shift in values. Astonishingly, young people today actually defer to rather than castigate their elders when it comes to morals: while only "about a quarter of the public (26%) says there is strong conflict in society today between the young and old," over two-thirds of those under age thirty believe that older adults have a stronger work ethic, a stronger sense of morality, and more respect for others (Taylor and Morin). Indeed, "Hope I die before I get old" has lost its taunting edge as rockers themselves have aged and their music has become the soundtrack of our everyday lives.

The shift toward the acceptance of rock has irrevocably redefined the genre's meaning as a cultural signifier. As an aside in the Pew study, authors Paul Taylor and Richard Morin note the irony that "while the music has largely stayed the same, its generational and cultural context has flipped. For boomers, rock was rebellion. For their children, it's mainstream" (Taylor and Morin). The Pew study emphasizes what should be evident to music critics: rock is part of living history. As such, its rhythm, its timbre, and its volume cannot simply be assigned a static and unchanging meaning based on past associations. Rather, the context of its present reception and distribution helps determine how it is consumed, who buys it, where and how it's listened to, and what role it plays in public social spaces. The fact that both Paul McCartney and The Rolling Stones have performed NFL Super Bowl half-time shows in the five years before 2011, for example, indicates how far the culture has come from the sixties, when so many adults actively disliked the music. Now it routinely serves the soundtrack for one of the largest rituals in American popular culture: who could watch these shows and imagine that the artists are somehow staging rebellion? In such arenas, we chart what Thomas Frank described as "bohemian cultural style's trajectory from adversarial to hegemonic" (8). From Frank's perspective, the aging hippies didn't simply abandon the revolution; rather, their countercultural style became dominant as "the way American capitalism understood itself and explained itself to the public" (26). In short, the bohemians won the cultural revolution, but in victory their style— particularly the distinctive signature of sixties music – lost much of its formerly radical political and social valence.

Teenage Symphonies to God

Given that rock has become the favorite genre for most people, it's not surprising that many contemporary artists have turned to the sixties for inspiration. Indeed, the Pew study indicates that The Beatles are popular across a wide swath of the culture, landing among the top four most popular artists for every age group studied (Taylor and Morin). And of course rock bands have consistently flaunted their indebtedness to their sixties heroes well before 9/11. Examples include everything from R.E.M.'s covers of Velvet Underground tunes to Oasis' collage of Beatles' ephemera to the multitude of tribute albums devoted to bands such as The Rolling Stones, The Kinks, and The Who. But the particular adaptation of sixties style after the 9/11 terrorist attacks bears special attention in this context. Contemporary rock artists do continue to draw heavily on the stylistic innovations of their sixties forebears, and in this sense share with many critics a deep nostalgia for the era. What recent artists don't generally seem to do, however, is see protest as an integral part of what they have inherited.

Indeed, if the legacy of sixties protest were to appear in recent music, we might well expect to see it in bands who came of age in the wake of the terrorist attacks and whose music is richly evocative of the earlier generation. Two illustrative contemporary examples are Grizzly Bear and Fleet Foxes. More so than many of their peers, these bands ground their aesthetics in the folk genre (with its rich link to the protest tradition), while also exhibiting the signature harmonic and studio experimentation of earlier artists. The members of Grizzly Bear all attended New York University, and the band released its first recording, *Horn of Plenty*, in 2004 (Goodman). Their West Coast peers Fleet Foxes debuted as a band in 2006, and released their initial effort, the *Sun Giant* EP, in 2008, when main songwriter and singer Robin Pecknold was twenty-two years old (McNair, James). Along with reaching maturity in the age of terrorism, both bands—although not remarkably similar in their sound—share the distinctive influence of sixties music. In particular, Grizzly Bear was tagged with the label "freak-folk" in their early days (Bemis). As for Fleet Foxes, Pecknold tells stories of family sing-a-longs to Crosby, Stills, and Nash tunes, and claims, "I was obsessed with Dylan ... The first song I learned was 'The Times They are A-Changin'"" (Scaggs; Simmons 86). With such a pedigree, Pecknold in particular might be expected to take up the finger-pointing cause.

Ultimately, though, Grizzly Bear and Fleet Foxes share a debt to another, decidedly apolitical strain of sixties rock music: both bands reflect the formative influence of Brian Wilson and The Beach Boys; in fact, they are frequently linked to the genre of chamber pop, the heir to the baroque pop of such sixties luminaries as Phil Spector and Brian Wilson (Gendron 172). As producers, Spector and Wilson helped widen the palette of rock by employing classical instrumentation and emphasizing complex choral rather than solo vocals. With its venerable heritage, baroque pop has long fascinated aspiring rock musicians, and chamber pop itself can be traced back at least to the mid-1990s and artists such as Sufjan Stevens and Eric Matthews. But it wasn't until the first decade of the twenty-first century that the choral vocal style came to prominence and Fleet Foxes arrived at commercial success (Frere-Jones).

Of the two bands, Grizzly Bear reflects a more pronounced indebtedness to Brian Wilson, and their musical style is anything but community-minded or politically engaged. The songs echo with reverb, and often sound as if you are overhearing a piano played in a distant room or inhabiting a house that is musically haunted. The effect is the opposite of clarity or an obsession with fidelity. Indeed, the music often features "found sounds," instruments that do not sound like themselves, or ones that are paired in unexpected ways – all tactics famously explored by Wilson on *Pet Sounds* (Lambert 3). Moreover, Grizzly Bear seems to have taken vocal cues from the complex fugato style of Wilson's arrangements, in which multiple, independent melodic lines are successively introduced and interwoven (Lambert 19). In short, the songs are not rousing or rebellious, but complex, layered, and multivalent.

Given the dream-like quality of much of this music, it is no surprise that the lyrics, too, downplay communal feeling, instead offering brief meditations on isolation and introversion. Edward Droste's home recording project—which became the first Grizzly Bear record, *Horn of Plenty*—opens with the song "Deep Sea Diver" and an image of submersion: "I'm a deep sea diver with my fins / and underneath your current I do swim"; driving home a sense of disconnection, the final lines refer to "losing air" and "sad swimming" while the object of affection simply doesn't care. As he calls up images of suffocation and loss, Droste distills Brian Wilson's self-consciousness to its essence, and seems to drown in the waters that The Beach Boys once surfed. Although the lyrics Wilson set to his music often exhibited introspection and longing ("Caroline, No," "I Just Wasn't Made for These Times," or even "In My Room"), the singer never seriously voices defeat, even if he at times feels dejected, and for listeners there is always the promise of a rousing chorus on the next track. In contrast, Grizzly Bear revels in tentative, desolate moods that hang like thick fog, and which are underscored by lyrics that have so far been sparse in the extreme. On their first full-length recording as a proper band, *Yellow House*, the singers deliver a total of 624 words, with the longest song, "Marla," offering 148 words and the shortest, "Colorado," featuring a mere twenty-two. Here self-expression fails to console, as language remains minimal, fragmentary, and suspect.

So what can we make of Grizzly Bear's oddly enchanting but disconsolate music as a response to the post-9/11 world? The band seems less interested in offering a lyrical message than in establishing a musical mood and enhancing it with brief, suggestive phrases. This spare tone is enhanced by the lack of verbal coherence, reflected in the jarring syntax of the lines. The first track on *Yellow House*, "Easier," includes the lyrics "I know, I know, the doors won't close, the pipes all froze, just let it go. Argue with me." The disjunctive grammatical structure and frequent parataxis open spaces in meaning, akin to the spaces separating the people who inhabit this relationship. And the songs themselves are generally offered as shards, blending into one another, with fragmented lyrics that confirm a shattered sense of personal identity. On *Yellow House*, the lyrics are presented underneath the disc in the jewel case, run together without titles or line breaks. If Grizzly Bear's music can be read as a response to the post-9/11 world, then, it does not function as a call to protest or urge us to adopt a strident pose in the face of assault; rather, the band offers an evocative, harmonically dense dissection of anguish, self-doubt, and loss.

In a similar vein, Fleet Foxes eschew activism, though they don't escape the present so much by looking inward as by looking backward. The melodic inventiveness of The Beach Boys stands out as a primary influence on their music, too, but the vocal interplay of The Band and the folk melodicism of Fairport Convention loom large as well. Fleet Foxes open the breakthrough EP *Sun Giant* with the largely a cappella tune "Sun Giant," which only briefly introduces a plinking mandolin after the singing has ended. Their first full-length offering, *Fleet Foxes*, opens in a similar vein, with an a cappella verse of "Sun it Rises," before breaking into characteristic acoustic strumming and lilting, bell-like guitar lines. With little sign of strident posturing from the male lead vocalist, the records feature harmonized vocals often awash in reverb. The intricate choral arrangements underscore the sense of this music as a hearkening back.

The timeless feel of Fleet Foxes' music is also reflected in the archaic language and subjects of their lyrics, which helped establish the band's popularity. The very song titles, such as "Tiger Mountain Peasant Song," "White Winter Hymnal," and "Sun it Rises" (with its poetic inversion), suggest a bygone era. And, throughout, the themes invariably wind their way to a celebration of the natural world. In "Blue Ridge Mountains," for example, the singer invites his brother to "drive to the countryside / leave behind some green-eyed look-alikes" so that "no one gets worried, no." And in "Meadowlarks," you're assured of the meadowlark "singing to you each and every day." The closest approximation to this style in the sixties might be The Beatles' "Mother Nature's Son." With their shimmering vocal texture and assurance of finding solace in nature, Fleet Foxes achieved some measure of popular and critical success: *Fleet Foxes*, for example, was selected by *Mojo* readers as the best album of 2008 and wound up on many critics' best-of-the-year lists as well (Simmons 80; Clayton). Such success indicates that their music expresses a sentiment or evokes a mood that is shared.

But the communal feeling does not incite action or express a common political vision. In this sense, Fleet Foxes and Grizzly Bear help us chart the evolution of folk music away from hard-line social activism. For many, folk music of the late fifties and early sixties signified communal resistance, with the singer as the mouthpiece exposing political corruption and highlighting social ills. The music thus functioned as a social conscience, often supported by a rigid morality, and it offered a clarion call to awakening. Bob Dylan's "The Times They Are a-Changin'" encapsulates the general tenor of folk poetics in this tradition, as it puts conservative and morally stunted adversaries on notice that they had better get out of the way if they "can't lend a hand" in remaking the culture. Although Grizzly Bear and Fleet Foxes adopt some of the stylistic markers of the tradition— hence the label freak folk—they reject the very element that made it explicitly political: its finger-pointing morality. In this sense, the bands are as heretical as Dylan, the infamous turncoat who abandoned folk and picked up an electric guitar.

In the brooding introspection of Grizzly Bear and the poignant lyricism of Fleet Foxes, we hear the search for solace in the face of loss and the attempt to recover of a sense of enduring, mystical beauty. From a literary standpoint, such themes are essentially Romantic. In setting such longing to music, both bands do adapt a variety of styles associated with the sixties and situate themselves as prodigal heirs to the folk tradition that they have proceeded to reimagine. But as a response to the chaos and threat of the post-9/11 era, their music reminds us that, for contemporary artists, the sixties represent far more than protest and rebellion. Startling musical inventiveness, studio experimentation, dense harmonic layering, and the general quest for individual identity in an indifferent cultural landscape, these markers of sixties style fire the imagination of younger musicians much more than the protest themes of topical songs.

The Future of the Sixties

Fleet Foxes and Grizzly Bear, of course, do not represent the only way that sixties musical styles have been adapted in current music. And I am not suggesting that all rock lyrics and music have become apolitical. As was made clear above, much music of protest was released in the first decade of the twenty-first century, particularly as the invasion of Iraq stalled and President Bush's popularity sank to a remarkable low. But Fleet Foxes and Grizzly Bear do represent the complex legacy of the sixties in their adaptation of earlier musical styles. Along with many other rock bands in the post-9/11 world, they did not give the political response that critics may have hoped for. Indeed, the most prevalent wish of those seeking political meaning in rock music is that it retain (or recover) a sense of community that it supposedly solidified in the sixties. It's telling, for example, that Ray Pratt opens his book *Rhythm and Resistance* with an evocation of the soundtrack to Oliver Stone's Vietnam film *Platoon* juxtaposed with an account of a 1985 concert by Bruce Springsteen and the E Street Band; in the book, Pratt goes on to explore this music as "significant and deeply moving examples of mass popular culture consumed and experienced by millions of people that may, some say, function simultaneously as a national and perhaps even international language" (2). This desire to read music as a "national language" suggests how deeply we want to believe that the music so many find personally meaningful must have a larger political effect. And the *Platoon* example—wed as it is to the sixties—underscores the search not just for communal meaning, but for the supposed political activism of an earlier age.

The problem is that sixties music presents anything but a coherent message when it comes to political action. Contrary to the image handed down to us, protest music was not a pervasive or popular genre then. And the more general rebelliousness expressed through rock was directed at a specific target: the adult authority of that era. Furthermore, the model of communal engagement called upon by recent critics seems strikingly out of key with much of the music produced in the wake of 9/11. In bands seemingly well positioned to wake up the echoes of sixties protest, we hear the homage to past styles, but not the dream of community. In short, the music offers not a feeling of empowerment or solidarity, but confusion and a growing sense of isolation and introversion, which makes a unified, politicized community increasingly hard to imagine. Moreover, the dream of collective action is difficult for contemporary music to inspire given the increasing fragmentation of audiences. As music critic Elijah Wald hyperbolically states, "For the first time in history, nobody has the faintest idea of who is listening to what" (Wald). For contemporary music, there is no simple equivalent to the record sales charts of days past. While sales figures can certainly tell you how many listeners are snapping up the latest Justin Timberlake offering, they are especially awful at indicating the distribution of independent artists. For those deeply invested in music as a reflection of their identity, listening and trading largely happens underground, electronically and illegally. Only in high-profile file-sharing lawsuits do you get a sense of the enormity of the problem, or how difficult it is to track listening habits.

If for many contemporary artists the legacy of the sixties is not protest, and the very idea of a community of listeners has been challenged by fragmented audiences, what might be the enduring legacy of that decade? One tentative answer comes from John Lennon (who, incidentally, only turned to consistent political activism through his music in the early 1970s, after the break-up of The Beatles). In his song "God," Lennon alerted us that "the dream is over," meaning the dream of The Beatles, gurus, hippies, Dylan, or any other supposed savior. In this context, I read the "dream" as a belief in the value of countercultural protest for its own sake.

In other words, Lennon recognized that style is not political substance. Wearing your hair long, or appropriating the folky stylings of early Bob Dylan, or stepping on your distortion pedal has no inherent political valence. To think otherwise is to succumb to a nostalgia that, in fact, distorts history. Through his own political commitments, Lennon demonstrates that such nostalgia obscures a clear-sighted engagement with the present. Consequently, Lennon's ever-vigilant attempt to wake up to the present moment—that might be the most valuable legacy of the sixties.

Works Cited

Altschuler, Glenn. *All Shook Up: How Rock 'n' Roll Changed America.* Oxford: Oxford UP, 2003. Print.

Bemis, Alec Hanley. "Folk, Without the Beards." *L.A. Weekly.* Feb. 15, 2007. Web. Oct. 16, 2009. Print.

Clayton, Richard. "Fleet Foxes Are in Harmony with Success." *Times Online.* Mar. 29, 2009. Web. Oct. 27, 2009.

DiFranco, Ani. "Self-Evident." *So Much Shouting, So Much Laughter.* Righteous Babe, 2002. CD.

Doggett, Peter. *There's a Riot Going On: Revolutionaries, Rock Stars and the Rise and Fall of the '60s.* Edinburgh: Canongate, 2007. Print.

Dope Poet Society. "War of Terrorism." *ProIntelPro.* Justus, 2007. CD.

Earle, Steve. "John Walker's Blues." *Jerusalem.* Artemis, 2002. CD.

Fleet Foxes. "Blue Ridge Mountains." *Fleet Foxes.* Sub Pop, 2008. CD.

——. "Meadowlarks." *Fleet Foxes.* Sub Pop, 2008. CD.

Frank, Thomas. *The Conquest of Cool: Business Culture, Counterculture, and the Rise of Hip Consumerism.* Chicago: U of Chicago P, 1997. Print.

Frere-Jones, Sasha. "Boys' Choir." *The New Yorker.* May 11, 2009. Web. Oct. 16, 2009.

Garofalo, Reebee. "Pop Goes to War, 2001–2004: US Popular Music After 9/11." *Music in the Post-9/11 World.* Ed. Jonathan Ritter and Martin Daughtry. New York: Routledge, 2007. 3–26. Print.

Gendron, Bernard. *Between Montmartre and the Mudd Club: Popular Music and the AvantGarde.* Chicago, IL: U of Chicago P, 2002. Print.

Gitlin, Todd. *The Sixties: Years of Hope, Days of Rage.* Toronto, ON: Bantam, 1987. Print.

Goodman, Liz. "Grizzly Men." *New York Magazine.* May 3, 2009. Web. Oct. 15, 2009.

Grizzly Bear. "Deep Sea Diver." *Horn of Plenty.* Kanine Records, 2004. CD.

——. "Easier." *Yellow House.* Warp Records, 2006. CD.

Hentoff, Nat. "The Crackin', Shakin', Breakin' Sounds." *The New Yorker.* Oct. 24, 1964: 64–90. Print.

Klinenberg, Eric. *Fighting for Air: The Battle to Control America's Media.* New York: Metropolitan Books, 2007. Print.

Lambert, Philip. "Brian Wilson's Pet Sounds." *Twentieth Century Music* 5.1 (2008): 109–33. Print.

Lennon, John. Interview with David Sheff. *The Playboy Interviews with John Lennon & Yoko Ono.* Ed. G. Barry Golson. New York: Berkley Books, 1981. Print.

McNair, James. "On the Hunt for Meaning with Seattle Band Fleet Foxes." *The Independent.* June 13, 2008. Web. Oct. 16, 2009.

McNair, Janis. "Make Music, Not War." *Center for Political Song.* Glasgow Caledonian University. May 2003. Web. Sept. 9, 2009.

Nuzum, Eric. "Crash Into Me, Baby: America's Implicit Music Censorship Since 11 September." *Shoot the Singer!* Ed. Marie Korpe. London: Zed Books, 2004. 149–59. Print.

Pratt, Ray. *Rhythm and Resistance*. New York: Praeger, 1990. Print.

Roessner, Jeffrey. "We All Want to Change the World: Postmodern Politics and the Beatles' White Album." *Reading the Beatles*. Ed. Kenneth Womack and Todd F. Davis. Albany: SUNY, 2006. 147–58. Print.

Scaggs, Austin. "Fleet Foxes' Perfect Harmony." *Rolling Stone*. Nov. 13, 2008. Web. Sep. 29, 2009.

Scherzinger, Martin. "Double Voices of Musical Censorship after 9/11." *Music in the Post-9/11 World*. Ed. Jonathan Ritter and Martin Daughtry. New York: Routledge, 2007. 91–121. Print.

Simmons, Sylvie. "Smile." *Mojo*. Aug. 2009: 80–88. Print.

Street, John. *Rebel Rock*. Oxford: Blackwell, 1986. Print.

Taylor, Paul and Richard Morin. "Forty Years after Woodstock, a Gentler Generation Gap." *Pew Research Center*. Aug. 12, 2009. Web. Sept. 11, 2009.

Ten Years After. "I'd Love to Change the World." *A Space in Time*. Chrysalis, 1971. CD.

Wald, Elijah. Interview with Laura Fitzpatrick. *Time*. June 24, 2009. Web. Oct. 22, 2009.

Weinstein, Deena. "Rock Protest Songs: So Many and So Few." *The Resisting Muse: Popular Music and Social Protest*. Ed. Ian Peddie. Burlington, VA: Ashgate. 3–16. Print.

Chapter 10

A New Morning in Amerika: Conservative Politics and Punk Rock in the 2000s

Matthew Siblo

Considering the profound impact of September 11, 2001 and subsequent military efforts in Iraq and Afghanistan had on American culture, the reaction from the punk community was cautious, if not muted. It was not until the beginning of the 2004 presidential election cycle where musical protestation, be it from punk artists or otherwise, became increasingly pronounced. At that point, President George W. Bush's approval ratings were dropping, particularly regarding his handling of war, ultimately dipping below 50 percent (Arak). The outsized presence of musicians during the election was "notable for both the unprecedented amount of direct political action and activity occurring within popular culture *during* the campaign and the interactions that took place *between* the formal campaign and these various cultural venues and actors" (Jones 196). Political engagement occurred on a large scale with *MoveOn.org*'s Vote for Change tour featuring Bruce Springsteen and Pearl Jam, along with genre-tailored outreach focused on youth-centric musical niches. Music for America collaborated with indie rock bands like Death Cab for Cutie and Modest Mouse, while Punk Voter mobilized the punk audience, a group traditionally resistant to large-scale advocacy (Ventre).

Punk Voter was the brainchild of 'Fat' Mike Burkett of the popular punk band NOFX—and partially funded by Silicon Valley mogul Andy Rappaport—who intended to "build a coalition of kids 18 to 25" including "punks and other disenfranchised young people to vote as a bloc, which no one has ever done before" to defeat President Bush (Garofoli; Wiederhorn). Punk Voter's Rock Against Bush campaign was all encompassing, featuring nationwide tours and two successful compilations on his record label Fat Wreck Chords, which reportedly sold over 650,000 copies, the proceeds subsidizing billboards in northern swing states and full-color ads in *US Magazine* (Pedersen; Wiederhorn). At the peak of its popularity, *Punkvoter.com* received 15 million hits a month and helped raise more than one million dollars, as Burkett entertained the organization becoming "a lobby group like the AARP or the NRA" (Garofoli; Winter 7). Given their historically anti-authoritarian leanings, punk musicians rallying against the Bush administration was not surprising; Punk Voter's engagement with mainstream political activism was more remarkable, especially from Burkett, whose band's pointed anti-MTV stance made him an unconventional spokesperson alongside popular left-leaning musicians such as Springsteen and Pearl Jam's Eddie Vedder. Thus, the group had its critics. Though the press provided ample, largely positive coverage to Punk Voter, singer Stephan Smith-Said wrote in an editorial for *The Progressive* that MTV initially declined to cover the Rock Against Bush campaign, claiming it was "not relevant" (Smith-Said). Propagandhi, a politically outspoken Canadian punk band signed with Burkett's label, requested that its contribution to the first *Rock Against Bush* compilation include the statement "this message was not brought to you by George Soros" in the liner notes (Aubin). The comment was a swipe at the controversial billionaire who donated heavily to progressive causes but had a long-standing history with the controversial Carlyle Group. Burkett, skittish about alienating partnering groups who received funding from Soros, asked that the band be placed on the second *Rock Against Bush* album, where the note would receive less immediate attention. They declined (Aubin). The reticence by Propagandhi to make this concession also occurred within Washington, DC punk activist group Positive Force, some members feeling like supporting Punk Voter meant acting as a spokesperson for mainstream politicians (Andersen and Jenkins 412).

The criticism stemmed from Punk Voter's collaboration with an unusual ally: the Democratic Party. In an interview with Greg Winter of *CMJ*, Burkett said his goal for Punk Voter was to register 500,000 young people, an idea that came from NOFX's playing a show in Florida shortly after the controversial result of the 2000 presidential election (Winter 6). He felt like it had become his "civic duty" to use his influence since it could have helped alter the outcome. Burkett, who famously refused to do interviews with his band, was a guest on nationally syndicated talk shows and attended Democratic National Committee meetings, even sitting down with the Democratic nominee himself, Sen. John Kerry of Massachusetts (Garofoli).

In the wake of Punk Voter's widespread visibility and, for some, disagreeable alliances, "conservative punk" emerged as an ideological counterpoint within the hyper-partisan and deeply divisive political landscape. *Conservativepunk.com* and others like it found their way into the *BBC*, *The New York Times*, *USA Today*, and *The Washington Post*, vocalizing its disdain for Punk Voter's codified view of punk politics. The coverage of these websites focused on the seemingly paradoxical impulse of punk fans and musicians aligning themselves with conservative politics, a development leading to great consternation among punk's most ardent and vocal followers. But how novel is this combination? Time has shown the conservative punk movement of 2004 to be little more than a countercultural Potemkin. At the time of writing, nearly six years later, the movement is nearly invisible, and the clandestine majority purported by its founders revealed itself to be nonexistent. But why couldn't conservative politics be understood within the traditionally rebellious youth culture, given its tendency to perseverate on the glories of the past? Were conservative punks distilling its movement's initial spirit by bucking convention, or do these political associations somehow betray punk's fundamental principles of independence and disobedience?

A Riot of Their Own

Andrew Wilkow was instrumental in making conservative punk a reality through his New York talk radio show. He explains:

> The idea of conservative punk was born on the air when I said that I can't be the only one who likes punk rock and conservatism. Let's create something for young people to let them know they're not alone. Their favorite bands were telling them that they couldn't think this way. The first time I went to a punk show, it was about energy and music. Who are you to tell me this genre of music has a cemented political leaning?

In his tome "Punk Rock, Diversity, and the Gonzo Conservatives," Dave Smalley, *Conservativepunk.com* columnist and member of seminal punk bands Dag Nasty and Down by Law, articulates the contradiction of a regimented political belief system within punk. Chiding those claiming to promote an open-minded atmosphere while reinforcing ideological absolutism, his principles of so-called gonzo-conservativism described those "punk rockers who believe in the government staying as small as possible, keeping taxes low and acting when necessary to defend the country" (Smalley). Smalley's vision comes closer to the individual freedoms promised under libertarianism—which are similarly fetishized within punk—rather than traditional conservative principles, particularly since many identifying as conservative punk shied away from the hot-button social and cultural issues that dominated much of the Bush reelection campaign.

Like Punk Voter, those involved with conservative punk did not receive direct funding from any political party, but its goals were far narrower. Whereas Burkett regularly met with politicians and political action committees, the conservative punk movement, if it can be described as such, was a loosely assembled group of fans intent on obtaining visibility. Here, conservative-minded punks appropriate the idea that "there exists in the electorate a hidden conservative majority; that the social division with the greatest political significance is not that between the 'haves' and 'have nots' but between the liberal elite and everyone else" (Kirkpatrick 103). Most of *Conservativepunk.com*'s media coverage, fielded by founder Nick Rizzuto and Wilkow, reiterate that very point: We are not alone (St. John). Rizzuto hoped to "discredit the stereotype that aligns punk voters with liberalism by informing young people of more conservative ideals through punk music," a forum "more welcoming to conservatives" (Shea and Green 189). In an interview with Dorian Lynskey for *The Guardian*, Rizzuto referred to himself as a "fearless voice of a silent majority" and claimed support from anonymous musicians he did not feel comfortable mentioning, "especially in a European newspaper" (Lynskey).

Speaking with Dave Segal of *The Washington Post*, Rizzuto claimed that *Conservativepunk.com* received over one million visits as of October 2004, though he admitted much of the attention stemmed from the "freak factor" of his beliefs and that half of the emails he received from the site were "hostile" (Segal).

Borrowing the phrasing of the controversial ban on gays in the American military, Rizzuto claimed that before the existence of his site "it was almost don't-ask, don't-tell (in the punk scene). If you were conservative or libertarian and not a bleeding-heart liberal, you almost felt like a bit of an outcast" (Ross). As well as Wilkow and Rizzuto, former Misfits lead singer Michael Graves spoke on behalf of *Conservativepunk.com*, which according to Rizzuto, resulted in the cancellation of Graves' European tour after a promoter read about his right-leaning views in *The New York Times* (Lynskey). In an essay published on *Conservativepunk.com*, Graves wrote that the punk political left "seem to indulge themselves in voguish conspiracy-mongering and an increasing belief that they are persecuted from all directions" (Graves). Echoing Rizzuto's post-9/11 political awakening detailed in *The Washington Post*, Graves goes on to say:

> Rebellion against the center of society and its politics is nothing new to punk rock. The stakes, however, have become much higher ... what happened on September 11, 2001 forever changed the dynamic of not only our country, but our lives, and if not paid proper attention to, the politics and anti-politics of the young will become more and more dangerous to everyone and everything. (Graves)

Like others on the right, Graves utilized the lingering anxieties of the 9/11 attacks to propose a life-threatening ultimatum: it is our way or impending catastrophe. The events of September 11, 2001, providing the very real threat of terrorism, changed the familiar script of the culture wars. Flipping the narrative, Republicans controlled all levels of Congress until 2006 by perpetuating an underdog mentality that capitalized on persecution from "the other" (Tiefer 234). This allowed for an ideological upper hand (pro-American, us vs. *them*), where they maintained control by positioning themselves as besieged by threats, both authentic and imagined. Identifying as the minority against *them* (defined as the terrorists, the non-patriotic), the right was given the platform of persecution from outside sources while retaining dominance. Though the political circumstances were largely different, this mentality resembled the neo-conservative movement of the 1990s, in which politicians tapped into the frustration and anger of an encroaching threat to middle-class values while upholding the advantages afforded to them through gender, socioeconomic status, and education.

    Punk rock and conservative politics overlap in their branding of outsider status to the decidedly privileged worldview of the white middle-class male, a profile that makes up a majority of those who now consider themselves punk (O'Hara 40). Punk rock conservatives in 2004, fashioning themselves as a minority within both their own liberal subculture and society at large, are afforded the self-identity of the ultimate outsiders while enjoying the insider benefits of the social and political majority. For conservative punks, their marginalized status derives from a principled stance against subcultural conformity, defying the hegemony of Punk Voter's liberalism. According to them, the result of their convictions—

cancelled tours, supporters too scared to reveal themselves—was irrefutable proof of persecution and justifiable righteousness. Prioritizing their rebellion against the punk community's ideological expectations diffuses the contradictions that emerge from an alignment with conventional authority.

Given Burkett's claim that "the punk scene is very united. We're gonna get every punk-rock band together, and I think we can take over the country and change the world," categorizing oneself as a conservative punk, and supporting the policies of the President of the United States, can be seen as daring (Wiederhorn). When punk conservative Johnny Ramone thanked George W. Bush on stage at The Ramones induction to The Rock and Roll Hall of Fame in 2002—itself a conservative enterprise—it might have been the most audacious gesture he could make (Fowler). Furthermore, *Rolling Stone*'s Anthony DeCurtis told the BBC, "In a lot of ways in the United States, the Republicans have gotten much more punk rock than the Democrats. The right has become more punk than the left: they're much more pugnacious, much more aggressive and much more forceful about putting out their ideas and drawing a line in the sand" (Fowler). Yet, considering the paucity of artists actively supporting the conservative punk movement, DeCurtis' assessment was more theoretical than prophetic. In Liz Worth's profile on conservative punk for the zine *Punk Planet*, the previously unknown Atilla and the Huns is the only band interviewed to identify with the label. Though not nearly visible as *Rock Against Bush*, *Crush Kerry: A Conservative Punk Compilation* was released in September 2004 on the now defunct American Streak Records. It featured two songs by The Undead, a new project from Bobby Steele of The Misfits, otherwise compromised little-known but colorfully named bands like The FlipFloppers, and Smart Bombs and Apple Pie. Yet, even if the few conservative-leaning punk bands failed to match the cadre of Punk Voter's anti-Bush allies, punk's intersection with right-leaning politics is far more complicated than Rizzuto and his cohorts let on.

A Conservative History of Punk Rock

One well-known example is The Ramones' Johnny Ramone. A staunch conservative, he did not believe the band should incorporate political issues into their music, preferring that it be "fun and entertaining" (Melnick and Meyer 163). This led to a spat with Joey and Dee Dee Ramone over the lyrics on "Bonzo Goes to Bitburg," a song decrying Ronald Reagan's controversial trip to Germany in 1985, where he attended a wreath-laying ceremony for forty-nine SS troops (Weinraub). The title was eventually reduced to a parenthetical phrase on the 1986 album *Animal Boy*, since Johnny considered Reagan "the best president of our lifetime" (Gillespie and Doherty). The proliferation of hardcore—punk's harder, punchier offshoot—in the 1980s resonated with a largely white, working-class audience, and the politics of its most popular bands—Fear, Murphy's Law, and The Cro-Mags—had a semblance of right-wing rhetoric. New York hardcore band

Agnostic Front's song "Public Assistance," written by Peter Steele, who went on to front metal band Type O Negative, is explicit in its mistrust of immigrant groups and social programs by lambasting the "crying minorities" who receive subsidized abortions but should be "cleaning the sewers" (Blush 192).

Ideologically, antipathy toward governmental intrusion is a unifying thread between punks and conservatives, both groups balking at the imposing reach of federal authority. Worth argues that this resentment and the importance of "thinking for one's self" is common ground between the two, but remained skeptical whether both could peacefully co-exist (70). Fueled by the economic inopportunity in the UK during the late 1970s, punk's vitriol stemmed from diminished expectations and resentment toward immigrant populations, with whom many young people had to compete with for work. In the UK, "Pakis" (a derogatory term for Pakistanis and other South Asians) were often targets. The far-right group the National Front, to cite just one example, made use of this resentment to gain credibility in the burgeoning punk culture (Barker and Taylor 270). Mark Anderson of Positive Force believes:

> There's a conservative aspect present through punk's various movements but it's always clearly the minority. Someone like Ian Stewart of Skrewdriver quickly moved his band in a very hard right direction in the early 1980s. He found an audience within parts of the English working class where more right wing politics flourished. A band like Sham 69, who was not in that scene necessarily, had their gigs interrupted by skinheads. Is skinhead punk? It is certainly identified with it but it's not the dominant strain.

Straight edge became its own distinct punk-related subculture in the 1980s, taking its inspiration from a song of the same name by Washington, DC hardcore band Minor Threat. Straight edge was a popular musical movement advocating temperance, where "participants develop [sic] personal identities grounded in an ascetic lifestyle of not doing drugs and not engaging in promiscuous sex," partly developed in response to the self-destructive impulses of early punk (Williams 176). Those classifying themselves as straight edge—mostly white, middle-class males aged fifteen to twenty-five—cultivated a complex subcultural code comprising both lifestyle and musical genre, with the rules of both seen as dogma: There are no exceptions and membership must be consistently reinforced for life (Haenfler 409).

At different points in its complicated history, straight edge has had pockets of followers who expanded it to include militant animal-rights activism, devout Christianity and Hare Krishna, but rarely traditional political perspectives. While straight edge often dovetails with punk's fierce individualistic mindset, the perceived homogenization of its music and participants has made it an easy target for criticism in light of punk's aspirations toward open-mindedness. Ian MacKaye, the influential singer of Minor Threat and Fugazi, has since distanced himself from the movement:

A lot of the people who really sign on with straight edge, or even hardcore, are really conservative. They are essentially the same as greasers, guys who still want to look like Elvis. We're talking about people who are saying "this is the way it should be done." They may have felt that within their context, within punk rock, they were being reactionary, but they are essentially lining up with the whole of America, or at least a significant part of it.

He finds the injection of conservative politics into punk unsurprising:

Personally, I thought you'd see it sooner because someone like Johnny Ramone was conservative since day one. But there was always this slight kind of irony about it, like the "We love America" thing, which in the late '70s made sense. At that time, to be even remotely patriotic was considered not cool. Punk rockers, being antagonistic as we were, we would say things like "Fuck Iran!" I was also 17 years old. What is surprising to me is that many of these conservative punk people are grown men and women.

True to punk's reactionary tone, Andersen recalls, "the very first band MacKaye was in, The Slinkees, had a song called 'Conservative Rock.'" This type of enmity is typical, punk being riddled with contradiction since its formation in the mid-late 1970s. With the initial influence of glam, David Bowie's blond Fuehrer is one of the first examples, however extreme, of right-wing imagery being used by one of the genre's predecessors as a shock tactic (Hebdige 60). Swastikas were de rigueur among certain crowds in the late 1970s, including bands like The Dead Boys, though its intent belied a desire to antagonize and not necessarily to sympathize with Nazi politics (McNeil and McCain 248).

These provocations reflected the era's increasing joblessness and shifting moral standards, with punks dramatizing the idea of crisis to make the mood tangible (Hebdige 87). Aspiring to commercial success while glamorizing nihilism, punk called for revolutionary upheaval and utter depravity, sometimes within the same breath (Barker and Taylor 265). Nearly forty years later, ascribing a definitive meaning to punk is a quixotic task, with its usage now more diffuse but a firm meaning no less obscure: a word that could appropriately describe a lifestyle, a guitar line, or a haircut. The semiotics of punk style was an intentionally outlandish representation of rebellion against the middle class. It resembled other subcultures, but a process of commoditization gradually developed, neutering its outlandishness by uniformly adhering to a singular representation. In *Subculture: The Meaning of Style*, Dick Hebdige describes this process as "taking two characteristic forms: (1) the conversion of subcultural signs (dress, music, etc) into mass-produced objects (i.e. the commodity form); (2) the 'labelling' and re-definition of deviant behavior by dominant groups—the police, the media, the judiciary (i.e. the ideological form)" (94). The other is then turned into "a pure object, a spectacle or a clown" (94). The irony—an anti-establishment youth movement guided by regimented standards of behavior and dress—is compounded by the broader culture's co-option of these semiotic indicators, stripping the gestures of their intent as a means of reducing its power in the same way MacKaye describes the misappropriation of the greaser sixty years after the fact. That some segments of punk style have remained mostly static since its inception in the late 1970s heightens the sense of compliant nonconformity.

These traditionalist tendencies are fitting since, as a musical genre, punk's effectiveness is often judged against narrow parameters. Songs abiding by a punk template—specific chord progressions played at a specific speed with specific instruments—have followed an easily identifiable structure nearly for the genre's entire existence. The success of the music comes in its listener's ability to recognize the sound (loud, fast, and angry) and respond with preordained behavior (jump, push, punch). In this rigidity, a creative tension emerges, with various approaches and dichotomies that continue to this day: Is Punk Voter's goal of ideological coherence an uncomfortable but necessary push toward self-definition, or is it another example of punk's conflicted inner dialogue? Does clothing and musical preference make one punk, or is it the absence of artistic restriction? Is it the eternal outsider, the snarling kid in the corner flipping off The Man, defined by its distance from the mainstream, or should it be part of a broader movement aiming to remake the mainstream, to overtake and transform society? (Andersen and Jenkins 414).

Flex Your Head

By its very nature, punk rejects coherent ideology, which is the point; its existence is a direct negation of prevailing societal belief systems. "Mass movements are always so unhip. That's what was great about punk. It was an anti-movement," proclaims *Punk* magazine founder Legs McNeil (McNeil and McCain 275). In Stephen Blush's *American Hardcore: A Tribal History*, the lead singer of hardcore band TSOL Jack Grisham put it bluntly, professing that "one of the things I think people get wrong is that they try to classify hardcore as a big social movement. The majority of the kids were dropouts and they had no plans. It was just a bunch of jerks. We were for anarchy because anarchy was fun" (352). This is partly true. It is difficult enough to construct a cohesive understanding of what punk "is" or "means," never mind a governing political affiliation. Punk's mobilization of youthful frustration began as an amalgam of -isms, borrowing from numerous vaguely leftist ideologies, anarchy being the most prominently espoused. Punk's partnering with Rock Against Racism in the late 1970s introduced an explicit social commentary and political criticism reinterpreted within a wide spectrum of progressive politics in the 1980s by bands like Crass, Conflict, and Discharge (UK), The Ex, and The Dead Kennedys (Widdicombe and Woofitt 12; O'Hara 71).

The majority of bands in the 1980s rallied against President Reagan's America with crude, blistering precision. Punk's objectives, once culturally transformative, focused toward a more insular, underground audience. In doing so, it embraced an ethos of do-it-yourself (or DIY), eschewing major labels, thereby changing the modes of production and distribution. The genesis of this underground network is well chronicled in Michael Azerrad's *Our Band Could Be Your Life*, highlighting how zine culture and record labels such as SST, Dischord, and Touch & Go helped to forge a thriving network outside of the industry. "It was sort of a conservative era, money conscious, politically nasty and Republican," Mission of Burma drummer Peter Prescott asserts in the book's introduction, "And that usually means there's going to be a good underground" (Azzerad 9). By the 1990s, punk's increased acceptance in the wider culture, coupled with the country's economic stability, provided bands an opportunity for commercial success that formerly eluded them. Two of the biggest, Nirvana and Green Day, broke through to larger audiences by harnessing punk's aggressive, anti-establishment bent in a largely apolitical manner. Politically inclined punk continued to thrive in certain circles, yet many subsects developed under the "person is political" ethos of mainstream liberalism, focusing on the dominant issues of the day, which, according to Craig O'Hara's *The Philosophy of Punk* included environmentalism, vegetarianism/veganism, sexual identity, and gender politics.

Punk's pre-eminent source for politics during the 1990s was Tim Yohannan's *Maximumrocknroll* (*MRR*), a popular Bay Area zine operating since the late 1970s, which has long provided explicit declarations for proper punk living. As its influence steadily grew, *MRR* did "what the web would later do for the culture at large: It removed the limitations of place and substituted for them an unplumbable pool of information and discourse" (McNett). At the height of its popularity, the zine "received criticism for promoting specific politics … that *MRR* has too much power over the punk scene. Too many punks now depend on *MRR* to inform them of who to support and who to boycott" (O'Hara 67). In 1997, Burkett's band NOFX recorded a song entitled "I'm Telling Tim," in which the narrator threatens to report all non-punk indiscretions to Yohannan. Despite Yohannan's intentions— to shield the underground from an encroaching mainstream—*MRR* developed an orthodoxy of ideological certitude with actions put forth for the *right* reason, which is at the heart of modern conservatism (Tanenhaus 22).

Growing up in the Bay Area, Hutch Harris, lead singer of Portland punk band The Thermals, was familiar with *MRR*'s formidable presence. "It was in the mid 1990s when *Maximumrocknroll* laid down that they were only going to review a certain type of record. It was the bible for so many people for so long but there were now so many rules," Harris explains. He continues:

> To me, the more rules that you have, the more you reflect the mainstream, having to categorize everything. Where I was coming up, I didn't have a conception of punk as a leather jacket and a mohawk. It meant DIY to us. We'd always call it a punk show but if someone heard the music, it would be confusing. "That's a punk show? That's not like The Sex Pistols!"

One response to this sense of imposed inflexibility, both artistically and ideologically, was punk adopting an increasingly constructivist lens. "Those who take a constructivist position," writes Maxine Green, "will reject the notion that there exists a representable set of phenomena the same for everyone" (112). By generating internal schemas based on one's own experiences, this position "rejects the idea that a truth corresponds to some objective state of things ... to refuse the visions of a self-sufficiently and idealized real," challenging definitive declarations of what is or isn't punk (Green 110). With her Riot Grrrl band Bikini Kill, Kathleen Hanna was interested in "taking the idea of punk rock and not thinking of it as a genre, but as an idea [which can then be applied] to different styles of music you're making up" (Oakes 126). Illustrating this malleability, Harris concedes that, "as liberal as I am, it would be unfair to say that a punk couldn't be conservative."

In the absence of defining criteria, Wilkow interprets punk's DIY work ethic as an extension of a conservative institution: the punk band as the embodiment of the American small business. Inspired by his father's work ethic, Wilkow gained an appreciation of free enterprise where hard work was prized and rewarded. In punk, he saw musicians personify that same independence and perseverance. Indeed, for many within the independent music scene in the 1980s, "the definition of independence came down to one thing: work. Making music was work. Touring was work. Booking shows was work" (Oakes 44). Rizzuto remarked to the BBC, "I would see the conservative viewpoint as being more punk than a liberal one, because a conservative viewpoint places a lot of emphasis on personal responsibility" (Fowler). This sense of responsibility extended beyond just the bands. Punk's egalitarianism broke down the divide between performer and the audience, strengthening the authenticity of punk's message by dismantling the traditional rock and roll hierarchy. Its artists could be trusted to tell you how they saw things (Barker and Taylor 271). It also offered opportunity: If you were inspired, why not start your own band? By valuing gumption and passion over proficiency, punk reinforced its own authenticity, touting that those without musical talent could produce something more meaningful than those who knew how to play their instruments (289). "It's one thing to pour your heart out to a crowd when you're making a million dollar payday, but it's another to pour themselves out for a smaller audience," says Wilkow. "I was so attracted to the fact that somebody genuinely gave a damn whether you personally applauded. You were so close that you were right there in it."

These ideals are easily reconciled with the tenets of Kirkpatrick and Wilkow's conservative philosophy: anti-elitism and free enterprise. The barriers to success—the privilege accompanying one's ability to access instruments, and the time and the money or status to acquire lessons—no longer exist. Cheap equipment played poorly provided entry into a culture that rejected normative indicators of musical talent. Artists found inspiration in the hope that if they demonstrated the will or conviction to start a band of their own, success—however defined—was possible. Substantial monetary gain being unrealistic for most punk bands, a common indicator of success to a group has been the opportunity to have its message heard.

This was certainly Burkett's intent with Punk Voter, a venture he was willing to lose money on because he felt passionately about the cause (Wiederhorn). However, this mentality illustrates a generational shift; a miscalculation by Burkett in assuming that today's punk fan was interested in heeding the ideas behind its best-selling compilations.

Chris McEvoy, the executive editor of *National Review*, decried the political nature of music in 2004 as an environment where artists acted as political tools. He argues, "In the Reagan 1980s, you could have loved The Clash and not sided with the Sandinistas" but that "political rock is an entity now, a true genre ... [It] has more than policy suggestions—which rock is filled with, from the inane to the plausible—it has a candidate. It is a partisan political machine. Don't think otherwise" (McEvoy). The increased political consciousness of musicians led to a countrywide debate played out on op-ed pages and cable news round tables regarding the merits of artists expressing their political views. "Someone plays a song, so that qualifies them to speak out on any cause, regardless of their knowledge? Do they even know what they are talking about?" asks Wilkow. "I like bands that have no agenda. Because you like music, that doesn't mean you care what they think. When bands get political, I get turned off." MacKaye, whose highly regarded band Fugazi is known for its steadfast dedication to DIY ethics, experienced this contention from his audience, challenging the notion of a universally receptive underground:

> I think the conservative punk thing closely follows what's happened in mainstream America. The first really brilliant and devious thing in Reagan's revolution was fucking with language. I think the surge in irony was a direct descendent of that. A term that sprang from the Reagan era that I find particularly offensive is "politically correct." Somehow, it became wrong to care. It's a complete inversion. It started to manifest within punk with bands not stating their intentions because it was uncool. Punk is as susceptible as anything else because it spread through the whole culture. You were ridiculed if you advocated for anything.

Within the volatile climate of the 2004 election, separating an artist's politics from their music had shifted from preference to an imperative, with McEvoy concluding his editorial with the statement, "We'll listen to the bands we like that still play rock and (for the most part) shut-up about politics. We already know how we're going to vote."

In *The Fort Collins Weekly*, Burkett admitted that he doesn't "actually read as much as I should, because the more I read the more bummed out I get, when I read political books. I don't want anything to do with this garbage" (BurnSilver). The necessity to get involved trumped any reservations: "I just thought somebody in the punk rock music scene had to step up. There's too many people in rock 'n' roll bands who don't want to go out on a limb, because they'll get Dixie Chicked. You might say something and lose a lot of your audience" (Garofoli). Dennis

Lyxzén, lead singer of the Swedish band The (International) Noise Conspiracy, a band upfront about its politics in songs like "Capitalism Stole My Virginity," was surprised at the opposition he encountered during a 2004 tour with the multi-platinum punk band The Offspring: "People got really, really offended that we talk about politics and the fact that if you elect the president in the United States, it's going to affect everyone. People get pissed off and this is at a punk rock show, it doesn't make any sense" (Green). The disconnect Lyxzén highlights—punk bands discussing left-wing politics being met with indifference or worse—illustrates the potentially large rift between those who see punk as a lifestyle or creed, as dictated through adherence to governing bodies and subcultural norms à la *Maximumrocknroll*, and those who simply enjoy hearing The Offspring play loud, fast music. The difference is not easily accounted for since there is no way of gauging one's commitment to a subculture. Outside of their preference for a certain style or type of music, that person might otherwise be quite conventional (Widdicombe and Wooffitt 27).

Particularly with advancements in technology making "the demarcation between the mainstream and indie unrecognizable," and as Ramones songs pipe through football stadiums and Sex Pistols t-shirts are sold at major department stores, Burkett's idea of a voting bloc made up of dyed-in-the-wool liberal punks reveals a sizable theoretical leap (Oakes xiii). Punk's considerable advances within the popular consciousness and its increased appeal have led to a broader swath of listeners, many of whom are either unaware of or uninterested in punk's historical relationship with politics. Paradoxically, an obscurity like the *Crush Kerry* compilation arguably hems closer to punk's sense of defiance and DIY attitude than Burkett's sheepishness over Propagandhi's insulting George Soros and taking meetings with Sen. Kerry. Burkett's effort to rally the troops, with its tinges of Sham 69's anthem "If the Kids Are United," disregards the continuing difficulty of promoting collective action in an era still defined by identity politics' individualized resistance, where every struggle against dominance is valid, regardless of legitimate distinctions. Why should people attend a rally or call their congressional representative, when their lifestyle choices have become an adequate replacement (Buechler 452)? Only four years after the 2004 election, the success of Barack Obama's presidential campaign would be credited for its ability to seize young voters' current preference for passive engagement via social media and micro-donations, demonstrating how the nature of political participation has changed. That said, the efforts of *Punkvoter.com* and other like-minded organizations undoubtedly helped the youth turnout in 2004, bringing approximately 20.1 million 18–29-year-olds to the polls, a dramatic increase from the 2000 presidential election and a demographic Democratic nominee Sen. John Kerry won by 9 percent (Dahl).

Searching for a Former Clarity

Conservativepunk.com and *Punkvoter.com* had no active presence in the 2008 presidential campaign, their founders apparently burnt out on its experimentation with national politics. In 2011, Wilkow hosts the right-leaning "The Wilkow Majority," on Sirius/XM satellite radio in New York, which Rizzuto produces. He is not currently involved with conservative punk, stating that he was glad to have "lit a spark and let someone else continue it." *Conservativepunk.com* went offline in 2010, though *www.conpunk.com* has replaced it, describing itself as "the misfits of the misfit crowd" ("About"). Burkett's connection to Punk Voter is one of distance. "I want to keep *Punkvoter.com* going. Put news stories up there. I will always be politically active, but not like I was in 2002 to 2004," he told *The San Francisco Chronicle* in 2007 (Garofoli). Proud to have spearheaded a coalition of artists against the Bush administration, he added that "Democrats are not the dream party" and that his time campaigning was too much work and "not fun" (Garofoli). As of the time of this writing, the domain *Punkvoter.com* is not currently active.

Outside this foray into electoral politics, punk has begun to settle into an increasingly conservative pose in its middle age, finding consolation in "identif[ying] itself as the guardian and advocate of a vanishing past and present, and a righteous bulwark against loss" (Brown 699). If the incessant drumming of punk's demise has grown tiresome, the willingness of its most exciting artists to slide within the safe confines of the rock and roll canon has been dispiriting, particularly as new bands continue to look to the past for preordained modes of acceptable behavior. "Usually the dudes, because it's almost always dudes, who are the conservative ones essentially spend a lot of time discussing the back in the day type of crap," asserts MacKaye. "'That's when things were really happening.' I'll go fetch my slippers and pipe." That conservative punk stirred such an impassioned response from the punk community speaks to the necessity for a continued discourse, one that fosters ideological growth and internal critique. Punk doesn't thrive in the absence of agitation. It requires an external catalyst to fend off stagnation and sustain relevance. By 2010, those who once fought against the musical dinosaurs of its era recount their rose-colored antics in copious books and documentaries. Perhaps Mark Anderson said it best when describing a series entitled "Punk Pioneers" at Boston's Institute of Contemporary Art. "This tribute," Anderson says, "however well intended—carried a slight aroma of death; the prophet safely entombed, now ready to be honored, if not really heeded" (Andersen and Jenkins 403). Despite punk's backwards-looking lens, MacKaye is focused and optimistic about the future. "Punk is always going to be in the factions. I see it as the free space where new ideas get to come out. It may not even be called punk, but that's the idea. And there will always be a new idea," adding "I'll be goddamned if I ever declare punk dead. I only want to declare something alive."

Works Cited

"About." *ConPunk.com*, 2010. Web. Jan. 31, 2011.

Agnostic Front. "Public Assistance." *Cause for Alarm*. Relativity Records, 1986. CD.

Andersen, Mark. Telephone Interview. Sept. 3, 2009.

Andersen, Mark and Mark Jenkins. *Dance of Days: Two Decades of Punk in the Nation's Capital*. New York: Akashic, 2009. Print.

Arak, Joel. "Poll: Bush's Approval Sinking." *CBS News*. Jan. 17, 2004. Web. Dec. 30, 2010.

Aubin. "Fat Mike / Propagandhi Clarify Situation." *Punknews.org*. Mar. 16, 2004. Web. Feb. 11, 2011.

Azerrad, Michael. *Our Band Could Be Your Life: Scenes from the American Indie Underground 1981–1991*. Boston: Little, Brown, 2002. Print.

Barker, Hugh, and Yuval Taylor. *Faking It: The Quest for Authenticity in Popular Music*. New York: W. W. Norton, 2007. Print.

Blush, Steven. *American Hardcore: A Tribal History*. Port Townsend: Feral House, 2001. Print.

Brown, Wendy. "American Nightmare: Neoliberalism, Neoconservativism, and De-Democraticization." *Political Theory* 34.6 (2006): 690–714. Print.

Buechler, Steven M. "New Social Movement Theories." *The Sociological Quarterly* 36.3 (1995), 441–64. Print.

BurnSilver, Glenn. "Punk the Vote." *The Fort Collins Weekly*. Jan. 14, 2004. Web. Dec. 30, 2010.

Dahl, Melissa. "Youth Vote May Have Been Key in Obama's Win" *Msnbc.com*. Nov. 5, 2008. Web. Dec. 30, 2010.

Fowler, Damian. "George W. Bush: Punk Icon?" *BBC News: Home*. May 18, 2004. Web. Dec. 30, 2010.

Garofoli, Joe. "Beyond PunkVoter: 'Fat' Mike Burkett Built a Legitimate Interest in Politics among Apolitical Punk Listeners, but Who'll Carry That Torch in 2008?" *The San Francisco Gate*. May 27, 2007. Web. Dec. 30, 2010.

Gillespie, Nick, and Brian Doherty. "I Dreamt I Saw Joey Ramone Last Night." *Reason.com*. Aug. 1, 2001. Web. Jan. 26, 2011.

Graves, Michael. "Conservative Punk Rock?" *Intellectualconservative.com*. Mar. 3, 2004. Web. Dec. 30, 2010.

Green, Stuart. "Bad Religion: Rocking For the Free World." *Exclaim!* July 2004. Web. Dec. 30, 2010.

Greene, Maxine. "A Constructivist Perspective on Teaching and Learning in the Arts." *Constructivism: Theory, Perspectives and Practice*. 2nd edn. Ed. Catherinine T. Fosnot. New York: Teachers College, 2005: 110–31. Print.

Haenfler, Ross. "Rethinking Subcultural Resistance: Core Values of the Straight Edge Movement." *Journal of Contemporary Ethnography* 33.4 (2004): 406–436. Print.

Harris, Hutch. Telephone interview. Aug. 20, 2009.

Hebdige, Dick. *Subculture: The Meaning of Style*. London: Routledge, 2001. Print.

Jones, J. P. "The Shadow Campaign in Popular Culture." *The 2004 Presidential Campaign: A Communication Perspective*. Ed. Robert E. Denton, Jr. Oxford: Rowman & Littlefield, 2005: 195–216. Print.

Kirkpatrick, Jeane J. "Why the New Right Lost." Excerpted in Sam Tenenhaus, *The Death of Conservatism*. New York: Random House, 2009. Print. 103–104.

Lynskey, Dorian. "Pro-Bush Punks Giving Republicans an Unlikely Lift." *The Guardian*. July 7, 2004. Web. Dec. 30, 2010.

MacKaye, Ian. Telephone interview. Sept. 19, 2009.

McEvoy, Chris. "Political Rock, 2004. Kissing Cousins Go All the Way." *National Review Online*. Aug. 9, 2004. Web. Dec. 30, 2010.

McNeil, Legs, and Gillian McCain. *Please Kill Me: the Uncensored Oral History of Punk*. New York: Grove, 1996. Print.

McNett, Gavin. "April 3rd 1998, The Day Punk Died." *Salon.com*. Apr. 17, 1998. Web. Dec. 30, 2010.

Melnick, Monte, A., and Frank Meyer. *On the Road with The Ramones*. London: Sanctuary, 2003. Print.

NOFX. "I'm Telling Tim." *So Long and Thanks for All the Shoes*. Epitaph Records. 1997. CD.

Oakes, Kaya. *Slanted and Enchanted: the Evolution of Indie Culture*. New York: Holt, 2009. Print.

O'Hara, Craig. *The Philosophy of Punk: More than Noise!!* Oakland, CA: AK, 1999. Print.

Pedersen, Erica. "The Day the Music Voted." *AlterNet*. Oct. 25, 2004. Web. Dec. 30, 2010.

Ross, Michael E. "Music-powered Web Sites? Not Just for Liberals." *Msnbc.com*. June 3, 2004. Web. Dec. 30, 2010.

Segal, David. "Punk Rock's New Colors: True Blue." *Washington Post*. Oct. 13, 2004. Web. Dec. 30, 2010.

Shea, Daniel M., and John C. Green. "Young Voter Mobilization Projects in 2004." *Fountain of Youth: Strategies and Tactics for Mobilizing America's Young Voters*. Ed. Daniel M. Shea and John C. Green. Lanham, MD: Rowman & Littlefield, 2007. 181–208.

Smalley, Dave. "Punk Rock, Diversity, and the Gonzo Conservatives." *scooterbbs. net*. Apr. 19, 2004. Web. Jan. 26, 2011.

Smith-Said, Stephan. "Why Neil Young Is Wrong." *The Progressive*. July 2006. Web. Dec. 30, 2010.

St. John, Warren. "A Bush Surprise: Fright-Wing Support." *The New York Times*. Mar. 21, 2004. Web. Dec. 30, 2010.

Tanenhaus, Sam. *The Death of Conservatism*. New York: Random House, 2009. Print.

Tiefer, Charles. "Congress's Transformative 'Republican Revolution' in 2001–2006 and The Future of One-Party Rule." *The Journal of Law & Politics* 23.3 (2007): 233–82. Print.

Ventre, Michael. "Musicians Use Their Talent to Further the Cause." *TODAYshow. com*. Sept. 24, 2004. Web. Dec. 30, 2010.

Weinraub, Bernard. "Reagan Joins Kohl in Brief Memorial at Bitburg Graves." *The New York Times*. May 6, 1985. Web. Dec. 30, 2010.

Widdicombe, Sue, and Robin Wooffitt. *The Language of Youth Subcultures: Social Identity in Action*. New York: Harvester Wheatsheaf, 1995. Print.

Wiederhorn, Jon. "Good Charlotte, Green Day, NOFX To Rock Against President Bush." *MTV*. Sept. 22, 2003. Web. Dec. 30, 2010.

Wilkow, Andrew. Telephone interview. Aug. 13, 2009.

Williams, J. Patrick. "Authentic Identities: Straightedge Subculture, Music and the Internet." *Journal of Contemporary Ethnography* 35.2 (2007): 173–200. Print.

Winter, Greg. "Fat Mike: Doin' It For the Cause." *CMJ New Music Report*. Mar. 15, 2004: 6–7. Print.

Worth, Liz. "From the White House to the Punk House." *Punk Planet*. March/ April 2006: 68–70. Print.

Chapter 11

"Agony & Irony": Indie Culture's Sardonic Response to America's Post-9/11 Devolution

S. Todd Atchison

9/11 exists as a distorted event in both sensory and cognitive terms: the sounds of planes flying too close, collisions, and explosions sending sonic shockwaves. We felt the impact from thousands of miles away while attempting to find meaning within the hyper-reality of the event—a catastrophe far removed from our conceptual framework. We relied on mass media to define the event and devise the plot. The resulting fallout created a meta-narrative reliant upon quick soundbites and Internet headlines. America's growing dependence upon the twenty-four-hour news cycle allowed corporate capitalism to exploit the commodity of identity—where everything is reduced to a simplistic formula of redundancy exemplified by the mass-produced representations of the "war on terror," the bumper-sticker phraseologies of "Roll On," "No Fear," and the co-opted "NYPD/FD." Our political personalities mirrored the pundits of CNN or Fox News. In the months that followed, citizens were advised to revitalize the national spirit by embracing economic freedom, therefore boosting consumerist-driven democracy and capital. Americans embraced a similar blind-faith sense of nationalism, accepting the authoritarian grand narrative and its ensuing isolationist xenophobia.

In the early 1980s at the core of the punk culture movement was a desire to critique such cultural stagnation and sameness beyond the boundaries of mainstream media. These critiques involved delving into the taboo, the forbidden, to bring these ideals forth in dark satiric art. Such measures also provided a means of warning society concerning the regressive herd mentality that reverberated through market-driven media. In this chapter I explore how today's alternative/indie rock subculture perpetuates punk culture's anti-corporate caveat by employing a parallel strategy that emphasizes its own consciousness of its marginality, and thus holding to "its position on the edge of the narrative" (Gray xvii). This alternative status remains driven by its satirically ironic representation railing against the status quo in a self-conscious refusal to be defined (much like Jon Stewart's refusal to have *The Daily Show* taken seriously, while simultaneously confronting real political figures and issues).

Subcultures are reactionary, relying on what is reviled as a part of their identity. Several bands that were highly critical of President George W. Bush and his administration's ensuing "war on terror" entered the political fray. Indie culture's resistance surfaced with the likes of punk band NOFX's political album

The War on Errorism and similar performances by heavy hitters like Alkaline Trio and Green Day during the 2004 Rock Against Bush tour. Indie rock's post-9/11 response offers a localized narrative that opposes the hegemonic discourse put forth by the Bush administration. In this chapter I address how these counternarratives operate in multiple ways: by amplifying the "death drive" and fear reflected in current American culture; countering the meta-narrative put forth in the mass-media post-9/11 that perpetuates consumerist-driven democracy; examining how the late-punk response found in the dark satirical lyrics of bands like Alkaline Trio remonstrates the consumer-capitalist ideals of isolationism as well as the "idiocracy" of mainstream America. Finally, I demonstrate how Green Day's *American Idiot*—a rock opera that has made the transition from recording to stage show—produces a spectacle of revolt through its self-reflexive critique of America's media-saturated culture. I draw from Guy Debord's *Society of the Spectacle* to demonstrate how *American Idiot* (the musical) attempts societal change through subverting mainstream culture.

Shock and Annoy: The Dark Dawn of Punk

"If it's popular, it ain't culture!"
Vivienne Westwood[1]

When punk culture erupted to the surface, the movement was an irrational, brash, knee-jerk disruption of social norms with the initial intent to shock and annoy. Punk's pathos portrayed a deliberate outsider aesthetic with an ironic stance: to have a good time meant to have a bad time (Savage xiv). Yet for punk to remain reactionary it also had to remain fluid and undefined through its attacks or critiques on multiple fronts—sexual taboos, gender politics, fashion, classism, and racism— to agitate through overkill. Punk worked best through a symbolic subversion of mundane items or areas found in our everyday lives. Dick Hebdige demonstrates how punk embraces dissent through manufacturing contradictions that contain a "series of subjective correlatives for the official archetypes of the 'crisis of modern life': the unemployment figures, the Depression ... converted into icons (the safety pin, the rip, the mindless lean and hungry look) these paradigms of crisis could live a double life, at once fictional and real" (65). Punk distorts real phenomena, common commodities, and it violates social codes in order to resituate meaning within the dominant framework. Doing so amplifies the subordinate versus dominant tensions found within forbidden contexts, such as class-consciousness and sexism, in an attempt to disrupt hegemonic discourse.

---

[1]   Quoted in Rabid, "V. Vale Interview Part 1" 115.

Today we nurse hangovers from weapons of mass destruction while gridlocked in Washington due to knee-jerk political punditry delivering pre-emptive strikes. One tactic to disarm such pre-emptive strikes is to embrace the right's absurdity and to build resistance through an alternative position—a cynical one that demonstrates and disrupts the official discourse. One such example within late-punk culture is the satirical side-project from Devo's Jerry Casale, dubbed Jihad Jerry & the Evildoers, where Casale reinterprets the symbolic representations of religious extremism. Jihad Jerry is a turban-wearing middle-aged white male who exploits the media's portrayal of Muslim extremists. In doing so, his detached irony reveals that there is little truth behind the dominant ideological fantasies. Through a sardonic stance, one can deflect the right's pre-emptive accusations of treachery by mirroring their fantastical constructs, and show the absurdities within their misinformation and punditry. Punk turns media against itself with a self-aware ironic parody in the distortion of representation, thereby using media as a means to define the subculture's rejection of dominant structures. Punk reframes experiences through the signifiers within our mainstream ideologies. Political pundits use media under similar terms by turning fantasy into reality through social frameworks—in other words, situating order and organization as the formation of stabilized identities. The Bush Administration built the resulting post-9/11 grand narrative on such fantasies by refusing a representation of fact-based reality, to mislead the American people through a base rhetoric of hatred and fear. As a nation in mourning, the US looked for easy answers that yielded complacency in the comforts of simplicity. Bush's cowboy code offered a revenge fantasy entailing a "Coalition of the Willing" destroying an "Axis of Evil" that danced in Americans' heads as they occupied Iraq.

Lee Edelman demonstrates how diverse political positions compete for the power to define and reshape collective identity through the shaping of signifiers that instill their own symbolic reality (7). We strive to define ourselves through social and linguistic codes that set us apart from the Other, yet this self-reflexive stance cannot bridge the gap between us and the ideology we choose to embody because we become signified as well—this works in ways similar to how punk's subculture exists through representations of representations. Edelman argues that queerness as a means of existence embraces a "death drive" that stands in contrast to the parent culture's hope for future within the dominant hetero-procreative drive. Edelman's death drive, like punk's pathos, embraces a Lacanian *jouissance* as "a violent passage beyond the bounds of identity, meaning, and law … undoing the consistency of a social reality" (25). Mary Harron, editor of *Isis*, similarly articulates this manifestation, reflecting that punk culture captured the "nihilism in the atmosphere, a longing to die. Part of the feeling of New York at that time [circa 1975] was this longing for oblivion, that you were about to disintegrate, go the way of this bankrupt, crumbling city" (quoted in Savage 133). Harron's statement eerily acts as a harbinger of when the Towers fell: within the falling ash and embers, the once-removed threat of terrorism blanketed us; the threat became distorted reality. Within *jouissance* there lies presence in absence, where the death drive manifests itself through fetishized objects that help shape symbolic realities. Punk's obsession with death and annihilation serves to rupture cultural signifiers through a juxtaposition of social contradictions (e.g., the current obsession with vampire culture and goth styles of the walking dead delivers a presence in absence, a living with no future; or the dominant ideology of American democracy that results in a capitalist-feudal state); these ruptures offer a self-reflection that resists definition. Punk's subculture strives to defy definition through the chaos of creativity—a nihilistic reaction toward popular culture and politics. This method is best exemplified by publicist Val Vale, known for his zine *Search & Destroy*, who envisions punk as owning a "negative dialectics": a philosophical negation that blasts the fakery of commerce and explores the taboo to rail against cultural authoritarianism. The acerbic stance of punk culture's post-9/11 counternarratives serves as a warning to shock us out of our complacency for misinformation.

American post-9/11 culture has devolved through its appetite for distraction toward an antithesis of a democracy—what once embodied the ideals of tolerance, education, and progress has digressed toward a herd mentality that ceases to think critically. The "millennial generation"—those born between 1980 and 2000—were raised on information overload, multitasking, and texting without vowels. English professor Mark Bauerlein deplores the distractive amount of "screen time" wasted by this generation. His basic argument holds that, while these digital natives are tech-savvy, ironically, they cannot use their technical abilities to glean pertinent information. Bauerlein notes that their reading scores fall flat, that "employers complain about the writing skills of new hires ... college students [majoring] in math [are now] a rarity, remedial course attendance [is] on the rise, and young people worry less and less about *not* knowing the basics of history, civics, science, and the arts" (109). Ultimately, Bauerlein complains that we have become ethnocentric, self-centered consumers who no longer consider civic responsibility nor seek accurate information regarding science, the environment, or health. And this is exactly the point about post-9/11 American society that I want to critique: that we have devolved into self-centered apathy.

Devo's Jerry Casale, in an interview with Jack Rabid, discusses the devolution of American society: "in the struggle between democracy—democratic ideals: humanitarianism, egalitarianism—and capitalism, democracy was a clear loser" (Rabid and Freilich 63). The basis of democracy holds that every citizen is educated enough to take on leadership roles and governance, and that every citizen should care about the community we inhabit. Casale's remarks illustrate how we have become devoid of personal responsibility because we prefer someone to bear the burden of providing it for us. And while we've become obsessed with reality television and social Internet sites, Bush turned America into a "corporate, feudal state, beholden to the world global system" (Rabid and Freilich 65). Bush used the crisis of 9/11 and the resulting "war on terror" to further coerce us to embrace capitalism as the steadfast solution. The deregulation of the private sector and the Bush administration's unwillingness to provide a real governmental solution caused the economic system to collapse. The damage is done. Hope and change should have occurred in 2004, not 2008.[2] Hope and change have become commodified and vacuous terms as well. Hope and change are hard terms to embody, especially when change enacted through protests no longer matters. Like Plato's cave analogy, if one informs people of how they've been duped and misinformed, it results in a silencing and a marginalizing of enlightenment. Today it's difficult to get people to rise up and take to the streets; today conformity is cool (Rabid and Freilich 67). Conformity to democratic capitalism has allowed a "manufacture of consent" where the ruling class—the top 2 percent, who own the wealth—delegates common interests and shapes public opinion through propagandistic representation in mass media.

If punk's ethos is to shake us from our complacency, to rail against the status quo by remaining on the boundaries of society, what happens as these boundaries shift and become more accommodating of consumer identities? With the increased popularity of Alkaline Trio and Green Day occupying the shelves in mainstream stores, what exactly is being consumed? Both bands cut their teeth on late-punk culture, grown from modest record sales to corporate recognition, thereby transitioning from small independent labels such as Asian Man Records (Alkaline Trio) and Lookout! Records (Green Day) to sign deals with Columbia Records' Epic imprint and Warner Brother's subsidiary label Reprise. Alkaline Trio currently record on their own Heart & Skull label, and Green Day, at least for now, retains indie-rock's purist ideals even while recording for a corporate label. Green Day holds to their position on the periphery because of their ability to use media's spectacle as a means to revolt.

Popular media thrives on market saturation and trending to create demand and control. And this raises a very interesting issue: as subcultures become more accepted, what was once held as taboo comes to the forefront in commercialized culture.[3] What was once reactionary has become a commodified conformity. The gothic styles that were once found only in underground S&M stores now can be found in chain stores in suburban malls. Does the mere commodification of subcultural styles serve to demystify these countermovements? Punk fashion is still striking, even if it's easily attainable at a mainstream store. The resistance remains subverted within popular culture—bright pink hair-dye retains its astonishing affect. Though punk's initial intent was to succeed through failure, ironically the movement still succeeds because nothing has changed; there is still inauthenticity everywhere. Rabid and Vale continue to demonstrate how a DIY mentality remains an essential element for combating the devolution of culture, even if it is through subversion. Rabid and Vale finally determine that punk's ultimate contribution,

---

[2]   See Rabid, "Autopsy".

[3]   This progression strikes a similar chord with Vale, as he tells Rabid: "All the supermodels have bellybutton piercings and all this crap, like the tattoo right above the low pants line above the butt that every suburban woman has now. These things are just a new kind of conformism! [sic]" ("V. Vale Interview Part 2" 102).

and this idea they borrow from William S. Burroughs, reminds us to question the reality they give you, to think critically, look longingly, and analyze.

The American Scream: Alkaline Trio

> And early on they saw the warning signs and symptoms all day long
> Wonder how far from here we'll fall before we hit the ground running on empty.
>
> Alkaline Trio, "Warbrain"

Even before the *Twilight* saga and *True Blood* series resulted in a phenomenal obsession with the undead, goth-punk culture infiltrated teen suburbia, attracting awkward and standoffish adolescents (and eventually finding an audience among women in their thirties and forties). Independent stores doled out goth-infused fashions for lost teens seeking to define themselves, and reclaim a sense of bodily self amid a sea of school uniforms. The goth-punk culture of the naughts, especially post-9/11, embraced its commodified identities where everything's branded. So why not death? Perhaps just looking like the undead projects a sense of surviving a decade dominated by fear. Masculine mascara-laden bands like Alkaline Trio project dark carnival videos of forlorn love lost by sinister means as a caustic mimesis—one that talks back to a vacuous popular media by denoting a generational loss of innocence caused by the "war on terror."

Alkaline Trio's late-punk doom-pop approach seethes a sinister cynicism by reflecting the jaded lives of suburban kids raised on skull candy. Founded in 1996 around McHenry, Illinois, the band consists of Matt Skiba (guitar, vocals), Dan Andriano (bass, vocals), and Derek Grant (drums), who fall in line with punk's simple mantra of "form three chords, go start a band." Lyrically they're dark and ironic, even graphic at times (see tunes such as "Mr. Chainsaw" or "All on Black"). Most of their songs provide glimpses into a variety of societal breakdowns, such as substance abuse and the emotional entanglements that result from it. For example, the explicit metaphors of betrayal in "All on Black" portray the song's protagonist as being stabbed in the back, left bleeding on the floor, and mourning the loss of something inside the self. The song's chorus abruptly turns toward clichéd jokes such as "What's black and white? / What's read all over? / This tired book / This organ-donor" to sardonically show the complexities that lie in the ambiguities of life and loss. The dualities of religious imagery (both Christian and Satanic—a popular binary in gothic-punk) conveyed through the lines "Sweet blasphemy my giving tree … What's upside down? / What's coated in silver? / This crucifix is my four-leaf clover," yield images of sacrifice (an offering of self: "virgin ears") that are lost because of the knowledge that everything's too complex, re-emphasizing America's "idiocracy" through its desire to have everything readily defined in a period of post-9/11 uncertainty.

Religious hyperbole abounds in Alkaline Trio's songs through metaphorical twists that demonstrate tensions between life, love, loss, and faith: agony and irony. Tunes such as "Armageddon" and "Mercy Me" are two great examples. In "Armageddon," which is essentially a breakup song, the narrator receives a piece of mail with a photograph of a couple "arm in arm (up in arms again)." Its self-reflexive narrative is a beer-fueled rant on the aforementioned photograph which its writer fears everyone will hate. "Armageddon" not only signifies facing the demise of a relationship, it also forces the song's protagonist to find something to believe in, thereby portraying the tension between attempting to save your soul, to save something, before the "end times." In contrast, the song "Mercy Me" centers on the loss of love, faith, and fear as a result of being desensitized by an oversaturated culture. The emotional release once offered by goth-punk's obsession with darkness and death are now lessened by societal acceptance. The lines within the chorus, "Oh mercy me / God bless catastrophe," evoke an appreciation of the spectacle where we drive ourselves insane through obsessions with death and the fear exposed by media outlets.

Alkaline Trio are not overly political, although they released "Warbrain" on the *Rock Against Bush* compilation and accompanied several bands (the likes of Flogging Molly, Sum 41, and Green Day) on a tour to promote that album. "Warbrain" has nothing to do with President Bush per se, but falls in line with their other war-narrative lyrics in songs such as *Agony & Irony*'s "Over and Out" and *This Addiction*'s "The American Scream." Both songs portray characteristics of post-traumatic stress disorder (PTSD) in returning servicemen. "Over and Out" does so by demonstrating the dissolution within American society and its reflection in frayed long-term relationships. The lyrics consist of dialogic moments between a man and woman (though it is ambiguous whether it is referring to one single relationship). She suffers in a hospital bed. He deals with PTSD from Vietnam and ultimately decides to commit suicide. The universal nature of the song conveys a sense of shared trauma that extends well beyond this relationship. Ultimately, the band offers itself, even this song, as solace and consolation, to "run for cover and you'll find us there / To take on the anger, make it disappear ... Let this candle burn 'til you get home / Never forget your face, never lose hope," as a means to keep a vigil, and keep memory.

The song "The American Scream" is based on a news story Matt Skiba read about a serviceman who committed suicide at his mother's grave after returning home from the Iraq War. The narrative plays out this soldier's experience and serves as an anti-war song that delivers a cynical critique of our nation's failure to properly remember military men and women. The opening lines make reference to yellow ribbons around oak trees—a standard symbol for remembering soldiers—that eventually yield to worn-out prayers and faded hopes. The second verse mirrors the first by describing a tourniquet wrapped, like the yellow ribbon, around a pipeline—metaphorical for both oil and blood—that "carries all the pain in this world," to the American public that remains isolated from a war far removed. The chorus comes across as both simplistic and hyperbolic—"And that's where they found me / in the cemetery / a smoking gun in my hand now I'm damned for the land of the free / Sing with me / The American Scream"—conveying a critique of our society's forgetfulness that portrays us "blindly [clapping] from the sidelines," outwardly demonstrating a symbolic parallel with the yellow ribbons on SUVs. This war, once narrated by embedded reporters, now offers very limited coverage concerning the veteran's dire needs: financial assistance, health care, and transitional issues for those who risk their lives for our "freedom." From both the White House and the corporate media, there has been little sacrifice asked of the American people in support of this war in monetary terms, like tax cuts (while the national debt mounts), nor in energy usage to derail the country's dependence on foreign oil supply.

Perhaps Alkaline Trio's best assault on divisive punditry comes through in "We've Had Enough." Ironically, this was *Good Mourning*'s first single, an anti-radio song to premiere on the airwaves. The song seemingly lashes out at Clear Channel's corporate monopoly and its list of censored songs in the days following 9/11. Musically, the tempo is a concussive staccato with a bemoaning end-gong that echoes in the background. The narrative meanders through dark passages of mourning with shadowed images of heads hanging low, hearing the cries of angels with voices "reminding you to breathe." The protagonist comes to rest on a bed of concrete stating, "That's all we live for ... we're only second-handed sick and lonely / fighting back the tears / and every urge to Van Gogh our ears," symbolic of our residual cultural trauma. The "second-handed sick" represents our distanced experience through the media representation of a shared traumatic event where the coverage of the catastrophe becomes a banal commentary stuck in a repetitive loop. The protagonist moves toward an angst-fueled rant against corporate radio, exclaiming, "That's it we've had enough / please turn that fucking radio off / ain't nothing on the airwaves of the despair we feel." Skiba cautions against the media insulating the public with the distraction of a grand narrative where uncertainties become readily defined. He reminds listeners that the radio cannot articulate the anxiety nor fully frame the grief through quick soundbites. Punditry and popular culture appeal to us on a base level, meaning we do not have to think about the information (or lack thereof) we receive. Our minds are shut off; that's Skiba's biggest fear: "The only tunes that you hear / come via antenna through your car radio." To reiterate the epigraph from the previous section from Vivienne Westwood: "If it's popular, it ain't culture" (quoted in Rabid, "V. Vale Interview Part 1" 115). We live in a world that bombards us with (mis-)information wrapped in trumped-up fears of Ground Zero mosques and Qu'ran burnings. Alkaline Trio retains that role of art as a mimesis of life's dark ironies to evoke a response—to be a catalyst for change, to shake us from those apathetic diversions offered through vacuous corporate media.

Conclusion: Green Day's *American Idiot* and the Manufacturing of Dissent

I don't believe illusions
'cos too much is real
So stop your cheap comment
'cos we know what we feel.

Sex Pistols

Since 9/11, America has become an abysmal place with everything wrapped in ambiguity. The true complexities of American foreign policy, religious tolerance, and the acceptance of those marginalized have fallen to diversions of fear and hatred. Having things undefined can be very threatening, and the current role of corporate media is to create readily defined, simplistic narratives to ease the public's displacement and fuel their fear. Lisa Finnegan identifies the lack of honest reporting as an attempt to allow for "cognitive dissonance," a psychological term that denotes our need for our beliefs and actions to remain harmonious. When we suffer a national trauma it is befitting that "people avoid information that increases this distress and search for ways to relieve the discomfort" (33). The result, Finnegan argues, is a press reluctant to examine America's rogue foreign policy, which could have incited the attacks in the first place. Americans, she claims, simply do not want to consider their government's actions abroad (33). Bush's aphorisms—"They hate our freedoms: our freedom of religion, our freedom of speech"—quelled American discomfort, thereby enabling them to tune out and to displace their discomfort by obsessing over Brad Pitt and Angelina Jolie instead (34). Part of punk's ethos is to resist such cultural distractions and to shake us from complacently accepting what we are being given by corporate-fed pundits. Yet to enter the political fray is to take a position.

Billie Joe Armstrong, lead singer and guitarist of Green Day, seems obsessed with exploring how individuals can define themselves in an increasingly mass-marketed society—a theme that resounds within Green Day's album *American Idiot*. Armstrong states, "We were in the studio and watching the journalists embedded with the troops, and it was the worst version of reality television" (Hendrickson 43). Marred and desensitized by our society's obsession with sensational media, he relays how it has become inescapable: "Switch the channel, and it's Nick and Jessica. Switch, and it's *Fear Factor*. Switch, and people are having surgery to look like Brad Pitt. We're surrounded by all of that bullshit, and the characters Jesus of Suburbia and St. Jimmy are as well. It's a sign of the times" (Hendrickson 41). *American Idiot* is Green Day's rock opera, with its protagonist, the Jesus of Suburbia, navigating through our post-9/11 landscape, finding solace within late-punk culture and guidance from St. Jimmy—self-described as a "product of war and fear that we've been victimized." The rock opera holds up the adage of "sex, drugs, and rock and roll" by portraying a female love interest in Whatshername and a landscape riddled with pot, heroin, and Ritalin. In the process, the work rails against the Bush Administration's "red neck agenda."

Armstrong, bassist Mike Dirnt, and drummer Tre Cool successfully convey what it is like to be part of a generation growing up under George W. Bush in a post-9/11 world consisting of ineffectual war coverage bombarded with the branding of CNN and Fox News. The lyrics within the album's title track admonish this knee-jerk-reaction nation under the thumb of television's trumped-up hysteria. We become so tuned-in that fear becomes a fad—"everybody do the Propaganda! / and sing along to the Age of Paranoia"—in corporate-ruled "Idiot America™." Here, Armstrong amplifies America's devolution under vacuous media with an emblematic trademark. We are proud to conform without question. Our blind nationalism leads to isolationist paranoia. Hawkish political pundits rebuke war protestors for supporting "faggot America's" emasculated diplomacy. These talking heads have their audiences amped up on anxiety. They warp reality to create real-time revenge fantasies.

Post-9/11 reality is paradoxical, ruled by the media—where the virtual is real, the real virtual. Stephen Duncombe suggests that the way to reach a sheep-like populace so easily distracted is by manufacturing dissent (9). In the case of Green Day, they successfully embrace the media spectacle of fantasy to mimic reality. *American Idiot*, being a concept album, illustrates America's irrational media, social, and political hypocrisy through its narrative structure. Armstrong wants to shake us out of complacency, to wake us from an apathetic stasis; as Armstrong says of making the album: "I made it to give people a reason to think for themselves. It was supposed to be a catalyst" (Fricke 141). Green Day strives to make a difference through subversion—leading a message of revolt through the mass production found in popular media.

Green Day carried the commercial success of *American Idiot* toward further spectacle by promoting a Broadway play based on the album's anti-war themes (along with tunes from their follow-up album, *21st Century Breakdown*). Directed by Michael Mayer and co-written with Armstrong, the adaptation works with *Idiot*'s ambiguities to recreate the album's narrative while filling in some of the spaces with an Iraq War veteran and set-pieces of broken-down urban landscapes—numerous television sets repeating a message of "Tune in. Zone out. Buy. Enlist" (Gardner 6D). Those messages mirror the distractions pulsing through the hegemonic discourse of revenge fantasy put forth by those Bushisms that embraced capital, commerce, and democracy—"They hate us for our freedom," "We'll be greeted as liberators"—concepts that echo in the show's rendition of "Holiday"; a number that best exemplifies an attempt to rein in reality from a media overdose. The protagonist begs to "dream and differ from the hollow lies" that distract our lives. He "hears the drum pounding out of time" with once well-intentioned protestors joining the other side because there is more money to be had by branding the war. He deciphers a news image consisting of "a flag wrapped around a score of men" as "a gag" that exists as insignificant as "a plastic bag on a monument." Media soundbites lead to simplistic bumper-sticker mantras that repress those discomforting ambiguities that arise from analyzing what led up to the attacks. These ideas resound through "Before the Lobotomy" with Tunny, one of the play's characters, who derides American society for our willingness to forget: "Dying / everyone's reminded / hearts are washed in misery / drenched in gasoline," it is the "brutality of reality" that prevents him from dreaming of a promising future. The characters within *American Idiot* (the musical) struggle to retain a sense of identity while trapped in a "static age" distorted by an oversaturation of media and readily defined patriots who wear trademarked slogans. Patriotism as branded by popular culture in consumable goods is a means to outwardly demonstrate the cause rather than actively take part in civic responsibility; with a yellow-ribbon magnet on the back of their SUVs people support the troops without truly considering their experiences in Iraq and Afghanistan. *American Idiot* (the musical) offers consumers the spectacle of revolt. It portrays our desire to reclaim localized personal identities from the hegemonic grand narrative.

American Idiot (the musical) works in similar ways to how Guy Debord defines the spectacle as a manifestation of "society's real unreality" through mass production (13). At first glance, Debord's argument seems to decry grand-scale representations for their capacity to only reify the ideologies prevalent within the parent culture, considering that such depictions "epitomize the prevailing model of social life" that yield a plastic reality (13). The plasticity of representation within grand productions reveal the "spectacle's essential character ... as a visible negation of life—and as a negation of life that has invented a visual form for itself" (14). Debord cautions against a society that is heavily influenced by the spectacle— events that he also deems as ineffective forms of art such as propaganda, protest, or entertainment—because spectators remain passive observers and not active participants. However, Debord then advocates the creation of a "transformative action" through events that correlate actors with their larger society toward an active engagement with a text, a work of art, or a dramatization (Duncombe 130). The implication of Debord's treatment of transformative action is that artistic representations should be avant-garde works of negation, thereby calling attention to their own act of representing (135). The spectacle of *American Idot* (the musical) works in similar ways through self-critique. The musical production negates the media's influence by using its own amplification of those plastic realities created on the stage. The multiple screens flashing repeated consumerist mantras serve to remind audiences that they are, in turn, watching a production. The information overload alienates spectators in ways that mimic the all-intrusive modes of diversion forced upon the post-9/11 generation. Ironically, *American Idiot*'s success is also Green Day's failure. For a band that began writing songs mostly concerned with marijuana and self-effacement, Green Day evolved a political conscience. The more critical they became of American society—dating back to the 2000 album *Warning*—the more popular they have become. Jon Savage brilliantly illustrates the ironic post-punk tensions of success when he writes: "To succeed in conventional terms meant that you failed on your own terms; to fail meant that you had succeeded" (195). Yes, Green Day sold out, but at least their spectacle *says something* through subverting popular culture.

Punk's detachment was engineered to fail. It was built to spill as an antagonistic, anarchistic approach without a center. The movement shocked and illuminated a consumer society through a harsh cultural critique of corporate influence. Devo's Jerry Casale tells Jack Rabid that "just by questioning the idea of progress and culture getting better—that is, more and more people having a better life, just by questioning that—we scared people" (Rabid and Freilich 63). Similarly, Mark Motherbraugh argues to NPR's Guy Raz that punk's abrupt confrontational reaction began to lack affect because it became predictable ("Devo"). He views cultural change as coming through subversion—to find the means for disruption from within the established media outlets. Punk, by necessity, has a short shelf life. Perhaps this explains the Sex Pistols' legacy as the eternal "what could've been," an ironic stance of abruptly ceasing artistic production at the pinnacle of success. Within that dismantlement of the distortion is the inability to comprehend. In several ways, this is similar to our cultural memory of the catastrophic events of 9/11. The tragedy of the Towers disrupted our lives. 9/11 exists as event that remains on the periphery, it resists definition, and remains distorted in a realm that cannot be fully understood nor articulated. The music and message of the late-punk bands covered in this chapter reside in a stance of "agony and irony," as an ambiguous open-ended betrayal, culminating in a chaotic interruption without closure, with no coda—only a dark, ironic reverb that generates reflection and resonates alongside us.

Works Cited

Alkaline Trio. "The American Scream." *This Addiction*. Heart & Skull/Epitaph Records, 2010. CD.

——. "Armageddon." *From Here to Infirmary*. Vagrant Records, 2001. CD.

——. "Mr. Chainsaw." *From Here to Infirmary*. Vagrant Records, 2001. CD.

——. "All on Black."*Good Mourning*. Vagrant Records, 2004. CD.

——. "We've Had Enough."*Good Mourning*. Vagrant Records, 2004. CD.

——. "Mercy Me." *Crimson*. Vagrant Records, 2005. CD.

——. "Over and Out." *Agony & Irony*. Epic Records, 2008. CD.

——. "Warbrain." *Remains*. Vagrant Records, 2007. CD.

Bauerlein, Mark. *The Dumbest Generation: How the Digital Age Stupefies Young Americans and Jeopardizes Our Future (Or Don't Trust Anyone Under 30)*. New York: Penguin, 2008. Print.

Debord, Guy. *The Society of the Spectacle*. Trans. Donald Nicholson-Smith. New York: Zone Books, 1995. Print.

"Devo: Back in Focus, Tongue in Cheek." *All Things Considered*. Host Guy Raz. National Public Radio, June 27, 2010. *NPR.org*. Web. July 10, 2010.

Duncombe, Stephen. *Dream: Reimagining Progressive Politics in an Age of Fantasy*. New York: The New Press, 2007. Print.

Edelman, Lee. *No Future: Queer Theory and the Death Drive*. Durham, NC: Duke UP, 2004. Print.

Finnegan, Lisa. *No Questions Asked: News Coverage since 9/11*. Westport, CT: Praeger, 2009. Print.

Fricke, David. "Billie Joe Armstrong." *Rolling Stone*. Nov. 15, 2007: 140–42. Print.

Gardner, Elysa. "'American Idiot' Elevates Hope Above Nihilism." *USA Today*. Apr. 21, 2010: 6D. Print.

Gray, Richard. "Introduction." *South to a New Place: Region, Literature, Culture*. Ed. Suzanne W. Jones and Sharon Monteith. Baton Rouge: Louisiana State UP, 2002: i–xxiii. Print.

Green Day. *American Idiot*. Reprise Records, 2004. CD.

——. "Before the Lobotomy." *21st Century Breakdown*. Reprise Records, 2009. CD.

Hebdige, Dick. *Subculture: The Meaning of Style*. New York: Methuen & Co., 1979. Print.

Hendrickson, Matt. "Green Day." *Rolling Stone*. Feb. 24, 2005: 40–44. Print.

Rabid, Jack. "Autopsy of a Recession: Big Takeover Readers Were Warned!" *The Big Takeover* 64 (2009): 10–14. Print.

——. "V. Vale Interview Part 1," *The Big Takeover* 62 (2008): 109–117. Print.

——. "V. Vale Interview Part 2," *The Big Takeover* 63 (2008): 100–106. Print.

—— and Claude Freilich, "Devo Interview Part 1." *The Big Takeover* 63 (2008): 62–7. Print.

Savage, Jon. *England's Dreaming: Anarchy, Sex Pistols, Punk Rock, and Beyond.* New York: St. Martin's Griffin, 1991. Print.

Sex Pistols. "Pretty Vacant." *Never Mind the Bollocks, Here's the Sex Pistols.* Warner Bros. Records, 1977. CD.

PART IV
Idle American, *American Idol*: Mainstream Media and Ideology

Chapter 12

Post-Dixie Chicks Country:
Carrie Underwood and the Negotiation of
Feminist Country Identity

Molly Brost

"Watch out, boys," journalist Jessica Yadegaran cautioned in the May 20, 2007 edition of the *Contra Costa Times*. "The new women of pop, rock, and country don't bother with getting mad. They skip to getting even" (Yadegaran). Citing Lily Allen, Beyoncé, and Carrie Underwood as examples, Yadegaran declared that "music's new seven-letter word is *revenge*," and that while "it would have been a risk for a female performer ... to sing songs like these twenty-five years ago," revenge songs were becoming increasingly common among mainstream female performers. Yadegaran was not the only reporter to pick up on this trend; in July of the same year, the *Philadelphia Inquirer*'s Dan DeLuca similarly noted that "in pop music in 2007, the ladies [were] wielding the most powerful weaponry" (E1). Though he cited many of the same examples listed by Yadegaran, he noted that, for country singers like Underwood and Miranda Lambert (who had a hit the same year with the revenge anthem "Gunpowder and Lead"), the success of such songs was particularly noteworthy: "It's not as though angry women have commandeered the country music industry" (E1). In the week his article went to press, in fact, only one of the top ten songs on the *Billboard* country charts was sung by a woman; industry trends indicate that this is not an anomaly. Since the Academy of Country Music began holding an annual awards show in 1966, there have been only seven female acts to win the coveted Entertainer of the Year award, and when Underwood accepted the award in 2009 she was the first to win it in nine years (Gerome). While it would be easy to point to many female country singers who would be considered successful—Shania Twain, Reba McEntire, and, of course, Dolly Parton—when compared to their male counterparts, these women receive only a small fraction of country music's commercial success and critical acclaim.

Country-music scholars indicate that this gender imbalance might have something to do with the prescribed dictates of authenticity to which country musicians are expected to adhere. As Gabriel Rossman notes, "Country music has always been associated with pastoral white America and its values, such as independence, patriotism, and religion" (68). Clearly, revenge anthems do not embody these values. Lesley Pruitt further suggests that there is a gendered component to this construction: "In American country music, certain gendered discourses dominate, wherein men are expected to exhibit traits considered masculine, such as aggressiveness, reason, rationality, and protection; women should demonstrate the corresponding feminine attributes: peacefulness, caring, emotion, and vulnerability" (86). Pruitt also suggests that these expectations are "more binding" than they might be in other genres like rock and folk, leaving female country performers little room for deviation from the traditional country model (86).

Much like any attempt to achieve cultural authenticity, the dictate that female country singers should always and everywhere embody "traditional" femininity can be impossible to fulfill. As Pamela Fox notes in "Recycled 'Trash': Gender and Authenticity in Country Music Autobiography," women in country music must first and foremost "embody 'home'" (244). She continues, "From its inception in the late 1920s, traditional country mythology has made the family its centerpiece, envisioning distinctly gendered roles for that institution's maintenance and protection" (244). Ironically, when a female country musician embarks on a career, the demands of touring often require that she leave that home. Success, then, as Fox argues, renders female country musicians "distinctly gendered 'failures' of country authenticity ... By 'choosing' the tour bus ... they lose their claim to 'home' altogether" (244). While this Catch-22 situation has somewhat loosened its grip in an age where country musicians often travel in tour buses large enough to house their husbands and children, many female country performers still find themselves confined by domestic demands. In interviews, contemporary country singers, such as Faith Hill and Martina McBride, have discussed arranging concert tours around their children's school schedules, an issue that is rarely brought up in interviews with male country singers. Additionally, scholar Jocelyn Neal notes that interviews with such singers often work to reposition them in the home; interviews with Hill, for example, frequently emphasize the singer's "devotion to her family," as well as "the influence of her love life on her musical productivity" (112).

Given this context, Carrie Underwood's success seems rather extraordinary. How did Underwood not only have a hit song with a decidedly anti-domestic revenge anthem like "Before He Cheats" but also attain a level of success in mainstream country music that few women ever achieve? My contention is that Underwood's skilled use of the mainstream media has allowed her to reposition herself within more traditional country discourses of home, family, and respect for tradition, which has bolstered her perceived authenticity—an authenticity that allows her the space to perform songs that would otherwise be considered risky for a female country performer. Furthermore, as evidence that a country singer's popularity has as much to do with his or her perceived authenticity as the songs he or she performs, I place Underwood in contrast to the Dixie Chicks, who similarly had a hit with a revenge anthem, 1999's "Goodbye Earl," only to be effectively banned from country radio when lead singer Natalie Maines criticized President George W. Bush, the archetypal American cowboy of the new millennium.

First, it is worth tracing Underwood's biography as a means of excavating her roots—her authentic roots, as it were. The daughter of a paper mill worker and an elementary school teacher, Carrie Underwood grew up in Checotah, Oklahoma and pursued a major in broadcast journalism at Northeastern State University in Tahlequah, Oklahoma ("Carrie Underwood Biography"). She was catapulted to fame in the country music community in 2005 after winning the reality competition show *American Idol*. Her debut album, *Some Hearts*, was the best-selling album by a female country singer in 2005, 2006, and 2007; as of 2010, it is also the best-selling debut album by an *American Idol* winner ("Biography"). In 2006, she was awarded the Country Music Association's Horizon award, which is given to a promising new artist each year, as well as the Country Music Association's Female Vocalist of the Year award. In the same year, she similarly won the Academy of Country Music's Top New Female Vocalist and Top Female Vocalist awards ("Carrie Underwood Awards"). She continued to find success in the country music community, winning the same award from the Country Music Association in 2007 and from the Academy of Country Music in 2008 ("Carrie Underwood Awards"). Most significantly, in April 2009, she became the first woman since 2000—and the seventh female act in history—to win the Academy of Country Music's Entertainer of the Year award (Gerome). While her debut album included songs, such as the title track, that were decidedly more pop than country, Underwood emphasized to the press upon the release of her second album, *Carnival Ride*, that she would be targeting an exclusively country audience.

In spite of her geographic and economic links to America's heartland—that expansive space that is allegedly home to "real Americans"—her authenticity as a country artist has been called into question. Since the country music community traditionally favors hard-won rags-to-riches and pay-your-dues-to-play-the-blues stories—stories, it should be noted, that are in keeping with the ideology of the American Dream—Underwood's success on a television game show has rendered her illegitimate in some critics' eyes. Furthermore, *American Idol* is a decidedly commercial venture. As scholar Joli Jensen notes, commercialization itself often renders an artist or work as "inauthentic" in the public eye:

> The charge of commercialization imagines an uncommercialized past that produced culture naturally and spontaneously. This past—like the hills and honky-tonks and (after much rhetorical work) the Nashville recording studio of the early 1960s—is the origin of cultural material that "comes from the heart." These allegedly more natural places, and processes, are imagined in contrast to contemporary life ... where professionally created material is manufactured and disseminated through commercial channels—insincere production, for the market, false, empty, *not* "from the heart." (137)

While Jensen does qualify these claims, noting that "it does not necessarily follow that commercially mediated culture is worse than communally constructed forms," it stands to reason that, regardless of the quality of the music performed by

American Idol contestants, that music might be labeled as "inauthentic" by those who feel that art should not be created or performed for an explicitly commercial purpose (137).

For that reason—and even though Underwood is careful to express gratitude to the show that made her a star (often thanking the show itself and her fans in awards show acceptance speeches, as well as making appearances on subsequent seasons of *Idol* and at *Idol* publicity events)—she also sometimes appears almost apologetic for having achieved success that way. While accepting the Country Music Association's Female Vocalist of the Year award in 2008, she thanked the country music community for accepting her, noting that she took an "unconventional route" to country music success, and that they certainly didn't have to welcome her with open arms. Underwood is aware, then, that her reality show past might make her seem less legitimate to some fans and critics, and she makes consistent efforts to circumvent such criticisms.

Furthermore, she often emphasizes how important belonging to the country music community is to her: "I want to be a country artist in a country world with country fans," Underwood told *Entertainment Weekly*'s Dave Karger. She continued, "You can call me 'not country' until your face is blue, but I sing country music" (Karger). As evidence, she cited the fact that though "Before He Cheats" had crossover success on pop radio, she refused to allow the song to remixed as a pop song; the version heard on pop radio stations was exactly the same as the version released to country stations—fiddle, steel guitar, and all (Karger). Jensen highlights the importance of these qualifications, noting that, traditionally speaking, "to 'crossover' into pop music was to perform, record, and promote country music in a way that would appeal to a larger audience and, thereby, increase radio air play and record sales. But such success would also lead to accusations of having 'abandoned' country music" (5). To put it another way, Underwood plays up the fiddle, the steel guitar, and its musical brethren, to maintain her ties to authentic country music—not allowing her music to be fiddled with in the (re)mixing booth, that space of artificial studio constructionism.

Underwood also frequently positions herself within traditional country discourses of rural life, home, and family. She does this primarily by invoking tropes of blue-collar, middle-American life. For example, her song "Jesus Take the Wheel," in keeping with the popular bumper-sticker slogan "Jesus is my copilot," finds her singing about turning to Jesus in trying times. Likewise, in "Don't Forget to Remember Me," she wistfully recalls the family members (parents, siblings, and a grandmother) that she left behind at home while she took off in pursuit of her dreams. Even in the edgier "Before He Cheats," Underwood specifies that she is trashing her boyfriend's "pretty little souped-up four-wheel-drive," evoking images of a pick-up truck that might be used to traverse country roads on the way to work at a blue-collar job.

However, perhaps more powerful than these gestures to rural life are Underwood's repeated reminders of her continuing ties to her rural roots. Though Underwood often refers to her Checotah, Oklahoma upbringing in interviews, she has also immersed herself in charitable causes in her hometown. In August of 2009, it was widely publicized that Underwood returned to Checotah to donate $120,000 worth of musical instruments to the town's elementary and high school music programs. When presenting the instruments during a school assembly, she invited a student onstage to sing with her (Witten). During the visit, she announced that this was "only the beginning" for her new foundation, Checotah Animal, Town, and Schools (quoted in Witten). While Underwood presumably performs such philanthropic work with the intention of giving back to her community, this work has the dual function of reminding country fans that she is from a small, rural community, and that she has not forgotten where she came from.

It is also worth noting here that Underwood's philanthropy establishes the basis for seemingly direct—and seemingly authentic—connections between her and her fans. As Neal notes:

> Within the tradition of country music, artists are expected to connect with their fans through shared biographical experiences and the relevance of their personal backgrounds to a stereotyped country identity. These tokens of authenticity amplify the genre-identity of an artist's output—Loretta Lynn's coal mining roots, Merle Haggard's time on the wrong side of the law, or Dolly Parton's Smoky Mountain upbringing are all frequently invoked as synonymous with the content, meaning, and impact of their music. (111)

By reminding fans of her small town roots, Underwood reinforces her identity as, in her words, "a country artist in a country world with country fans." When she releases a song that might be considered a bit more provocative than is typical for country music (such as "Before He Cheats," "Last Name," or "Cowboy Casanova"), audiences may be more accepting of it because they see it as coming from someone whose background and experiences closely match theirs.

As edgy as Underwood might seem in comparison to the themes of most contemporary country music, it is important to note that Underwood is not the first or only country singer to balance more provocative fare with an emphasis on her rural roots and more traditional values. As Mary A. Bufwack and Robert K. Oermann note in *Finding Her Voice: The Saga of Women in Country Music*, Loretta Lynn, who had her first hit in 1960, "created a whole new subgenre of country song" with music written, in Lynn's words, "from the women's point of view" (309). As Lynn states in her autobiography *Coal Miner's Daughter*, "There's plenty of songs about how women should stand by their men and give them plenty of loving when they walk through the door, and that's fine. But what about the man's responsibility? ... I feel there's better ways to handle a woman than whipping her into line. And I make that point clear in my songs" (quoted in Bufwack and Oermann 309). Such songs were sometimes met with controversy, as Bufwack and Oermann note: "[Lynn] got by with 'Rated X' (1973), which condemned people who look on divorced women as used goods and sexually easy, but her birth control celebration 'The Pill' (1975) created a furor" (311).

Her continued success rested, Bufwack and Oermann assert, "in her proud-to-be country attitude and her assertive woman's stance" (313). As Underwood would do decades later, she balanced more controversial song choices with firm expressions of pride in her working-class roots.

In the years between the height of Lynn's popularity and Underwood's mainstream popularity, other mainstream female country singers would have success with songs handling more provocative subject matter—even, in some cases, revenge anthems. Both Yadegaran and DeLuca note the example of the Dixie Chicks' "Goodbye Earl," in which the trio gleefully recount the story of Mary Anne and Wanda, who band together to kill Earl, Wanda's abusive husband. The Dixie Chicks, like both Underwood and Lynn, can count themselves among the seven female acts to win the Academy of Country Music's Entertainer of the Year award, and to this day, they remain the best-selling female group in any genre. Moreover, their music can arguably be seen as fitting even more firmly in the country genre than Underwood's, with band members Martie Maguire and Emily Robison playing the fiddle and banjo, respectively. Yet the Dixie Chicks are no longer part of the mainstream country community, nor do their songs receive significant airplay on country radio, for reasons having nothing to do with their music itself and everything to do with a statement made by lead singer Natalie Maines at a 2003 performance at the Shepherd's Bush Empire in London, England: "Just so you know, we're ashamed that the President of the United States is from Texas."

In the aftermath of that statement, the group was effectively banned from country radio. Some radio stations, like Kansas City, Missouri's WDAF, set up trash cans and organized events for listeners to throw away their Dixie Chicks CDs. Similarly, Houston, Texas's KILT-FM and Talladega, Alabama's WTDR-FM suspended play of the Dixie Chicks' music. The fact that these responses were provoked by a comment a band member made while espousing a personal and political belief—and *not* in response to anything that the group was doing musically—illustrates that being accepted in the country community has as much to do with demonstrating a shared background and values with the audience as it does with producing "authentic" country music. Scholar Claire Katz reaffirms this notion, claiming that the Chicks were viewed by many as betraying not only their country but also country music: "[The Dixie Chicks'] version of country music [was] simply not country enough" (142–3). This response, however, was largely contradictory. As Katz notes, "Prior to the 'incident,' they were viewed as too country for country," largely due to the prominence of the fiddle and banjo in their songs (143). However, since Maines' comments seemed to signal a treasonous act among the group's fan base, it became clear that country music ultimately "becomes a claim about politics—country music stands for certain ideologies" (Katz 143). Given this context, it is pretty clear why Underwood takes such pains to identify with her audience. If she isn't with them, then, apparently, she must be against them.

It would, of course, be a generalization to suggest that all country music fans share the same political and ideological views. As scholar Randy Rudder chronicles, when music journalist Chet Flippo claimed in an anti-Dixie Chicks column that "country music fans are largely conservative and patriotic," author Bill Malone "took [him] to task," stating, "I am sorely offended by your attempts to argue that the country music audience is monolithic, or that some of us are more patriotic than others because of our attitudes toward [George W. Bush]" (211). Indeed, journalist Chris Willman observes that "it's worth remembering that country music is massive in plenty of blue-collar states in the north and Midwest where, unlike the nearly union-free South, labor has a strong political presence and the Democratic party hasn't completely squandered the double-digit advantage it's enjoyed in union areas" (9). Even some contemporary country artists have spoken about the need for country music to cross political party lines. For example, Gretchen Wilson has argued that "Country music is supposed to unite people. And we all do our own things and we have different opinions, but we all get along and have so many things in common that I don't see red and blue" (quoted in Willman 9). Thus, certainly not all country fans would have seen Maines' statement as a "betrayal."

However, it is noteworthy that Maines' statement made much more of a stir than similar statements made by other celebrities. As Rudder notes, anti-Bush comments made by public figures such as Pretenders' lead singer Chrissie Hynde and actor Jennifer Aniston did not get nearly as much public attention (208). Dixie Chicks member Martie Maguire has stated that she believes that the reaction to Maines' comment is "all about the fact that we're in country music" (quoted in Willman 41). It is also worth noting that other country musicians have expressed liberal political views on different occasions, both in interviews and in song. Martha Hume, editor of the *Journal of Country Music*, argues that perhaps the stir over Maines' statements comes from the fact that the Chicks had not expressed similar political opinions in the past:

> To the fans, their statements came out of left field. Willie [Nelson] and Merle [Haggard] can sing anti-war songs or anything they want and even audience members who are voting for Bush will say, "They're good men, they can do it." But when the Chicks did it [...] There's something there, and I don't know if it's sexism. My feeling is that it's because their politics are not otherwise reflected in their work, and with [Johnny] Cash and those guys, their politics *were*, so when you hear what they're saying, it's consistent with the character they've put out there. (quoted in Willman 33)

Conservative Dixie Chicks fans might have reacted in such a manner because they were surprised to learn that the Dixie Chicks did not share their political views. Willman suggests that this is not terribly surprising. He states:

The polarization of America has resulted in an atmosphere where red types and blue types tend to emigrate where they feel the most camaraderie—if not literally uprooting and moving across borders … then certainly selecting churches, private schools, and workplaces where like minds are the norm … And if your neighbors all fall in line, why not assume that the Dixie Chicks, talent and good looks aside, are *just like you*? That's the very cornerstone of country music: that the entertainers are no different from their audience, a rule not found in any other genre. (33)

Therefore, there might somewhat understandably be a backlash when a country artist espouses viewpoints that are inconsistent with those held by many of their audience members. It is not only the case that certain audience members might be offended by hearing a contradictory viewpoint but also that they would feel (as Katz observes) betrayed to learn that the artist held a contradictory viewpoint in the first place. As Willman explains, "In the Chicks fracas, some country fans may have been wounded by the realization, subconscious or otherwise, that they aren't really so tight with the people who they believed gave a voice to what was in their hearts after all" (33).

Moreover, fairly pronounced changes in country radio have occurred since Loretta Lynn's voice first graced the airwaves. As Lynn notes, even though her song "The Pill" was controversial:

The *women* loved it. But the men who run the radio stations were scared to death. It's like a challenge to the man's ways of thinking. See, they'll play a song about making love in a field because they think that's sexy, from a man's point of view. But something that's really important to women, like birth control, they don't want no part of, leastways not on the air. Well, my fans … forced most of the radio stations to play it. (quoted in Bufwack and Oermann 311)

Fans, then, played a large part in making sure that the song got radio airplay. However, the radio consolidation that followed the Telecommunications Act of 1996 (which lifted caps on radio ownership) led to a radio industry in which, as journalist Alec Foege notes, "most commercial stations … measure their success primarily by advertising revenue, not listenership" (114). Therefore, the support of advertisers became more important than the preferences of individual listeners, leaving many individual radio stations far less power to promote individual artists than they might have in the past.

It is not surprising, then, that the political climate following September 11 also played a large part in the Dixie Chicks' reception. As scholar Aaron A. Fox notes, following September 11, "Traditional working-class patriotic nationalism had emerged from the wreckage at Ground Zero" (173). Country music, perhaps by default, became a place to assert "a privileged claim to speak for the nation in the voice of (white) working class experience" (172). Thus, the Dixie Chicks' statement emerged in a political environment where their views were counter to the values that largely conglomerate-controlled country radio was espousing. Though their viewpoint might have been tolerated at one time, in a post-9/11 radio environment it was difficult, if not impossible, for them to get support from radio stations.

With these events in the background, it is perhaps unsurprising that Underwood would present herself as endlessly respectful of the traditions of country music. During her time as a contestant on *American Idol*, she cited Martina McBride as both a favorite and an influence; on the show, she performed country songs whenever possible, including McBride's "Independence Day" and "When God Fearin' Women Get the Blues." Similarly, in 2009 she had a hit with a cover version of country mainstay Randy Travis's "I Told You So." She then returned to the *Idol* stage to perform the song as a duet with Travis during the week he served as the contestants' mentor. She also often shows a great deal of humility and reverence for veteran country singers. In an article publicizing her 2008 appearance on *Saturday Night Live*, she discussed her experiences at country music awards shows—where, as previously noted, she is a frequent winner—stating, "I still don't feel like I'm supposed to be there … because I'm looking around and all of the people around me are the musicians I was listening to and seeing in concert when I was in high school and college" (quoted in Baca E-01). She further exhibited her humility in a reflection on her co-headlining tour with Keith Urban: "We're co-headlining, but he's been doing this for much longer than I have, so he should play last. I love watching him night after night, and picking out things I like" (quoted in Baca E-01). She likely gains favor not only with country fans but also with the mainstream country music community as a whole by showing respect for country singers who have been in the business for a long time. In doing so, she sends the message that even though she might not sing country music exactly like they do, or about topics that they might choose to sing about, she is not interested in replacing them—or in disrespecting anything they have done in the past. She also makes it clear that she is not interested in doing anything that flies in the face of the values of such singers, or of her fans.

In contrast, the Dixie Chicks made a more aggressive effort to distance themselves from the country music community in the fallout from Maines' comment. In 2006, Maguire told *Time* magazine, "I'd rather have a smaller following of really cool people who get it, who will grow with us as we grow and are fans for life, than people who have us in their five-disc changer with Reba McEntire and Toby Keith. We don't want those kinds of fans. They limit what you can do" (quoted in Tyrangiel). While Underwood consistently expresses her solidarity with both other mainstream country artists and with country fans, the Chicks are now equally emphatic about their unwillingness to adhere to the gender- and genre-specific expectations of the country-music community. Regardless of their music's sonic ties to traditional country sounds, their offstage comments make it clear that they would prefer not to be associated with the genre.

Despite their lack of interest in remaining part of the country music community, it is impossible to deny that the Chicks have had an influence on the female singers who have appeared on the scene in the years since 2003. Indeed, without the example of "Goodbye Earl," it is hard to say whether "Before He Cheats" would even have existed. "Nobody can for one minute say that they aren't believably talented and that they haven't broken down doors," Gretchen Wilson acknowledges (quoted in Willman 52). She continues: "The Dixie Chicks made it easier for me to say 'Hell yeah' on the radio—there's no doubt about it" (quoted in Willman 52). Thus, while the Chicks themselves are no longer part of the mainstream country community, their musical example lives on in singers like Underwood, Wilson, Lambert, and even Taylor Swift, who had a hit with the revenge anthem "Picture to Burn."

That being said, such artists might do well to acknowledge the issues that the Chicks' 2003 incident brings to light. For example, it is fairly clear that the criticisms leveled at the Chicks were gendered in nature. As Katz reminds us, "The Dixie Chicks were not simply called unpatriotic, they were called 'Dixie Sluts' and 'Dixie Bitches,' terms reserved only for women and, in particular, women who, in almost every case, act contrary to the prescribed passive role assigned to them" (151). Pruitt underscores this, noting that "traits typically deemed 'feminine' have been used in several ways to construct a negative portrayal of the Dixie Chicks. Following the notion that women are immature and unable to think rationally, the Dixie Chicks were represented as irrational and childlike" (90). This—and the Chicks' 2003 incident as a whole—suggests that, for a female country performer, the consequences of stepping outside prescribed genre boundaries can be especially harsh.

However, some scholars remain optimistic that these boundaries are widening to make room for a country woman who does not so closely adhere to traditional, prescribed gender roles. Alena Horn, for example, cites Wilson, along with Underwood's "Before He Cheats," as examples that indicate that "boundary-pushing song lyrics … are being embraced by the industry" (471). If nothing else, female country musicians have a wider range of roles available to them than those described by Jensen. In her words, traditional female country musicians "are either angels (waiting at home, patient and loving) or fallen angels (sitting in honky-tonks with tinted hair and painted lips)" (30). As Carrie Underwood, who would just as easily smash up her boyfriend's car as she would ask Jesus to drive it, indicates, today's female country musicians need not divert solely to either extreme.

Works Cited

Baca, Ricardo. "Carrie's Success Story: Underwood's Crossover Appeal Evident in the Millions of Albums Sold, *SNL* Appearances." *The Denver Post.* March 9, 2008: E-01. *LexisNexis.* Web. Sept. 21, 2009.

"Biography." *The Official Carrie Underwood Site.* Web. Sept. 21, 2009.

Bufwack, Mary A., and Robert K. Oermann. *Finding Her Voice: The Saga of Women in Country Music.* New York: Crown Publishers, 1993. Print.

"Carrie Underwood Awards." *CMT.com.* Web. Sept. 21, 2009.

"Carrie Underwood Biography." *CMT.com.* Web. Sept. 21, 2009.

DeLuca, Dan. "Songs of Revenge, Rage Rule Charts." *Chattanooga Times Free Press.* July 13, 2007: E1. *LexisNexis.* Web. Sept. 21, 2009.

Foege, Alec. *Right of the Dial: The Rise of Clear Channel and the Fall of Commercial Radio.* New York: Faber and Faber, 2008. Print.

Fox, Aaron A. "'Alternative' to What? *O Brother*, September 11, and the Politics of Country Music." *Country Music Goes to War.* Ed. Charles K. Wolfe and James E. Akenson. Lexington: The University of Kentucky Press, 2005. 164–91. Print.

Fox, Pamela. "Recycled 'Trash': Gender and Authenticity in Country Music Autobiography." *American Quarterly* 50.2 (1998): 234–67. Print.

Gerome, John. "Carrie Underwood Wins ACM Entertainer of the Year." *The Associated Press.* Apr. 6, 2009. *Lexis Nexis.* Web. Sept. 21, 2009.

Horn, Alena. "'Keepin' it Country': What Makes the Lyrics of Gretchen Wilson Hard?" *Popular Music and Society* 32.2 (2009): 461–73. Print.

Jensen, Joli. *The Nashville Sound: Authenticity, Commercialization, and Country Music.* Nashville, TN: Vanderbilt UP, 1998. Print.

Karger, Dave. "The Confessions of Carrie Underwood." *Entertainment Weekly.* Oct. 18, 2007. Web. Sept. 21, 2009.

Katz, Claire. "'The Eternal Irony of the Community': Prophecy, Patriotism, and the Dixie Chicks." *Shofar: An Interdisciplinary Journal of Jewish Studies* 26.4 (2008): 139–60. Print.

Neal, Jocelyn. "The Voice Behind the Song: Faith Hill, Country Music, and Reflexive Identity." *The Women of Country Music: A Reader.* Ed. Charles K. Wolfe and James E. Akenson. Lexington: The University of Kentucky Press, 2003. Print.

Pruitt, Lesley. "Real Men Kill and a Lady Never Talks Back: Gender Goes to War in Country Music." *International Journal on World Peace* 24.4 (2007): 85–106. Print.

Rossman, Gabriel. "Elites, Masses, and Media Blacklists: The Dixie Chicks Controversy." *Social Forces* 83.1 (2004): 61–79. Print.

Rudder, Randy. "In Whose Name? Country Artists Speak Out on Gulf War II." *Country Music Goes to War.* Ed. Charles K. Wolfe and James E. Akenson. Lexington, KY: The University of Kentucky Press, 2005. 208–226. Print.

Tyrangiel, Josh. "Chicks in the Line of Fire." *Time Magazine*. May 21, 2006. Web. Mar. 14, 2008.

Underwood, Carrie. *Carnival Ride*. Arista, 2007. CD.

——. *Play On*. Arista, 2009. CD.

——. *Some Hearts*. Arista, 2005. CD.

Willman, Chris. *Rednecks and Bluenecks: The Politics of Country Music*. New York: W. W. Norton, 2005. Print.

Witten, Kelsey. "Carrie Underwood Duets with Lucky 5th Grader." *People.com*. Aug. 28, 2009. Web. Sept. 21, 2009.

Yadegarden, Jessica. "R-E-V-E-N-G-E." *Contra Costa Times*. May 20, 2007. *LexisNexis*. Web. Sept. 21, 2009.

Chapter 13

Walking the Great Line: Underoath and Christian Fundamentalism in Punk Rock after 9/11

Gerrit Roessler

When dealing with the unimaginable—with an unimaginable catastrophe—a need for simple explanations arises. These explanations are often rooted in tested, familiar structures and ideologies. In *Welcome to the Desert of the Real!*, Slavoj Žižek argues that 9/11 shattered American reality, or, rather, "the symbolic coordinates which determine what we perceive as reality" like no other event in recent history (16). At the same time, the 9/11 attacks produced new fantasies, and affirmed old ones, about the self and the other. Around the time that Žižek made his observations, during the immediate aftermath of the events, many of the cultural and national narratives were already forming that now, ten years later, frame mainstream American perceptions of 9/11. The "us and them" dichotomy, established by the rhetoric of the Bush administration, seems to have found its continuation in the populist hubris of the Tea Party Movement and its self-appointed spokespeople, Glenn Beck and Sarah Palin. Moreover, the religious, predominantly Christian, basis of that dichotomy can be traced from Jerry Falwell and Pat Robertson's statements on *The 700 Club* immediately after the events, in which they blamed America's alleged hedonistic and immoral lifestyle for the attacks. Similarly, the more recent debates over the so-called Ground Zero Mosque—opponents of which argue that a Muslim cultural center so close to the "hallowed grounds" of the former World Trade Center is an insensitive, if not ill-willed, gesture toward the victims of 9/11—also reek of a kind of Christian egocentrism.

Žižek points out that the religio-political answer to 9/11 is at least problematic, if not entirely paradoxical. Muslim fundamentalism was accused of attacking the freedoms that characterize Western society in part by those who claimed that Western society had not adhered enough to the order of Christian fundamentalism (Žižek 84). In the case of the Ground Zero Mosque, for instance, the freedom of religious expression that the Taliban suppressed so violently in Afghanistan is not unequivocally granted in the society whose freedoms were allegedly at stake on 9/11.

However, not all post-9/11 narratives were religiously motivated. Writing for *Time Magazine*, Roger Rosenblatt proclaimed as soon as four days after the attack that "one good thing could come from this horror: it could spell the end of the age of irony." The unimaginable catastrophe had, in a way, renewed a need for metaphysical truths and absolutes and had shaken the postmodernist ivory tower. In a time that needed stability, the fantasies of free-market capitalism and liberal parliamentary democracy were more tempting than cultural relativism or deconstructionist *différance*. In response, Stanley Fish found himself arguing in the *New York Times* against a post-9/11 discourse that was "grasping for the empty rhetoric of universal absolutes to which all subscribe but which all define differently" (A19).

What these narrative reactions have in common is that they are based on dichotomies—us versus them, freedom versus fundamentalism, irony versus truth—intended to fulfill a desire for meaning, a desire to come to terms with the unexpected and unimaginable. What they also have in common, like all epistemological dichotomies, is that they are based on contradiction. As Jacques Derrida teaches us in *Dissemination*, we are unaware of these contradictions because one side of the pair is always privileged and dominant, while the other is subjugated and controlled. We operate under the illusion that these hierarchies are natural, stable, and inevitable. In other words, for such a dualism to become the structuring narrative by which we can make sense of the unimaginable—the catastrophe of 9/11, in this context—we have to choose sides, to put a halt to play and ambiguity, and submit to the law of what Derrida calls the "god-sun-father-capital" (1832). We have, to paraphrase Roger Rosenblatt, to put an end to irony.

If an alleged mainstream is constituted by contradictions, if its homogeneity is merely a fantasy, and if a sudden event reveals it as fantasy and contradiction, where do we situate those cultural layers that define themselves in opposition to this mainstream? It seems that countercultures would either have to find different, pluralistic strategies to cope with such an identity crisis or that they would have to embrace homogenous and absolutist discourses even more radically. In this essay, I will argue, using the example of the punk-rock band Underoath, that subcultures have historically been characterized by the same desires and contradictions as the mainstream. Moreover, I contend that it was the absolutist mainstream discourse after 9/11, rather than the postmodernist relativism of the pre-9/11 era, that opened the doors for fundamentalist ideologies to establish themselves within the anti-establishment punk subculture. By successfully negotiating the line between ideological uniformity and individualistic plurality, Christian punk rock demarcates the basic lines of the political and cultural discourses of the decade since 2001.

In 2006, Underoath's album *Define the Great Line* debuted at #2 on the Top 200 *Billboard* Album Charts; another, *Lost in the Sound of Separation*, reached #8 in 2008 ("Underoath"). That a band performing in a punk-rock variety often referred to as "screamo" entered the Top 200 at such a high position would be reason enough to examine the possible implications for the state of mainstream culture. In 2006, for example, Underoath found themselves in the neighborhood of Nelly Furtado, and her songs about a "promiscuous maneater," while in 2008, they shared the top ten with Detroit's Kid Rock ("Music Albums").

Even more remarkable is the fact that Underoath simultaneously made #1 in the Top Christian Albums list ("Christian Albums"). In the past, Christian popular culture existed with its own infrastructure for production, distribution, and marketing—an infrastructure that was strictly separate from, and deliberately alternative to, the secular mainstream. The few Christian bands who managed to cross over into the secular market—like Sixpence None the Richer and Creed, for example—either had to downplay their Christianity or formulate religious messages so vaguely that they would be lost on most non-Christian listeners. Other Christian artists would often limit their religious content to a general mention of God or "Him" but avoided reference to Jesus, the Lord, or other specifically Christian terms and motifs.

Simply put, Underoath does not do any of that. In interviews, lyrics, performances, liner notes, and the like, they unapologetically stand by their Christian beliefs. A number of questions immediately arise here: What is it about punk that enables it to harbor Christian beliefs without being a specifically Christian genre? What happens to the very idea of "genre" if its definition is so malleable that it can describe something that seems to be utterly other to it? And, along those same lines, what happens to the idea of "mainstream" if it can contain something that, like punk, defines itself in opposition to the mainstream?

I am using punk rock here as a somewhat fluid term that allows me to include hardcore punk, emo, and a plethora of other variations and subgenres. I believe this is appropriate, as they all share a common narrative of origin. The rules and conventions that define and delineate each variant are legitimized and authenticated by, sometimes rather incompatible, interpretations of punk's creation narrative, so to speak. I will return to the broader question of how to interpret shared narratives, as well as to the matter of authenticity, later in this essay. For now I will offer a very brief overview of its creation narrative and the ways in which it crosses paths with Christian popular culture.

By the mid-80s, the rock and roll of Jimi Hendrix, the flower-power of Scott McKenzie, and the art-rock of Emerson, Lake, and Palmer had become part of the cultural establishment. Former hippies now held Wall Street jobs and voted for Ronald Reagan. The commodification of high-profile symbols like Woodstock and the Vietnam Protests, in, for example, the musical *Hair*, and its subsequent film version, left a sense that the members of the 60s counterculture had betrayed their ideals. Punk emerged during the mid-1970s, first as an expression of British working-class culture, and then as a radical subcultural youth movement in deliberate political and aesthetic opposition to the baby-boomers in general and to hippies in particular. Always careful to avoid becoming part of the loathed establishment—or "selling out," as the term goes—the punk scene refused to participate in established structures of the music and fashion industries and, instead, developed an alternative subcultural infrastructure. Similarly, Christian popular culture, which emerged in the late 1960s and was also a reaction against hippies and the excesses of the "Summer of Love," kept its own record production and distribution, as well as journalism and fashion, independent of the commercial and cultural establishment. Christian popular music, however, did not intend to place itself in direct opposition to the mainstream music and fashion industries, as punk arguably did. Rather, Christian pop music attempted to mimic the fashion and music of the "flower-power" generation in an effort to redefine them in terms of the Christian faith. The "Summer of Love" was to be the "Summer of Love for Jesus."[1]

There are, of course, many different and often mutually exclusive Christian beliefs. Each denomination is based on its own reading of the Bible, and each denomination claims to know the one true reading of the Scriptures and does not accept other readings as equally valid. Characteristically, they share an imperative to "save" non-believers by winning them over to accept their particular interpretation. Bruce Lincoln calls these communities "maximalist," because they strive for a maximum of religious foundation (59). Religion serves as a stabilizing factor and normative corrective of cultural practice (Lincoln 59). Hence, Christian popular music is not a musical genre, but a revision of an existing genre according to a fundamentalist belief system. The genre's rules are slightly rewritten according to the code of conduct of a particular Christian viewpoint, based on the Bible as its fundamental document. The aim is as much to minister to a secular culture as it is to provide an alternative to it.

Punk, on the other hand, is not so much a belief system as an attitude, which started as rage against all social determinism, making it decidedly "antibürgerlich" ("anti-bourgeois"; Büsser 86, my translation). When punk threatened to become part of the commercial mainstream in the early 1980s, movements like straight edge and hardcore developed as ideological and stylistic radicalizations of the attitude. In order to continue identifying with the "punk idea," fans needed to create new labels that would signify a purified mode of the genre. This game of "I am more punk than you" pushed punk towards more and more specific political agendas. Hardcore, for example, was intended as a return to punk's mythical working-class and anti-establishment origins at a time when Johnny Rotten and Sid Vicious of the Sex Pistols had become fashion icons and when punk style was absorbed into the London art scene via Vivienne Westwood. As Martin Büsser points out, hardcore increasingly adopted fragments of a variety of other ideologies (120). Ecological, economical, racial, and feminist causes, to name but a few, were taken on, ultimately leading to straight edge, a near-ascetic lifestyle, whose proponents relinquished drugs, alcohol, and often even sex. The similarities to Christian culture reach beyond the asceticism: as each of the subgenres claims to be the most authentic and legitimate heir to the punk-rock idea, they become inevitably exclusive and dogmatic, or, one might say, fundamentalist.

---

[1]   Romanowski's "Roll Over Beethoven" is particularly strong on these subcultural connections.

This escape into ever more esoteric circles was also motivated by what Büsser calls pointedly the "Fehler im System" ("flaw in the system"; 86, my translation): if everybody were punk, what would there be to revolt against? Likewise, if there were nothing to rebel against, how could one still be punk? This systemic flaw requires any underground culture that defines itself in opposition to the mainstream to be constantly in flux. Punk as a subculture either denies any prescriptive value, because it opposes all types of ideology and thus cannot be pro-anything but only contra, or it becomes so radically prescriptive that it has to refract constantly into ever smaller subcultures. Today, aged punk veterans like "Fat" Mike Burkett of NOFX compensate for their commercial success with a mere gesture of loudmouthed juvenile rebellion against the alleged mainstream Other, while also professing nostalgia for the ultimate anti-attitude as Punk's mythical origin narrative. The compatibility of this gesture with mainstream culture is well illustrated by Green Day's Broadway success based on their 2004 album *American Idiot*, which, much like the musical *Hair* or the more recent *Rent*, represents yet another kind of commodified vision of anti-establishment feel-good rebellion.

Whether a mere gesture or an ideological foundation of the genre, the anti-dogma, anti-establishment attitude that constitutes the origin fantasy of punk is difficult to square with fundamentalist Christianity, particularly in a time like post-9/11 America, when Christianity seems to dominate the social, cultural, and political mainstream. However, as I have noted, Underoath is a band that is unwilling to hide or downplay their Christian beliefs, while simultaneously taking part in non-faith-based festival tours and providing interviews for non-Christian music magazines. In interviews, videos, and onstage, the band members emphasize the importance religion plays in their lives—thus blurring the line between their performative personae and their "real" lives offstage. On their website, discussions of social and political issues frequently take recourse to faith and concrete Bible passages, and their song lyrics deal with classical conversion stories, chastity narratives, and calls for the unconditional love of God. In doing so, they fulfill the conditions of fundamentalist religious practice as outlined above: Religion is the central domain of cultural practice. The reverse is true as well: All practices and preferences are secured by grounding them in religion.

They're Only Chasing Safety (2004) is the band's fourth album and the first with their current lineup. While Christian bands usually change to a secular mainstream label to obscure their faith-based origins, *Chasing Safety*, and all of Underoath's subsequent records, were released on the influential Christian record label Tooth&Nail. The song "Some Will Seek Forgiveness, Others Escape" explicitly contains the word "Jesus," a divergence from the customs of mainstream Christian bands, many of whom revert to the term "Him." In the song's lyrics, the lyrical "I" promises an "unfaithful" other to teach it the Christian virtues of forgiveness, love, and spiritual strength. "Jesus" is asked to welcome it back home. The constant repetition of the lines "Jesus, I'm ready to come home" and "I will love you" turn the song into a kind of prodigal-son story, in which the son earns his return by converting the unfaithful. Guitarist Tim McTague explains in an interview with the popular Christian periodical *CCM Magazine* that "the song is about realizing the error of your ways, asking for forgiveness and making a vow to start over and do what's right" (quoted in Jenison). Furthermore, McTague explains that the group did not want to "accommodate" and put "their beliefs on the backburner and [forget] why they started the band in the first place" (quoted in Jenison). Underoath are clearly setting up a contrast between themselves and other faith-based bands by suggesting that their religious integrity is greater than that of others. The band thus creates a narrative of authenticity based on the myth that their spirituality is radical and uncompromised. This narrative parallels punk's perpetual refraction(s) into a more radical, more "authentic" version of the genre.

The lyrics to the track "In Regards to Myself," from *Define the Great Line*, also deal with truth and authenticity. Here, the lyrics' religious connotations are not as obvious, although they do make frequent references to God. However, alongside the song's video by Linus Johansson, the Christian message becomes difficult to miss. The main theme of the song is the recognition of one's true self. This acknowledgment of truth is brought about by "light" that "is blinding to the naked eye." This line combines two Christian tropes: Jesus as "the light of the world" and the impossibility of looking upon God directly (John 8.12). It encapsulates the promise of salvation and the imperative of faith without empirical proof—the two central paradigms of Christianity. The line also alludes to a biblical passage in which Jesus heals a blind man on the Sabbath. As the story goes, Jesus is accused by the Pharisees of breaking the law, since no work must be done on this day. He responds by saying: "For judgment I have come into this world, so that the blind will see and those who see will become blind," suggesting that he will make those see the truth who believe in him and that he will blind those who only think that they can see (John 9.39). The lesson here is that authentic, true belief is not measured by following the law or going through the ceremonial motions. Underoath appropriate these concepts, suggesting in their own work that true faith can involve a critical attitude to established and institutionalized forms of religious practice.

Underoath extend these themes in their video for "In Regards to Myself," which criticizes the act of idolizing pop stars. Roughly halfway through the video, the band can be seen performing at the heart of a labyrinthine system of corridors. Three sevens appear suspended from strings and attached to a mesmerizing spiral behind the band. The spiral seems to have captured the audience and rendered them apathetic. One little girl breaks the spell as she takes the sevens and runs away. Toward the end of the video, the girl uses the numbers to unlock an escape door out of the labyrinth. In Christian popular culture, the triple seven has become a sign for positive Christianity as a symbolic counterpart to the triple six, which represents Satan. Whereas the latter is scripturally founded, the former is a very recent custom. Underoath also incorporates the triple seven into the URL for their website (www.underoath777.com), which allows the numbers to reverberate against an even larger set of reference points. The triple sevens now stand not only for God and Christianity but also for Underoath—a mediated product, issuing a warning not to be distracted from the gospel by false pop-cultural prophets. By establishing these connections, Underoath triangulate the realms of Scripture, Christian pop culture, and punk rock, rendering themselves authentic in each facet of that trinity, because, clearly, they reside at the center of it.

Heather Hendershot suggests that it is questionable whether or not evangelical youths actually listen carefully to the lyrics of contemporary Christian music and interpret them "properly" (71). She remarks that, although the Christian component of the music is almost exclusively evident in the lyrics, it remains uncertain whether "Christianized" lyrics produce more peaceful and chaste fans (71). With respect to Underoath, this remark is particularly relevant because the band's vocals—screamed loudly and aggressively—are almost impossible to understand. However, the lyrics are available online and, frequently, in the liner notes. Moreover, the band supports religious interpretations of the lyrics through the Christian symbolism of some of their videos, as well as in statements in interviews. They also provide increasingly theological reflections on their life and work on their blog. Not all band members offer the same amount of theological insight, but the blogs by Tim McTague are especially personal accounts of spiritual development. In particular, McTague expresses both personal religious reflections as well as suggestions about appropriate Christian behavior, based on his interpretation of the faith. For a band trying to woo an exclusively Christian audience, none of these gestures would be remarkable, since this kind of reflection is an integral aspect of evangelical religious practice. However, for a band that shared a concert bill on the 2009 Warped Tour with punk standard-bearers Bad Religion, Underoath's brand of good religion is nothing short of provocative.

Still, this does not mean that the band is singularly out to convert their secular audience. During the 2006 Warped Tour, "Fat" Mike Burkett of NOFX famously poked fun at the band from the stage, saying that "Underoath doesn't believe that dinosaurs existed" (quoted in Saitowitz). When Underoath left the tour for undisclosed reasons, speculations arose as to whether they had quit in response to the rejection by such an established and overtly secular punk band (Paul). In an interview with the Canadian online punk rock magazine *PunkTV*, two of Underoath's members, bassist Grant Brandell and drummer Aaron Gillespie, joked about an online game that would put Burkett and their own vocalist Chamberlain up against each other in a fight to the death. The game, released in 2006 as *Warped Tour Game* by *FuseTV*, features bloody battles of popular musicians with a Warped Tour background and blasts of music from the player who emerges victorious. Brandell and Chamberlain predicted good chances for their own combatant because Burkett is, in their opinion, old and fat (quoted in Christie). We can see that the overtness of the band's Christian message does not seem to contradict an otherwise ordinary decorum for a punk-rock band, as they display bawdy humor and an interest in video games with a jocular use of violence. Furthermore, the band regards itself as the next "real" thing in punk rock: a younger and newer counterpart to the aged and settled punk establishment.

In the October 2006 issue of *Alternative Press Magazine*, Underoath's McTague and NOFX's Burkett were confronted about their disagreements. In the story, Burkett expresses a number of problems he has with the opinions of individual band members. He refers, for example, to a conversation he had with McTague, where "[McTague] made himself very clear … He thinks homosexuality is wrong. He doesn't think gays should be able to get married. And he thinks that gay people are probably that way because they were molested as children" (quoted in Staddon 186). Burkett's response is emphatic: "I think that is backward thinking and I will ridicule [McTague] for that publicly" (quoted in Staddon 186). Burkett goes so far as to claim that Underoath proselytize in concert by saying that they perform in the name of Jesus Christ: "I think they're being evangelistic by doing that. They're trying to get kids to think it's cool to join an organized religious group. I don't think that's cool" (quoted in Staddon 186). Burkett's band emerged in the 1980s and has been politically outspoken, particularly against organized religion, ever since. In 2003, they released a record called *The War on Errorism*, punning on the rhetoric employed by the Bush administration in the immediate aftermath of 9/11, which featured a caricature of the president. In 2006, they released *Never Trust a Hippie*, ridiculing both Christianity and punk's original nemesis, with a drunken Jesus figure as the original flower child on the cover. As such, Burkett's comments are not entirely surprising.

Rather than spend his time defending the band's right to practice their faith openly, McTague's rebuttal mainly takes issue with the implied correspondence between Christianity and sociopolitical conservatism. Underoath frequently refers to the religious establishment as "Americanized Christianity," to emphasize how Christianity has been appropriated for political and social agendas, particularly in the post-9/11 environment. Spencer Chamberlain, Underoath's lead screamer, laments that the punk community "judge[s] us for something that Americanized Christianity has turned into, which is everything that we kind of stand against" (quoted in Silnicki). The terminological dissociation of America and religion implies a desire to untangle the conceptual unity of national and religious symbols that post-9/11 civil religion had revived so radically. Underoath explicitly want not to be "like your average Christian band," where "Christian" is synonymous with being pro-war, pro-life, and xeno- and homophobic (quoted in Reay). The mainstream political appropriation of religious symbols and rhetoric has, in the band's opinion, harmed the perception of their spiritual content. Mainstream religion is no longer about faith but is rather about a conservative self-image. Tim McTague sees mainstream Christianity in America as being homophobic, patriarchal and pro-war, whereas he identifies himself as "a mixture of red and blue, as far as my political color goes" (quoted in Staddon 184). The use of terms like "mixture," the detachment from institutionalized Christianity, and the emphasis on individual and personal articulations of faith seem to imply a relativist, anything-goes attitude. Yet, an analysis of the band's work and public statements, like those presented here, makes it clear that they maintain a fundamentally dualistic worldview based on the belief that Christian faith will ultimately reveal a truthful understanding of the world and will provide salvation from its troubles.

McTague's defense against Burkett's accusations makes it apparent that Underoath feel misunderstood and somehow unjustly persecuted for their beliefs. This is, of course, a biblical narrative as much as it is a punk-rock narrative. Criticism especially has strengthened the musicians' status as quasi-martyrs who risk their commercial success by refusing to downplay their spirituality, by resisting the temptation to sign a major record deal, and, ironically, by quarreling publicly with punk rock icons like Mike Burkett. Punk rock's inherent need for perpetual radicalization, and its concurrent push to oppose its own established structures, provides a perfect point of entry for this type of Christian self-perception. The dissociation from traditional images of organized religion and the association with punk rock values generates a novel image of Christianity: Christianity as underground—Christians as the underdogs of punk-rock culture.

At the beginning of my discussion, I suggested that Underoath is a Christian band that is successful in the secular American mainstream. Later, I situated Underoath within the punk-rock tradition and presented the band as a bastion of pseudo-subversive countercultural thinking. Which of these descriptions is true? Well, in a way, both are accurate. "Underground," like "punk," has become a commodified label. Martin Büsser writes that punk's "corpse" had already started to "smell" in the early 1990s, referencing the increasingly indiscriminate, and increasingly distasteful, use of the term *punk* for all kinds of pop-cultural phenomena (147). Certainly, there still is the self-administered community that does not strive for commercial success, but it no longer exists as an independent alternative to the mainstream. In fact, there is no homogenous mainstream anymore, and perhaps never has been, but rather a heterogeneous mix of marketable labels, all of which promise authenticity and originality. Tom Holert and Mark Terkessidis argue as much, claiming that stylistic and ideological deviance is no longer streamlined but has become a commodity in itself (10).

Underoath's unapologetic display of religious fervor secures the disapproval of the established punk community, and their punk decorum secures the disapproval of those religious conservatives, who, post-9/11, claimed to represent mainstream America. It is this double movement of marginalization which makes Underoath and similar bands—such as Mute Math, Switchfoot, and Norma Jean—particularly marketable. Their claims to authenticity makes them implicitly political without the need to take sides in the dominant political discourse.

The established cultural and political institutions failed to create a homogenous response to 9/11 precisely because homogeneity is not a quality of mainstream culture. The dyadic structures which characterized the dominant attempts at making sense of the events were too overtly revealed in their inherent contradictions by the events themselves. Given the choice between "us and them," the answer was, too often, neither. This "neither" was, it seems, not a rejection of metaphysical truth claims in favor of deferred meaning. On the contrary, as the phenomenon of Christian punk shows, the desire for "truth" has not lessened, but it is packaged inside an established genre repertoire which presents absolute truth as a choice and an expression of independence, freedom, and rebellion, rather than a totalitarian imperative. That Christianity sees itself in the position of the marginalized outsider is not new and not particular to Underoath or Christian punk. What makes this case special is that the label "Christianity" was used to describe both the mainstream and the subcultural response and that the ideological structures of these responses— the fundamental truth claim and the radically dyadic world view—were identical. Yet, in case of the mainstream, the knowledge of the alleged truth informed its choices, and, in case of the subculture, Christian truth was just one of the choices, even though it was clearly marked as the one that was more authentic and "punk."

Underoath's religious beliefs serve as an authoritative, moral foundation in which fans can ground their individual spirituality. It is this balance between essentialist absolutes and *laissez-faire* non-conformity that is so appealing to post-9/11 America, whose central cultural myths had just been revealed as mere fantasy, and whose central cultural and political institutions had failed to provide a satisfactory and stable framework within which to cope with the unimaginable. From its peculiar position of "knowing truth," Christian punk can provide answers in a more profound way than the fundamentalist evangelical discourse that dominated the public response to the attacks. By distancing themselves from the teachings of evangelical figureheads, and from the political establishment from both sides of the congressional spectrum, without explicitly specifying their own point of view on critical issues such as gay marriage, the "war on terror," abortion, and creationism, Underoath avoid the prescriptive didacticism of Jerry Falwell and the destructive polemics of secular figures like Michael Moore. The disastrous events of 9/11 did not, perhaps, put an end to irony, but rather opened a space for highly ironic articulations such as Christian punk. If Christianity, as I argue above, serves as a source of truth and absolute values, and punk rock as the antidote to the sociocultural dogmatism of the mainstream, the question remains at what point either label loses its credibility and at what point of commercial success this novel mode of an otherwise established genre can no longer—to use a variation on the title of Underoath's 2006 album—"walk the great line" between the ideologically dogmatic and the highly adaptable and individualistic.

Works Cited

The Bible. New International Version. London: Hodder and Stoughton, 2001. Print.

Büsser, Martin. *If the Kids Are United: Von Punk zu Harcore und Zurück*. 6th ed. Mainz: Ventil Verlag, 2003. Print.

"Christian Albums." *www.Billboard.com*. July 8, 2006. Web. Jan. 21, 2011.

Christie, Dixon. "Underoath Interview at Warped Tour 2006 with PunkTV.ca." *www.PunkTV.ca*. 2006. Web. Aug. 29, 2009.

Derrida, Jacques. "From *Dissemination.*" Trans. Barbara Johnson. *The Norton Anthology of Theory and Criticism*. 2nd ed. Ed. Vincent B. Leitch. New York: Norton, 2010. 1830–77. Print.

Fish, Stanley. "Condemnation Without Absolutes." *The New York Times*. Oct. 15, 2001, late ed.: A19. Print.

Hendershot, Heather. *Shaking the World for Jesus: Media and Conservative Evangelical Culture*. Chicago, IL: University of Chicago Press, 2004. Print.

Holert, Tom and Mark Terkessidis. *Mainstream der Minderheiten: Pop in der Kontrollgesellschaft*. 2nd ed. Berlin: Edition ID-Archiv, 1997. Print.

Jenison, David. "Underoath: A Hardcore Day's Night" *www.ccmmagazine.com*. 2004. Web. Feb. 13, 2011.

Lincoln, Bruce. *Holy Terrors: Thinking about Religion After September 11*. Chicago, IL: University of Chicago Press, 2003. Print.

"Music Albums, Top 200 Albums and Music Album and Charts." *www.Billboard.com*. 8 July 2006. Web. 25 Aug. 2009.

——. *www.Billboard.com*. Sept. 20, 2008. Web. Aug. 25, 2009.

Paul, Aubin. "Fat Mike Addresses Underoath Rumors." *www.Punknews.com*. July 31, 2006. Web. Aug. 29, 2009.

Reay, Cathy. "Interview with Underoath." *http://Europunk.net*. July 17, 2006. Web. Aug. 29, 2009.

Romanowski, William D. "Roll Over Beethoven, Tell Martin Luther the News: American Evangelicals and Rock Music." *Journal of American Culture* 15.3 (1992): 79–87. Print.

Rosenblatt, Roger. "The Age of Irony Comes to an End." *www.Time.com*. Sept. 24, 2001. Web. Aug. 25, 2009.

Saitowitz, Paul. "Punk Band NOFX Working Hard to Enjoy this Year's Van's Warped Tour." *www.pe.com*. June 29, 2006. Web. Aug. 29, 2009.

Silnicki, Graham. "A Grill of One's Own." *www.andPOP.com*. June 17, 2006. Web. Aug. 29, 2009.

Staddon, Tristan. "Sometimes You Walk the Line, Sometimes the Line Walks You." *Alternative Press Magazine* 219 (2006): 180–86. Print.

"Underoath Album and Song Chart History." *www.Billboard.com*. n.d. Web. Feb. 20, 2011.

Underoath. "In Regards to Myself." *Define the Great Line*. Tooth&Nail, 2006. CD.

———. "In Regards to Myself." Dir. Linus Johansson. Tooth&Nail, 2006. Video.
———. "Some Will Seek Forgiveness, Others Escape," *They're Only Chasing Safety.* Tooth&Nail, 2004. CD.
Žižek, Slavoj. *Welcome to the Desert of the Real! Five Essays on September 11 and Related Dates.* New York: Verso, 2002. Print.

Chapter 14
War Is Heavy Metal:
Soundtracking the US War in Iraq

Steve Waksman

Immoral behavior breeds immoral behavior. When a president commits the immoral
act of sending otherwise good kids to war based on a lie, this is what you get.

Michael Moore, *Fahrenheit 9/11*

Michael Moore's documentary on the Bush administration's response to the events
of September 11, 2001, *Fahrenheit 9/11*, has been alternately celebrated and
critiqued along multiple lines. Impassioned, and driven by Moore's characteristic
sympathy for those he considers political underdogs, the film uses footage drawn
from myriad sources to construct a dense montage in which political analysis
rubs up against emotional pathos, on one hand, and humorous punch lines on the
other. Moore's comments about the "immorality" of Bush's decision to send US
troops to war are meant to absolve soldiers of much of the responsibility for the
big-picture consequences of their actions; for the moral and political crux of the
film concerns the failure of leadership stemming from the highest echelons of US
government. Yet portions of the film show those same soldiers to be acting in full
accordance with US policy mandates and to be treating the Iraqi population as
something less than fully human. Thus, "this is what you get": soldiers laughing
at a dead Iraqi laying on the ground with a rigor-mortis-induced erection; soldiers
treating a Christmas Eve raid on a civilian as a mock visit from Santa; and, in one
of the more stirring bits of footage, a white male soldier singing directly to the
camera lines from the nu metal band Bloodhound Gang's song, "Fire Water Burn."
"We don't need no water let the motherfucker burn / Burn, motherfucker, burn,"
chants the soldier, eyes open wide and mouth crooked in a half-smile in apparent
glee at the imagined damage evoked by the lyrics he sings.

This last clip is one of several that Moore lifted from an earlier Iraq war
documentary, *Soundtrack to War*, by the Australian artist and filmmaker George
Gittoes. In Gittoes' film, the main subject of which is the musical practices of Iraq
War soldiers and Iraqi citizens, the scene in question occupies a particular pride
of place at the film's conclusion. It is also a more extended scene, taking some
two-plus minutes to play out. Gittoes, whose voice is audible but whose physical
presence is offscreen, interviews one final US soldier who introduces himself as
John Frisbee from Lebanon, Tennessee. Gittoes instructs the young man as to what
he wants: some indication of the music he most prefers and thinks is most suited
to the circumstance of being stationed in Iraq, and some recitation of sample lyrics

from that music. Such seemingly basic instructions lead to an unusually halting sequence, however, for the exchange between filmmaker and soldier is interrupted twice, first by a passing car that draws attention and then by Gittoes dropping his camera. Gittoes edits so that the pattern of stopping and starting the interview is on display in all its awkwardness, his mishandling of the camera stopping Frisbee mid-stream as the soldier is half-speaking, half-singing the words to the Bloodhound Gang song. By the final iteration of the scene, Gittoes is veritably feeding lines to his soldier-subject, telling him to simply say, "My favorite number one is the Bloodhound Gang and this is how it goes." Frisbee complies and then sings the notorious lines, after which he laughs at his own performance and asks to the camera, "Was that good?" An abrupt edit cuts to the end credit sequence, over which plays the commercial recording of the same Bloodhound Gang song.

Of the whole sequence recounted above, Moore includes only the penultimate moment in which the soldier—unidentified in *Fahrenheit 9/11*—sings the lyric in a direct, unencumbered fashion. Whether or not Moore's use of the clip is misleading is less of interest, though, than the way in which these two different uses of the same footage present two distinct versions of the connection between music, and specifically heavy-metal music, and the sensibilities of Iraq War soldiers. The first, foreshortened clip creates what appears to be a direct association between heavy metal and white male military aggression. Although Moore's overall portrait of American soldiers in Iraq is far from one-dimensional, this particular audio-visual soundbite clearly tips toward the less savory side of US military attitudes, showing a young man for whom the charge of destruction is akin to a satisfying burst of visceral sonic pleasure. In the second, longer sequence, by contrast, the soldier's aggression appears far more complicated. Indeed, Frisbee does not even choose the song he sings himself, but presents it only after another soldier whose voice is heard offscreen begins to sing it. Frisbee declares his own preference for classic rock, but explains that the Bloodhound Gang song suited the mind frame of him and his fellow soldiers at a time when they were trying to get "Saddam and his regime out." As such, "Fire Water Burn" comes across here as much an expression of military male camaraderie as untrammeled lust to crush the enemy. Moreover, Frisbee's rendition is more overtly performative in Gittoes' original sequence, rather than merely expressive: he is clearly playing to the camera, and his version of the lyrics only achieves resolution after much coaxing from the filmmaker. Heavy-metal music and military mayhem, then, are not so neatly sutured together, but the music is shown to be an integral part of the soundscape of US military engagement.[1]

Films about the war in Iraq have proliferated in the past several years, and one of the recurrent trends in these films is the use of heavy metal as an integral part of the cinematic soundtrack built around the war. Such use should not be taken for granted. After all, by certain logic, country music would be a more obvious

---

[1]   Pieslak has written the most thorough study of music in the context of the Iraq War to date. Also see Gilman for a revealing inquiry into soldiers' uses of music.

genre to employ in connection with the war in Iraq, as country musicians have produced the most overt and widely recognized expressions of musical patriotism in conjunction with the war effort.[2] Yet in both documentary and fictional films about the second Iraq war, country music has occupied a decidedly subordinate role, and heavy metal has vied with rap for a sort of musical hegemony in the aural world of the US soldier. Moreover, metal's role in these films has not been limited to its association with US combatants, but in one significant case—the documentary film *Heavy Metal in Baghdad*—has been positioned as an integral medium for a group of young Iraqis who are themselves living with the day-to-day stress of war and, later, geographic displacement and exile. As one key facet of the cinematic soundtrack to the Iraq War, heavy metal has not therefore given rise to a single sort of battle-ready subjectivity, but has been employed to project a surprisingly diverse range of subjects who occupy markedly different positions in relation to the larger field of conflict and of representation. Recognition of this diversity is not meant to celebrate a benign pluralism of musical identities where the war on film is concerned, but should awaken our attention to the complex cultural work that popular music is made to do in contemporary portrayals of warfare.

To explore these matters, I have organized this essay into three main sections. In the first, I consider the role of heavy metal in the soundtracks of two recent documentary films about the second Iraq war: the aforementioned *Soundtrack to War*, and *Gunner Palace*, an on-the-ground film focused on a group of soldiers who are housed in the former palace of Uday Hussein, Saddam Hussein's eldest son. The second section explores heavy metal's use in two fictional narratives, *The Hurt Locker* and *The Messenger*. The combined focus on documentary and fiction is strategic and meant to highlight a double-sided dynamic: the parallels between the music used in the two types of films lend greater realism to the fictional narratives, while the use of music in the documentary films has significant implications for the ways in which these films convey a sense of the subjective experience of warfare that is akin to their fictional counterparts. In the third section, I examine the documentary *Heavy Metal in Baghdad*, using the film to raise questions about how heavy metal operates on the war's "other side," where metal is alternately construed as a way toward freedom of expression and a symbol of a nation under attack.

In her astute survey of the first wave of Iraq War films, Susan Carruthers distinguished between two basic categories: "those that align their sights with the US military, and a smaller subset ... that strives to convey the texture of everyday life under occupation for ordinary, and extraordinary, Iraqis" (31). Pat Aufderheide makes a similar distinction in an essay concerning the different publics that Iraq War films seek to address, adding a category of films "about the legitimacy and logic of the war" (57). For both authors, *Gunner Palace* figures as a paradigmatic

---

2   See Schmelz on the alignment of certain country artists with US military objectives.

film of the first sort, a "grunt doc" in which documenting the war through the US soldiers' perspective is the first priority. Carruthers and Aufderheide both criticize the limitations of this documentary mode and are more favorable in their assessment of those films that make more effort to acknowledge the Iraqi experience of the conflict. It is unfortunate, then, that neither writer includes any reference to *Soundtrack to War* in her respective survey, for the film is distinguished not only by its focus upon the place of music within the war, but by demonstrating shared concern with both US combatants and Iraqis living amidst the conflict, and as such goes against the grain of critical classification.

There are several possible explanations for this omission, but in part it reflects a problem recently identified by Corey Creekmur that "the almost exclusive attention critics have paid to *images* (or language) in the 'War on Terror' threatens to return to a once common neglect of the role of *sound* ... in the production and reception of mass media" (84). Seeking to correct this oversight, Creekmur identifies what he calls a sort of "aural Orientalism" that has filtered into a range of film and television sources, which consists of "the sound of cultural difference mediated through questionable forms of expertise and ideological control" (91). This mode of aural representation can be heard in the way that spoken Arabic language is not accompanied by subtitles in several recent film works, so as to serve as a pure mark of sonic otherness for presumed English-speaking audiences; or in use of the sounds of Muslim prayer to convey a sense of narrative tension and even dread. Insightful as Creekmur's observations are, though, they are predicated on their own strange omissions; for he pays almost no attention to the ways in which Western popular music figures in the soundtracks of recent film works, fictional or documentary. The present chapter is a step toward filling that gap.[3]

Soundtrack to War opens with what has often been hailed as the ultimate "extreme" metal statement: Slayer's "Angel of Death," the opening track of the band's highly influential and controversial 1986 album *Reign in Blood*. With lyrics that seek to inhabit the mind of Josef Mengele, architect of the Nazi "final solution," "Angel of Death" is a song that deliberately blurs the line between celebration and critique where the portrayal of violence is concerned. It occupies a position from which genocide is treated not as immoral but as amoral, a position that is designed to elicit shock from the listener. Director George Gittoes employs the song in a highly edited fashion, rearranging bits of the Slayer recording (a mid-tempo breakdown that occurs halfway through the song, a squealing near-atonal guitar solo, singer Tom Araya screaming "Angel of Death" at song's end) over the film's title shot and then over a rapidly paced sequence of scenes taken from the streets of Baghdad, intercut with snippets of interview footage with US soldiers. "Saddam, what you doing, we'll be coming for you," says one African American soldier into the camera, accompanied by a frenetic blast of drums from the Slayer

---

[3]   Several of the essays collected in Ritter and Daughtry address uses of music on television in the months and years after 9/11, but none takes up the uses of music in film.

track. About forty-five seconds in, the music recedes as another white soldier holds up a compact disc while interviewed from within what appears to be a tank, and explains: "This is the one we listen to the most. This is the one, we travel, when we're killing the enemy, going through war, coming up here into Iraq, coming into Baghdad." Rather incongruously, given the preceding sounds, the soldier reveals this most listened-to selection to be not Slayer but Drowning Pool's "Bodies" (often called "Let the Bodies Hit the Floor") about which he further elaborates: "That was the motto for our tank, 'Let the Bodies Hit the Floor,' 'cuz it was just, it was fitting for the job we were doing." As a recording of the song enters the non-diegetic soundtrack, the soldier adds, "War itself is heavy metal, yes."

Heavy metal is hardly the only musical style featured in Gittoes' documentary. Rap music appears almost as frequently as does metal, typically in the form of original raps delivered by African American soldiers. Elsewhere, one can hear singer-songwriter styled music played with acoustic guitar and voice; an a cappella rendition of an original patriotic paean to America sung in the style of contemporary rhythm and blues by a white female soldier; a group of black soldiers collectively singing an old style gospel shout; and, in an especially poignant sequence, two Iraqi brothers—one of whom was a former prisoner at Abu Ghraib—harmonizing a version of the Bee Gees song, "New York Mining Disaster." Despite this relatively broad range of sounds, Gittoes' decision to bookend his film with bursts of heavy metal carries considerable weight; it appears as both a reflection of the musical preferences of many of the soldiers with whom he came into contact, and an aesthetic decision on the part of the filmmaker to draw upon the aural power of metal to serve as an index of the war's affective dimensions. "War itself is heavy metal" may be a line spoken by one of his interviewees (and, actually, by more than one, as we'll see), but it also seems indicative of an equation that Gittoes makes through his choices of what sounds to foreground. Yet the statement "war is heavy metal" is hardly as transparent as either the filmmaker or his subjects would seem to have us believe. What can it mean to say that "war is heavy metal"?

One possible answer to this question comes about twenty minutes into the film, through a short interview with soldier Bradley Corkins. Among the more offbeat personalities to appear in the film—so much so that he is pictured on the cover of the DVD release—Corkins first enters not through his image but through the sound of his amplified electric guitar, on which he plays a distorted, single-note low-end riff that hovers somewhere between heavy metal and surf music. As the camera pans toward him, we see Corkins playing a red Stratocaster-shaped guitar, with a small amplifier just in front of him. At his left side are two rifles poised standing against a wall; at his right is a fellow soldier who listens appreciatively.

After finishing his performance of the riff, Corkins notes that he plans to write some "gore metal" lyrics to go along with it—gore metal being a subgenre in which charging, brutal music is matched with lyrics that describe acts of physical violence in graphic, gruesome detail. He caps his brief statement by saying, "To me, war is heavy metal," and flashes one of the most recognizable signs of metal subculture, the devil horns, to the camera while sticking out his tongue.

His companion, who goes unnamed, builds on Corkins' proclamation: "War *is* heavy metal. It's fast paced, heavy and emotional. It gets your adrenaline going, it helps you feel what you got to feel, get it out of the way. Help you relax and end of the day, it can give you anything you need to feel." Gittoes does not let these statements go uncontested, but refers to Corkins' own encounters with "gore" during his deployment—he evacuated a convoy that was hit with an improvised explosive device (IED) and had bodies fall apart in his hands—and asks whether the soldiers' taste for such music might be "feeding on the pain" of those who have died. Corkins stands his ground, emphasizing that much gore metal is in fact about war, and that the graphic details of the lyrics explain what war is in an effective and convincing manner.[4] The segment concludes with Corkins' account of some lyrics he'd written, "I sold my soul to thee / And hell has started for me," using the conventions of metal word craft to express not his impressions of bodily dismemberment but his feelings of basic powerlessness in the face of his military duties.[5]

Power is an issue that comes up repeatedly in academic treatments of heavy metal. Deena Weinstein and Robert Walser, in their respective sociological and musicological analyses of the genre, both emphasize "power" as the central preoccupation of heavy metal in aural and visual terms. Power is audible in metal's stress upon extremes of volume, in the distorted timbre of the guitars, the magnified crash of the double bass drum, the vocals straining for either the highest of high notes or the lowest of low, depending on the subgenre. Power is visible, in turn, in the profusion of studded leather, the demonstrative virtuosity of metal instrumentalists, or the fascination with the trappings of masculinity. The presumption in these works and others is that metal's projection of power proves empowering for its dedicated listeners, and that metal often fosters a distinct sense of empowerment among those whose social position teeters between privilege and marginality—young white males of lower-class standing who yearn for a field in which to achieve some sense of mastery yet often experience frustration in these desires. As Lisa Gilman suggests in her study of the value of popular music among US soldiers in Iraq, it is precisely the "combination of real powerlessness and the necessity of being confident and physically dominant" under conditions of warfare that leads soldiers toward heavy metal as a preferred genre (8). Corkins' appearance in Gittoes' documentary exemplifies this maxim, and it is the tension

---

[4]   One example that Corkins references in this connection is the group Six Feet Under and its recording *Warpath*, which opens with the song, "War Is Coming." A sample lyric, from the second verse of the song, is as follows: "Blood's pouring from the hole in your side / Take the pain – it'll focus and strengthen you / Take the pain—or your life's fuckin' through / Face the pain—let it become part of you / Take the pain."

[5]   Corkins elaborates: "What I meant by that is by, uh, basically joining the Army I feel I sold my soul to the Army ... they're in charge of me until I get out, and uh, 'Hell has started for me' was the day we got out here, to Iraq." Pieslak addresses this scene briefly (115).

between the soldier's lack of power within the chain of military command and his need to feel empowered for the purposes of committing or otherwise dealing with acts of aggression that presents itself as one way to interpret the declaration, "War is heavy metal."

Within the terms of *Soundtrack to War*, though, this understanding of heavy metal's place in the scheme of the Iraq War is incomplete. Soldiers are not the only ones who find the sounds of metal emotionally resonant and culturally useful. This point becomes clear in a segment, ten minutes after the exchange with Corkins, where Gittoes leads us into the underground practice space of the Iraqi heavy metal band Acrassicauda. Some years later this band would be the subject of a separate film, *Heavy Metal in Baghdad*, to be discussed in a subsequent section. Here, the group is shown at an earlier stage of its history, with three members— drummer Marwan Riyadh, guitarist Faisal Talal, and lead guitarist Tony Aziz— playing through portions of their song "Massacre" and discussing the meaning of its sentiments, with an unnamed friend observing.

Not a song specifically about the US occupation of Iraq, "Massacre" addresses "the massacre all over the goddamn fucking planet, this miserable planet ... [in] Iraq, Afghanistan, Africa," in the words of drummer Riyadh, who quotes some of the lyric in piecemeal fashion: "It's talking about how the boy's crying, how the boy's starving, his mother's heart inside burning, they stole my land, they stole my home, they stole my flesh, they stole my bone." To this guitarist Talal adds, "This song is really talking about a tough thing, which is called the massacre, and really means that someone wants to smash your fucking home and you're really pissed off and you don't want them to smash it." Encouraged by Gittoes, the band moves into a performance of the song, preceded by a unison shout of "let's rock!" the lightheartedness of which offers stark contrast to the anger of the foregoing comments. The members of Acrassicauda never literally say "war is heavy metal," but their performance and surrounding remarks convey the different weight that such a statement carries when articulated from the position of the occupied rather than the invading forces. As Riyadh and Talal explain to Gittoes, "We are born in war, and we have lived in war, but we are not going to fucking die in the war. I mean, there have been three wars since I have been born [says Talal, but Riyadh corrects the number to four] ... Come on, for god's sake, I want to live, I'm young, I'm too young to die." Riyadh punctuates the exchange: "What we are looking for is a better place that can support us, where we can just go out for the people without being afraid from saying, 'Yeah, we are an artist, and we play heavy metal, so let's bang and shit.'"

Gunner Palace does not accord the same prominence to Iraqi perspectives as does Gittoes' film. The Iraqis that appear in *Gunner Palace* play a notably subordinate role, not only in the amount of screen time they are given—in this, the two films are not so different—but in their relationship to US military operations. Two such figures, going by the names "Roy" and "Super Cop," have made veritable careers out of cooperating with US forces; a title in the film tells us that together they have captured 300 Iraqi insurgents. Another, nicknamed

"Mike Tyson," appears to have a similarly cooperative arrangement until he is arrested and accused of photographing targets for the insurgents, an occurrence that leads filmmaker Michael Tucker to claim in somber voiceover, "Nothing is black and white here anymore." Otherwise, Iraqis mainly appear as the victims of nighttime raids or as anonymous background to the work of the soldiers. When music enters into the relationships between soldiers and Iraqi citizens it often does so in ways that reinforce the power of the former, most notably (and notoriously) in a brief scene introduced with the title "Scaring the Natives," in which a PSYOP (psychological operations) speaker truck projects loud heavy metal music at the local population while en route to the Baghdad airport.[6]

In this regard *Gunner Palace* differs from *Soundtrack to War*, but in other particulars the two films have marked similarities. Both make considerable use of first-hand interviews with the war's participants, shot in a close-up style that conveys the tenor of a personal exchange between filmmaker and subject (and, by extension, the viewer). The two films are episodic and largely non-narrative in structure. Most salient to the current discussion, although *Gunner Palace* is not ostensibly *about* the musical lives of US soldiers in Iraq, music is one of the primary features of the film, and its attention to the musical tastes and habits of those stationed in Iraq strongly echoes the emphasis of such matters in *Soundtrack to War*. As *Gunner Palace*'s co-director Michael Tucker explains, the film's focus on music occurred almost by accident; the music was so omnipresent among the soldiers he filmed, and so compelling, that became integral to the fabric of the work (Fuchs). The resulting film integrates music made by its soldier-subjects in a variety of ways, sometimes as explicit diegetic content and other times as non-diegetic source music that provides an aural backdrop to the soldiers' activities.

Musically speaking, *Gunner Palace* is narrower than *Soundtrack to War* in the range of styles featured. The film's soundscape is dominated almost exclusively by rap music and heavy metal, and, of the two, the former dominates. African American soldier/rappers appear intermittently throughout the film, their tone sometimes aggressive, sometimes more subdued, but in either case often remarkably lucid about such issues as the psychological effects of deployment, the conditions that shape wartime violence, and the discrepancy between their experience in Iraq and that of the average American back home who only sees images of the war through the news media. This latter theme dovetails with one of the main emphases of the film as a whole, which co-directors Tucker and Petra Epperlein develop throughout. Tucker's intonation two minutes into the film— "Most of us don't see this on the news anymore. We have reality TV instead.

---

[6] This scene is unusual among the films surveyed for showing direct evidence of the use of music as a part of combat operations, rather than an adjunct to combat, something used by US soldiers to mentally prepare for battle or to cope with the trauma of combat experience. For a pivotal discussion of music's utility in waging cultural and psychological warfare and the disturbing ethical implications this raises, especially with regard to processes of interrogation, see Cusick.

Joe Millionaire. Survivor. Well, survive this. A year in Baghdad without changing the channel"—is echoed almost an hour later by Specialist Richmond Shaw, who offers a low-key but harrowing rap that concludes: "When we take a dip, we try to stick to the script / But when those guns start blazing and our friends get hit / That's when our hearts start racing and our stomachs get woozy / 'Cause for y'all it's just a show but we live in this movie." In this instance and others, rap music stands as an ultimate mark of the film's authenticity, its street-smart accounts of everyday violence eminently well suited to the business of patrolling (or cinematically documenting) the war-torn streets of Baghdad.

War, then, is not heavy metal within the cinematic frame of *Gunner Palace*, which instead moves more commonly to the cadences of rap. Still, heavy metal plays an important supporting role in the film through the presence of Stuart Wilf, the youngest of ten soldiers with whom Tucker shares sleeping quarters during the time that he is embedded with the 2/3 Field Artillery. Only nineteen, Wilf is presented as part of the "new army" that has been recruited to serve in Iraq. A high school dropout from Colorado Springs—proximate to both "Columbine and *South Park*," Tucker tells his viewers—his cheerful demeanor and acerbic humor make him something of a comic foil for the filmmakers. Yet he also serves as a sort of moral compass in the film, someone who uses humor to cope with the mix of boredom and fear that constitutes day-to-day life in Baghdad, but who can also be more reflective when called upon to do so. When the viewer is first brought into the confines of the palace where the soldiers are housed, Wilf is shown holding a standard sized sheet of paper on which are printed the words "Gunner Palace," serving as a mock placard while caught in a fast tracking shot that zooms in on Wilf's fake-serious posture. At film's end, Wilf is given the last words. Asked by Tucker, "How do you rationalize the loss of life?" the young soldier shows no signs of his usual jocularity. "I couldn't even answer that question," says Wilf, who pauses and then continues, "There's not really any rationalization behind someone's child dying. I don't think [this war is] worth the death of someone's family member," gazing directly into the camera as the screen fades to black.

Alongside the other qualities he exhibits, Wilf is also a guitarist, and his playing on electric and acoustic guitars appears at several points. Indeed, in the final scene recounted above, Wilf holds his electric guitar in his hand while speaking, and his words are underscored by his strumming a minor-key progression on acoustic guitar, a fact made plain when the fade gives way to an image of him playing. This juxtaposition of electric and acoustic guitars matches the breadth of Wilf's persona as portrayed in *Gunner Palace*, the two instruments carrying rather different cultural connotations and used to convey distinct emotional registers. Here, the sound of the acoustic guitar projects a pathos that trumps the visual symbol of the electric guitar, which more commonly suits Wilf's more playful, ironic or even aggressive side.

Two earlier scenes in the film place Wilf's electric guitar more in the foreground, to contrasting effect. The first gives the best evidence of Wilf's metalhead leanings. It also offers one of the most peculiar exchanges in the film between a US soldier and an Iraqi citizen. Wilf wields his guitar on the outer steps of the palace, and plays a characteristic death metal riff concentrated on the instrument's lower strings, using fast staccato picking and a tone rich with piercing distortion. Directly in front of him stands an older Iraqi man who, we are told in a title, is Basil, "Attorney by Day, Interpreter at Night." Wilf directs his playing at Basil, putting his arm up in the air and grunting, "Basil rules!" while encouraging his compatriot to grunt with him (which he does). In a linked interview clip, Wilf stands beside Basil, calling him the "coolest Iraqi I've ever met" while sporting a t-shirt for the death metal band Exhumed, who are notable exponents of the same "gore metal" subgenre favored by *Soundtrack to War* interviewee Bradley Corkins. Another clip, nearer to the end of the film, shows Wilf playing a version of "The Star-Spangled Banner" on electric guitar. Here, the filmmakers clearly seek to evoke, if not entirely recreate, Jimi Hendrix's era-defining performance of the national anthem at the 1969 Woodstock festival. Wilf's rendition of the song lacks the aural fireworks of Hendrix's. He plays the melody fairly straight aside from the distorted guitar tone and a few chromatic flourishes at the end that have an identifiable heavy metal inflection. However, the framing and editing of the scene, in both visual and aural terms, stretches the boundaries of the song significantly. Wilf wears full combat fatigues, including a helmet strapped securely to his chin, and plays on what appears to be a rooftop, at times backlit by the sun and the orange Iraqi sky, at other times with shots of Baghdad visible in the distance. Meanwhile, his image is crosscut with that of a military helicopter flying through the sky, the churning sound of its propeller and at one point of automatic rifle fire intermixed with that of Wilf's guitar. Like Hendrix's potent act of musical deconstruction, the mix of sonic and visual signifiers here seems to connote something rather far from the untrammeled patriotism for which the national anthem is usually made to stand. Wilf appears and sounds, instead, like an American out of place, his guitar and his soldier's uniform sending contradictory signals about the soldier's role in the war on terror.

Taken together, these various scenes involving Wilf portray a figure possessing a distinctly mobile form of subjectivity, and his engagement with music is a crucial constitutive part of that mobility. This mobility, in turn, fosters what music and media theorist Anahid Kassabian has called an "affiliating" form of cinematic identification. Unlike "assimilating identification," which seeks to narrow the field of relations between cinematic perceivers and onscreen subjects, affiliating identification leaves that field more wide open, allowing for a broader range of engagement and a less finite sense of the personhood of who we are watching onscreen (3).[7] For Kassabian, this sort of identification is especially characteristic of recent films that use a "compiled" rather than a "composed" score, one that is put together from a collection of popular songs, often already familiar to the film's auditors in style if not in actual substance. Both *Soundtrack to War* and *Gunner*

---

[7]   "Perceivers" is Kassabian's preferred term over the more typical "spectators," as it admits that the perception of film is multisensory, involving more than the visual realm.

Palace present a distinctive form of compiled score, in which popular music styles enter the frame through soldiers' own modes of musical practice. In the former film, however, while "heavy metal" as a genre may be shown to have considerable social fluidity, the individual interview subjects tend to be defined by their stated musical preferences in a more straightforward one-to-one fashion. *Gunner Palace* gives its soldier-subjects more room to maneuver, musically and otherwise; and Wilf personifies this flexibility, his taste for heavy metal seemingly bringing him closer to the Iraqis around whom he serves, and his guitar playing providing a musical analogue for the ambivalence of his commitment to service.

Compared to their documentary counterparts, the fictional portrayals of the Iraq War under discussion—*The Hurt Locker* and *The Messenger*—have a much stronger tendency to foreground the individual over the collective experience of war, and to organize their narratives around a single main protagonist. *The Hurt Locker* starts from the premise that "war is a drug," as an opening title announces, and immerses the viewer in a high-tension series of events driven forward by the cannily named William James, whose apparent addiction to the rush of defusing explosives puts him and his two fellow squad members in harm's way. *The Messenger* concerns itself more with the after-effects of war, the lingering trauma that is magnified by lead character Will Montgomery's assignment to the task of notifying families of soldiers who have died in combat. Music is used rather sparingly in both films, but both use the sound of heavy metal at key moments to mark the subjectivity of their protagonists. In *The Hurt Locker*, the music seems to reinforce James's supposed "wildness," albeit with some potentially hidden undertones. *The Messenger* uses metal to amplify the lead character's struggle to connect with the world outside, a world from which he is distanced by his physical and emotional wounds.

Probably the most broadly acclaimed film about the Iraq War, with its Academy Award for best picture and director Kathryn Bigelow's historic award for best director, *The Hurt Locker* has also been criticized for its lack of open engagement with the politics of the war.[8] Like *Soundtrack to War* and *Gunner Palace*, *The Hurt Locker* places its focus not on macro-political matters but on the details of soldiers' experiences. More than those non-fiction works, *The Hurt Locker* is especially concerned with the intensity of combat and of soldiers' work in the field, elements it can represent more directly precisely by not having to "document" them. Yet it shares with the documentary works an overarching recognition that the lines between combat and non-combat experience become exceptionally blurry for the

---

[8]   In *Cineaste*, for example—a magazine known for placing much value on film as political engagement—Robert Sklar opened his review with the question: "Is it possible to make a film dealing with the US war on Iraq without condemning, or at least acknowledging, the mistakes, failures, and illegal acts committed by George W. Bush, Dick Cheney, and their cohorts?" (55). He does not quite go on to say that the film refuses politics entirely, but does argue that it deliberately avoids any sense of "ideological arm-twisting" in favor of a more "timeless and universal" approach.

contemporary soldier. Day-to-day life in Iraq is filled with dread, or at least with the potential for violent outbreak, even in moments of supposed downtime; and, while most soldiers wish for a reprieve from the relentless sense that something bad is about to happen, Will James thrives on that possibility and his power to defuse it.

Heavy-metal music arises at three instances in the film. Its first appearance coincides with James' entry into the film's narrative. He is sent as a replacement team leader for a squad charged with the responsibility of disarming explosives; his predecessor was killed by an IED found on a busy Baghdad street. When existing squad member J.T. Sanborn comes to welcome James, he finds the sergeant alone in his room with very loud, abrasive heavy metal music blaring. In Bigelow and director of photography Barry Ackroyd's framing of James' introduction, the music precedes the soldier's image; the screen is black for a moment, the darkness shortly giving way to a shot of James crouching in an unlit room, his head buried in his outstretched arms, almost in a position of prayer but for the cigarette he holds. When Sanborn enters, James turns the music off, and quickly enlists his colleague in removing the protective board from his lone window, his preference for sunlight over safety foreshadowing the recklessness of his combat demeanor. Their brief meeting concluded, James cranks the music back up, grinning at Sanborn with the declaration "home sweet home," which proves to be less ironic in James' case than it would first seem, the military front being the place where he feels most at home.

The coincidence between James' taste for heavy rock music and his approach to his military responsibilities becomes clear in the next scene, when he and his fellow squad members—Sanborn and Owen Eldridge—go on their first mission together. From the moment they reach their target destination, James acts with a bravado that catches his colleagues off guard. He refuses to rely on the robotic device used by the squad to investigate possible IEDs, choosing instead to venture into the field and put himself at risk. The protective suit he dons to exercise his task is one of the film's great elements, enclosing the character in a self-contained sensory world in which he is left alone with his heightened perceptions and the sound of his own breathing—which is prominently featured on parts of the soundtrack—his only contact with his fellow soldiers through a radio headset. This is James' true home, the scene reveals, the place where he is most himself, and his enclosure within the suit mirrors his immersion in the high-volume sound of metal within his military quarters. Making the connection all but explicit, James announces, "Let's rock and roll, man," as he leads himself forward to disarm the explosive, prompting his team members to label him alternately "rowdy" and "reckless."

The Hurt Locker is in many ways a film about the male-to-male chemistry between soldiers. As much as James seems to follow no direction but his own, his placement alongside Sanborn and Eldridge, and the conflicts and loyalties that ensue, are at the core of the film's drama. It is no surprise that heavy metal, a genre widely recognized for its masculine connotations, accompanies one of the film's most vivid scenes of male bonding through a mix of friendly camaraderie and competitive struggle for dominance. After a prolonged and successfully waged effort to flush out a group of snipers in the middle of the desert, the trio returns to James' quarters to let off steam. The charging metal music, strongly reminiscent of the sounds that first accompanied James' appearance in the film, marks the scene as taking place within his territory, literally and symbolically. It also matches the playful but aggressive wrestling bout occurring between James and the African American Sanborn, who trade punches while enacting a ritual of dominance and submission, the older and more highly ranked (and white) James making sure he keeps his black counterpart in his place.[9] Meanwhile, Eldridge, the youngest team member not just in age but in demeanor, largely acts as a combination spectator and referee, his own masculinity being too far beneath his fellow soldiers to be admitted into the fight.

James' masculinity is distinguished from his compatriots along several lines: age, rank, experience (he reveals in an earlier exchange that he also saw action in Afghanistan), and race, in relation to Sanborn. Not least among these factors is James' paternity. Unlike his younger counterparts, he has a son back home, whose picture he keeps in a box of his possessions that also contains souvenir parts from various explosives he has dismantled, and his wedding ring strung on a chain necklace (both of the latter he classifies, sardonically, as "stuff that almost killed me"). James' paternity supports the authority he wields over his men, but it also stands as his greatest point of vulnerability, because as a father James is flawed beyond repair. "Everyone's a coward about something," the older soldier says to the child-like Eldridge, who admits having been scared during the encounter with the snipers. For James, as for so many iconic American heroes, his fear is mainly stoked by the prospect of domestication and the responsibilities of fatherhood.[10]

In this light, the third moment in which heavy metal asserts its presence on the soundtrack consolidates the thematic trajectory wherein Will James flees from his domestic and paternal duties into the adrenalized masculinity of military engagement. *The Hurt Locker*'s penultimate sequence shows James at home, his tour of duty over. From the first glimpse of the character walking through the aisles of a supermarket as though in a stupor, it is made clear that James does not belong here. The benign, easy-listening background music that plays beneath the scene only reinforces the sense that James is out of place in a seemingly normal setting; amidst the undemanding routine of everyday consumerism, he loses his bearings. Later, putting his infant son to bed, he offers an unsettling monologue about how, as a person grows older, the field of things for which one can feel love continually shrinks. "By the time you get to my age maybe it's only one or

---

[9]   Whitsitt makes a provocative if heavy-handed argument regarding the integral role of the "interracial romance" between the white male James and the black male Sanborn, connecting *The Hurt Locker* to such archetypal American fictions as *The Adventures of Huckleberry Finn*.

[10]   Faludi discusses the imperilment of American masculinity in the wake of 9/11, and the corresponding cultural need to valorize heroic masculine saviors.

two things," he tells his son, "With me I think it's one." With that, the sound of a helicopter signals James' reenlistment and return to Iraq, a decision underscored on the soundtrack by the fluctuating sound of an Arabic woman's singing voice over a building mechanical drum beat. The film's final image is of James back in his protective suit, walking toward another thing that might kill him; as he does so, the texture of the music becomes increasingly dense, filled with the sound of distorted guitars, and then swells to maximum volume as the image dissolves to show the end credits, over which the song continues.

Like the other two metal-sounding songs heard earlier, this closing musical piece is by the industrial metal band Ministry. A longstanding force in the world of industrial music, with a career stretching back to the early 1980s, Ministry makes an odd choice to define the tastes of a soldier in the 2000s. One might take the presence of their music as a sign of Bigelow and writer Mark Boal's efforts to denote James' age. Yet such a reading is too literal and does not take into account another key factor concerning Ministry: that, as an ongoing entity in the 2000s, the group—and, specifically, creative figurehead Al Jourgensen—dedicated the bulk of its recent output to a thoroughgoing and relentless sonic critique of the Bush administration and its military aggression.[11] The Arabic voice in the film's closing song, "Khyber Pass," is therefore not used as simple mark of "aural Orientalism," in Creekmur's terms, but is meant to evoke the voices of those victimized by US policies, voices that may be alternately energized or at risk of being drowned out by the surrounding din. When James' taste for metal is shown to be a taste for contemporary Ministry—all three songs in the film come from the band's 2007 album, *Rio Grande Blood*, the title a play on Bush's Texas background—then the music's role in the film expands beyond its support for James' hyperbolic enactment of military manhood. The sound of metal also serves, however implicitly, as a critique of the larger military and political initiatives that convert masculinity into a vehicle for annihilation.

Unlike *The Hurt Locker* and the documentary films discussed above, *The Messenger* is set not in Iraq, but rather in the US, where Sergeant Will Montgomery has returned after becoming an injured and decorated soldier during his deployment in Iraq. Beset with an eye injury that prevents him from being able to cry, Montgomery carries some powerful inner conflicts within him. Labeled a hero for his service, he is haunted by the truth behind his supposed heroic acts: his injury occurred during a failed attempt to keep another wounded soldier alive. Beside this echo of his military service, he is emotionally torn by his relationship with Kelly, the young woman he left behind upon enlisting, and who has subsequently become engaged to another man. His assignment, upon his return home, to the Casualty Notification arm of the military only adds to the tensions within his character. Repeatedly confronted with the difficult task of telling others about the

---

[11]   Writing for *AllMusic*, Jeffries describes the three Ministry albums released after 9/11— *Animositisomina, Houses of the Molé*, and *Rio Grande Blood*—as a "George W. Bush hating concept trilogy."

death of their loved ones, Montgomery is made to face his own emotional isolation as a soldier who has "returned" in body but not completely in mind.

Despite the pronounced differences between *The Messenger* and *The Hurt Locker* in plot and setting, the films use music—and heavy-metal music in particular—in some markedly similar ways. As with Will James, so with Will Montgomery, the sound of metal becomes a marker of the connection between the character and his personal space. Through much of *The Messenger*, Montgomery's apartment is the place where he is left to himself, where the private dimensions of his romantic and military life become magnified by his set-apartness. The scenes that feature Montgomery in his apartment are almost always at night, dimly lit, and often accompanied by metal music on the soundtrack, sometimes clearly as part of the diegetic space, as music that he has chosen to hear. An early scene, immediately following his having learned of his Casualty Notification assignment, shows Montgomery brooding around his apartment in his underpants at night. On the soundtrack, moody, arpeggio guitar lines give way to a heavy, distorted melody as the soldier sits on his bed, the high volume shown to be internal to Montgomery's environment as we hear the sound of a neighbor's voice shouting through the wall, "It's the middle of the fucking night, turn that goddamn music off!" In a later scene, after a particularly difficult death notification, Montgomery returns to his apartment and listens to an emotionally painful phone message from Kelly, who retracts her earlier invitation for him to attend her engagement party. Montgomery responds by punching a hole in his apartment wall, and then turns on some music to accompany him in his anger, the same loud but somber metal song heard before.

If a particular species of heavy metal—marked by alternation between quiet and loud passages, minor-key guitar melodies, an absence of vocals, and an emotionally downtrodden affect—amplifies Montgomery's withdrawal from the world beyond his apartment walls, another sort signals the possibility of his reconnection with that world. Two characters in the film represent this possibility: Tony Stone, his accomplice and commanding officer in his Casualty Notification duties, and Olivia Pitterson, the widow of a deceased soldier to whom Montgomery becomes drawn, against the ethical standards of his assignment. In a pivotal scene involving the latter, Will spies Pitterson in a shopping mall with her young son Matt while he is helping to recruit young men into military service. Shopping for clothes to attend her husband's funeral, Pitterson interrupts the recruiting efforts in protest, shouting about the details of her husband's remains. Will immediately assumes a protective air toward Olivia; when she leaves the mall, he follows her in his car. As he drives up to offer her a ride while she waits at a bus stop, his car stereo plays a song by the upbeat, groove-heavy metal band Clutch, "Profits of Doom." Although the resulting interaction between them is filled with awkwardness, the song—with its propulsive, almost funky rhythm and gruff, spirited vocal by singer Neil Fallon—suggests a more optimistic direction that is realized in the film's final scene, when the two promise to stay in touch after Olivia relocates to New Orleans.

This narrative trajectory in *The Messenger* makes it into a very different portrait of military masculinity than *The Hurt Locker*. Whereas Will James leaves his family behind to return to the front, eschewing the heterosexual scene of married domesticity for the homosocial setting of the Army, Will Montgomery longs for some kind of familial connection. That Olivia is shown to be not just a widow but a mother is a crucial detail in this regard, indicating that she has a capacity for nurturance that is balanced by her own need for emotional healing. That heavy metal music plays a critical role on the soundtrack to the film at precisely the moments when Montgomery's desires take shape is equally crucial, and also, perhaps, unexpected. Metal has tended to be associated more with the kind of masculinity personified by Will James, demonstrative, reckless, and narcissistic. Yet its use to support the character of Will Montgomery is not an aberration so much as it is a demonstration of Robert Walser's assertion that, in heavy metal, "there are no 'real men,'" but instead a variety of ways of enacting manhood through engagement with the genre and its trappings (136).

Neither *The Hurt Locker* nor *The Messenger* has much to offer regarding the relationship between US soldiers and Iraqi citizens, or the Iraqi experience of the surrounding war. In this they suffer in comparison to their documentary counterparts, *Soundtrack to War* and *Gunner Palace*, however limited the latter may also be. Another strain of Iraq War documentary has placed Iraqis more squarely at the center, what Pat Aufderheide refers to as "Learning from the Iraqis" films that are directed to "a public that is called into being around its vivid awareness of common humanity" (61–3). *Soundtrack to War* displays traces of this tendency. A far more dedicated example of this branch of Iraq War cinema, though, is *Heavy Metal in Baghdad*, a film that parallels *Soundtrack to War* in its emphasis on music as a path toward understanding the experience and impact of war, but goes well beyond that earlier film in drawing attention to Iraqi protagonists first and foremost (albeit depicted through the lens of two Canadian journalists and filmmakers, Eddy Moretti and Suroosh Alvi, whose presence in the film is pronounced). Beginning with the effort to document a seeming anomaly— an Iraqi heavy metal band—*Heavy Metal in Baghdad* becomes something more than a standard-issue music documentary, and reveals much about the conditions of dislocation and displacement that have been produced by years of protracted conflict.

Writing about the place of rock music in Iran, where public culture is circumscribed by a combination of religious proscription and political repression, historian Mark LeVine has observed that life in general tends to happen "inside." "Inside you don't need to wear your veil, you can blast your music, dance, watch pirated copies of the latest Hollywood—or Bollywood—movies," claims LeVine, who expands on this notion regarding rock and other forms of "nontraditional music," which are heard "not just indoors, but quite literally underground, in basements, the storage rooms of apartment buildings, and parking garages" (175–7). These remarks appear to apply directly to the experience of the Iraqi heavy metal band Acrassicauda, who were shown in their "literally underground" practice space during a sequence in *Soundtrack to War*, and are the primary subjects of *Heavy Metal in Baghdad*. In the group's six-year history up to the time of the latter film's 2007 release, they had managed to play a total of eight public gigs, six in Baghdad—half of which occurred before the onset of war in 2003— and two more after their 2006 relocation to Syria. Acrassicauda is a band whose sense of togetherness has mainly been forged in their private rehearsals, and the film captures the group members' shared commitment to heavy metal music under the most trying of circumstances.

Alvi, a Canadian of Pakistani background who was a founding editor of *Vice* magazine, is the principal narrator of *Heavy Metal in Baghdad*, and from the outset his involvement with the group goes well beyond that of the usual relationship between filmmaker and documentary subject. The first major event portrayed in the film is a 2005 concert organized by *Vice* on behalf of Acrassicauda at the Hotel Al Fanar in central Baghdad. Alvi and Moretti, traveling through Beirut, got stuck in transit due to bomb explosions in Lebanon and so had to enlist the help of a Danish photojournalist friend to facilitate the concert and its filming. This was only the beginning of the hardships faced in seeking to offer Acrassicauda an opportunity to play, as shots of tanks and blast walls in the immediate vicinity of the hotel offer visual evidence of the security risk undertaken just to make the event happen.

Despite the band following all the required protocols, including subjecting their equipment to a scrupulous search, as show time approaches the security forces guarding the hotel refuse to admit any of the attendees, "probably because of their Iron Maiden t-shirts and so on." Luckily, a conversation with a soldier stationed nearby allows the band to proceed as planned, but the time leading to the show is full of other moments of uncertainty: at one point a power failure, at another the sound of a mortar round exploding nearby. When the performance finally begins, it is as though the band has won a victory against fate. The all-male audience's enthusiasm, evident in localized versions of headbanging and moshing and in the preponderance of t-shirts for a wide swath of metal bands, illustrates drummer Marwan Fiyadh's comments: "You just feel like you've been, like, caged, like there's chains all around you. So like, we just like, for two hours, three hours, the practice time or the live performance, we want to free ourselves from that chain." And the explosion of excitement that the band's music elicits makes all the more poignant Alvi's voiceover explanation at the end of the show that this would be the last concert Acrassicauda would ever play in Iraq.

Besides its focus on this unusual group of Iraqi heavy-metal musicians, *Heavy Metal in Baghdad* stands out in relation to the other films discussed so far by unfolding over a much longer period of time. Both the documentaries and the fictional narratives about the Iraq war have tended to happen over fairly compressed time frames, a matter of weeks or maybe of months, but rarely so long as even a year overall. *Heavy Metal in Baghdad*, however, moves across a span of years rather than months, and so the cumulative effects of the war are more fully apparent. Thus, when Alvi and Moretti travel to Baghdad in 2006, in what will be their first face-to-face meeting with the members of Acrassicauda, the circumstances of life in Iraq have changed dramatically, and not for the better. Of the group's members, only bassist Firas Al-Lateef and singer Faisal Talal remain in Baghdad. Guitarist Tony Aziz had moved to Syria almost a year earlier, just after the group's last concert, to escape the violence and try to earn money to support his family, and drummer Fiyadh had joined him some months later. Violence due to the surrounding civil war had become pervasive and all but inescapable. In these conditions, the band existed in a state of fractured, suspended animation best indicated by the fact that its rehearsal space of several years, where they had been filmed in 2003, had been blown up by an exploding missile. Alvi seeks to arrange a visit to the bombed-out space with Al-Lateef, but the dangerous conditions of the Baghdad streets only allow them to film at a distance while driving past. Instead, Firas shows his own homemade video of the wreckage taken shortly after the explosion, as he and Faisal vent about the anger and despair they feel at the senselessness of what surrounds them.

After another four-month ellipsis, Alvi and Moretti reconnect with the members of Acrassicauda, all of whom had now made the move to Syria. Alvi recites a set of statistics and news reports to offer a context for the band's situation: the Iraqi insurgency has placed even greater restrictions on musical activity in the country than had previously existed; the death toll from the combined occupation and civil war had risen to 655,000 by fall 2006; and, most notably, Iraqi refugees had dispersed widely to various surrounding countries, with Syria alone drawing 1.2 million. For its final half-hour, *Heavy Metal in Baghdad* becomes a story of this exodus as viewed through the experiences of four twenty-something Iraqi heavy-metal musicians. We see Acrassicauda play its first Syrian concert in a combined pool hall and Internet café, the first concert the band will have played together in almost two years, and an event around which their future as a band hinges. Marwan explains to the camera, upon surveying the sparse attendance in the hall: "We made a decision, all four of us, that this concert, if we made a big gig down here, we'll last forever, we'll keep playing music, because the whole situation is different for us right now [as Iraqi refugees in Syria] ... So, probably this is going to be the last gig for Acrassicauda." However, as with the earlier concert in Baghdad, the show is a minor triumph. The small crowd was won over by the band's convincing covers of Metallica songs, and the group eventually broke from its plan to play only covers, and finished with a number of its original compositions to a spirited reception, leaving Marwan to contradict his earlier pessimism and proclaim, "Metal up your ass," a phrase made popular by Metallica in that group's early career.

This sense of triumph is integral to the fabric of *Heavy Metal in Baghdad*, but it is not definitive or conclusive. Indeed, the film leaves its viewers less with a sense of uplift than of uncertainty filtered through the growing homesickness of the band members. A sequence in which Acrassicauda goes into a Damascus recording studio to record a demo, with assistance from the filmmakers, offers strong evidence that their musical aspirations remain intact. Yet when interviewed after the session has ended, their pride is undercut by an inescapable feeling of displacement. Firas reveals that, during the session, he got a phone call from his mother, who tells him, "Never come back." Marwan also describes his guilt about the family members he left behind. These sentiments become intensified in the final moments of the film, when the band watches rough footage of the film being made about them. Nostalgia for Baghdad informs the group's response to the footage from the start; but when the film reaches the scenes of their old, bombed-out rehearsal space, that nostalgia turns to open sadness, especially for Marwan, who had already left when the space was destroyed. His final address to the viewer echoes the words of the soldier/rapper in *Gunner Palace*, for whom the reality of war was impenetrable to the outside observer: "These are things that you lay your back on. These are things that you turn off the TV whenever or like change the channel when it's on. So for you fuckers down there, this is how it goes, this is the daily life in Iraq. This goes to all of you, fuckers. Pigs." Following this climactic note of indignation, *Heavy Metal in Baghdad* ends with a series of titles explaining that the band had to sell its instruments to pay rent, continues to live in limbo, and "is still trying to find its way to a place where they can live in peace, grow their hair long, bang their heads and play heavy metal again as loud as they want."

The reality stressed by Iraqi metal musician Marwan Fiyadh and that sung about by African American soldier Richmond Shaw may be viewed as two sides of the same proverbial coin, or as an indication that the Iraq War, like any other complex political event, has no single reality but assumes meaning through a variety of competing narratives that may be more or less commensurate with one another. One could say the same for the uses to which heavy metal music has been put in films about the Iraq War. Certainly, there are shared tendencies among these five films under discussion. The association between heavy metal and masculinity, for instance, is inescapable in all of the films surveyed. This includes *Heavy Metal in Baghdad*, in which the all-male constituency for Acrassicauda's concerts is openly recognized by the band members and explained as a mark of the country's "traditions." Yet this example also speaks to the circumstantial nature of heavy metal's relationship to masculinity, for Iraqi proscriptions on the ability of women to participate in public cultural events hardly explain the use of metal to support the construction of military male subjectivity in *The Hurt Locker* or *The Messenger*. That these latter two films contrast significantly over the values they attach to their white American male subjects only reinforces the larger point that, while heavy metal is a strongly masculinized musical form, there are a plurality of masculinities that find definition through the genre, in or out of a zone of combat.

Such diversification is also characteristic of heavy metal in a more fundamental sense. Like all music genres, metal is composed of a system of signs—sounds, images, aspects of discourse—in which those elements that confer the appearance of integrity are continually in dialogue with those elements that encourage differentiation. There has never been just one right way to play metal or one right sort of metal fan; and the variety of subgenres that collectively comprise the metal genre have expanded dramatically since the early 1990s. Films about the Iraq War offer much evidence of this diversification of the metal genre and the different sorts of meaning that might become attached to metal in different circumstances. For Bradley Corkins and Stuart Wilf, gore metal provides an important resource for grappling with the more extreme violence encountered in the course of combat. In *The Hurt Locker*, by contrast, the music of industrial metal band Ministry brings a politically critical subtext to what might otherwise seem a basic correlation drawn between musical and military aggression. *The Messenger*, in turn, plays two distinct kinds of metal sounds—one that might be classified as progressive metal, the other as blues metal—against each other to inform the multiple registers of its protagonist's emotional response to his return from war. Across these examples, we see that, despite the commonsense linkage between metal and the will to destruction provocatively posited by Michael Moore in this essay's opening example, heavy metal has not simply been used—either by soldiers or by filmmakers—to aurally represent the kind of power that clearly exerts itself over others. Instead, different types of metal have been employed to portray distinct forms of experience and subjectivity associated with the war.

Another dimension of this tendency toward variation in metal has been the genre's increasingly global reach. Studies of metal and globalization by Mark LeVine, Emma Baulch, Jeremy Wallach, and others have shown that, while metal may be a genre with clear roots in the US and Europe, it has been invested with considerable local significance as it has moved to other regions of the world. Keith Kahn-Harris has added an important comparative element to this line of analysis, and emphasizes that the current "extreme metal scene"—which encompasses most of the varieties of metal discussed herein, including that played by Acrassicauda—can best be understood as a "global scene that includes local scenes within it" (22). The significance of metal for the members of Acrassicauda is clearly an exemplification of this globalizing tendency, and reveals both the power and the fluidity of heavy metal as a term of identification. For bassist Firas Al-Lateef, heavy metal transcends any specific national or political interests; interviewed after the completion of *Heavy Metal in Baghdad*, he connects himself primarily to a "country" of metalheads, who themselves are global in scope (Capper and Sifre 151). However, heavy metal is integral to the continuing sense of connection that he and his band mates feel toward Iraq as they become exiled from their country of origin. Iraq is where they discovered heavy metal, and where they forged their connections with each other through their mutual attraction to the genre, which was fortified in underground spaces where the music seemed, temporarily at least, like all that mattered. For them, heavy metal has become the sound of Iraqis in exile, political casualties of the US "war on terror."

Works Cited

Aufderheide, Pat. "Your Country, My Country: How Films About the Iraq War Construct Publics." *Framework* 48.2 (2007): 56–65. Print.

Baulch, Emma. *Making Scenes: Reggae, Punk, and Death Metal in 1990s Bali.* Durham, NC: Duke UP, 2007. Print.

Bloodhound Gang. "Fire Water Burn." *One Fierce Beer Coaster.* Geffen, 1996. CD.

Capper, Andy, and Gabi Sifre. *Heavy Metal in Baghdad: The Story of Acrassicauda.* New York: MTV Books, 2009. Print.

Carruthers, Susan. "Say Cheese! Operation Iraqi Freedom on Film." *Cineaste* 32.1 (2006): 30–36. Print.

Clutch. "Profits of Doom." *Blast Tyrant.* DRT Entertainment, 2004. CD.

Creekmur, Corey. "The Sound of the 'War on Terror'." *Reframing 9/11: Film, Popular Culture and the "War on Terror."* Ed. Jeff Birkenstein, Anna Froula, and Karen Randell. New York: Continuum, 2010: 83–93. Print.

Cusick, Suzanne. "'You Are in a Place That Is out of the World …': Music in the Detention Camps of the 'Global War on Terror'." *Journal of the Society for American Music* 2.1 (2008): 1–26. Print.

Fahrenheit 9/11. Dir. Michael Moore. Sony, 2004. DVD.

Faludi, Susan. *The Terror Dream: Fear and Fantasy in Post-9/11 America.* New York: Metropolitan Books, 2007. Print.

Fuchs, Cynthia. "There Wasn't a Front Line: Interview with Michael Tucker and Jon Powers." *PopMatters* (2005). Web. Oct. 11, 2010.

Gilman, Lisa. "An American Soldier's iPod: Layers of Identity and Situated Listening in Iraq." *Music & Politics* 4.2 (2010): 1–17. Web. Oct. 9. 2010.

Gunner Palace. Dir. Michael Tucker and Petra Epperlein. Palm Pictures, 2005. DVD.

Heavy Metal in Baghdad. Dir. Eddy Moretti and Suroosh Alvi. Arts Alliance America, 2008. DVD.

The Hurt Locker. Dir. Kathryn Bigelow. Perf. Jeremy Renner, Anthony Mackie, Brian Geraghty. Summit, 2010. DVD.

Jeffries, David. Review of Ministry, *Adios … Putas Madres. AllMusic.* Web. Jan. 22, 2011.

Kahn-Harris, Keith. *Extreme Metal: Music and Culture on the Edge.* Oxford: Berg, 2007. Print.

Kassabian, Anahid. *Hearing Film: Tracking Identifications in Contemporary Hollywood Film Music.* New York: Routledge, 2001. Print.

LeVine, Mark. *Heavy Metal Islam: Rock, Resistance, and the Struggle for the Soul of Islam.* New York: Three Rivers Press, 2008. Print.

The Messenger. Dir. Oren Moverman. Perf. Ben Foster, Woody Harrelson, Samantha Morton. Oscilloscope, 2010. DVD.

Ministry. *Rio Grande Blood.* Megaforce, 2007. CD.

Pieslak, Jonathan. *Sound Targets: American Soldiers and Music in the Iraq War*. Bloomington: Indiana UP, 2007. Print.

Ritter, Jonathan, and J. Martin Daughtry (eds). *Music in the Post-9/11 World*. New York: Routledge, 2007. Print.

Schmelz, Peter. "'Have You Forgotten?': Darryl Worley and the Musical Politics of Operation Iraqi Freedom." Ritter and Daughtry 123–54. Print.

Six Feet Under. *Warpath*. Metal Blade, 1997. CD.

Sklar, Robert. Review of *The Hurt Locker*. *Cineaste* 34.1 (2009): 55–6. Print.

Slayer. *Reign in Blood*. American, 1986. CD.

Soundtrack to War. Dir. George Gittoes. Melee, 2006. DVD.

Wallach, Jeremy. *Modern Noise, Fluid Genres: Popular Music in Indonesia, 1997–2001*. Madison: U of Wisconsin, 2008. Print.

Walser, Robert. *Running with the Devil: Power, Gender, and Madness in Heavy Metal Music*. Hanover, NH: Wesleyan UP, 1993. Print.

Weinstein, Deena. *Heavy Metal: The Music and Its Culture*. New York: Da Capo, 2000. Print.

Whitsitt, Sam. "'Come Back to the Humvee Ag'in Will Honey,' or a Few Comments About the Sexual Politics of Kathryn Bigelow's *The Hurt Locker*." *Jump Cut* 52 (2010). Web. Oct. 10, 2010.

Index

Acrassicauda (band) 191, 201-205
Afghanistan xi, 15, 16, 75, 83, 84, 86, 87,
     115, 116, 129, 155, 173, 191, 197
   United States War in Afghanistan 15,
     75, 83, 84, 86, 87, 115, 116, 129,
     155, 173, 191, 197
   the album 7, 49. 57-68, 93-103
   digitization of album 66, 67
      downloading 66, 67, 96, 103, 117
   performed live in entirety 7
   physicality of album 66, 67, 93-103
   protest albums 57-68
Alkaline Trio (band) 9, 146, 149-152
   "All on Black" (song) 150
   "The American Scream" (song) 151,
     152
   "Armageddon" (song) 151
   "Mercy Me" (song) 151
   "Over and Out" (song) 151
   "We've Had Enough" (song) 152
America's Army (video game) 14, 17, 18
   as recruitment tool 18
American Airlines Flight 11 3
American Idiot (musical) 146, 154, 155,
     177
American Idol (television show) 5, 6, 9, 95,
     163, 164, 169
Anderson, Mark 9, 134, 141
Armstrong, Billy Joe 153, 154
Atta, Mohamed 2, 3, 70
Attali, Jacques 3, 4, 31-33, 35

Basinski, William 1, 2, 4, 7, 47
   The Disintegration Loops (album) 1,
     2, 4
Baudrillard, Jean 3n, 61
Beach Boys, The 118, 122, 123
Beastie Boys 108n, 117
Beatles, The 6, 34, 40, 61, 115, 118-121,
     124, 125, 128

The Beatles ["The White Album"] (album)
     6, 118
   "Revolution" (song) 115, 118-120
Bloodhound Gang (band) 185, 186
   "Fire Water Burn" (song) 185, 186
Braudel, Fernand 58, 59, 63, 64
   longue duree (Braudel concept) 58,
     63, 64
Burkett, "Fat" Mike 129-131, 133, 137,
     139-142, 177, 179-181
Bush, George H. W. 107
Bush, George W. xii, 9, 34-36, 40, 70, 94n,
     99, 109, 111, 113, 116, 124, 129,
     131, 133, 145-148, 151, 153, 154,
     162, 167, 185, 198
   administration of 13, 15, 34, 36, 94, 98,
     100, 129, 141, 145-148, 154, 173,
     180, 185, 195n, 198
   criticism of administration 94, 100,
     141, 145-148, 154, 185, 198
Butler, Judith 14, 16, 19

Cage, John 47, 80
Casale, Jerry (Devo) 147, 148
cassette tapes 7
Cassetteboy (recording artists) 8, 69-78
   "Fly Me to New York" (song) 69-75,
     77
   The Parker Tapes (album) 70,72-74, 76
Certeau, Michel de 62, 63
Cheney, Dick 36, 195n
Clear Channel 74, 96, 116, 117
   "questionable" songs list 116, 117
Clinton, William Jefferson (Bill) 35
code (with networks) 31-41, 102-104
the Cold War 17, 46, 51, 62, 87
Columbia Records 119, 149
compact discs xv, 59, 96, 100, 166, 189
conservativepunk.com (website) 130-132,
     141

counterculture 8, 34, 37, 39, 40, 61-63, 66-
      68, 111, 119-121, 130, 174
   activism and 103, 125
   in America 57
   in the 1960s 115, 120, 121, 175
   musical counterculture 40
country music 161-170, 186, 187
   revenge songs 161, 162, 170
"The Creed" (commercial) 20
Critical Art Ensemble (CAE) 35, 36
Cusick, Suzanne 16, 17, 192n

Dahlen, Chris 72-74
Danger Mouse (recording artist) 6, 39
   The Grey Album (album) 6, 39
Davis, Miles 7, 80
Debord, Guy 146, 155
Deleuze, Gilles 33, 39, 41, 94, 102
Derrida, Jacques 174
Desrosiers, Mark 4
digital downloading xv, 6, 25, 45, 49, 50,
      96, 117
Digital Millenium Copyright Act 95
Dirty Beaches 46, 51
discipline 33, 34, 37-39, 89
Dixie Chicks, The 9, 139, 162, 166-170
   controversy surrounding anti-War
      views 166-168
   "Goodbye Earl" (song) 162, 166, 170
Dylan, Bob 5, 7, 40, 57, 61, 62, 65, 75,
      118, 122, 124-126
   "The Times They Are A-Changin'"
      (song) 57, 122, 124

Edelman, Lee 147
Eminem 33-36, 112-113
   "Mosh" (song) 34-36, 113
Explosions in the Sky (band) xi-xvi, 5n
   All of a Sudden I Miss Everyone
      (album) xiv
   cover art for xiv
   The Earth is Not a Cold Dead Place
      (album) xiii
   impact of 9/11 upon xii
   Take Care, Take Care, Take Care
      (album) xv

*Those Who Tell the Truth Shall Die,
   Those Who Tell the Truth Shall
   Live Forever* (album) xi, xii, 5n
   controversy surrounding xi

Facebook 59, 60, 63, 65
Fahrenheit 9/11 (film) 185, 186
Fiasco, Lupe (rapper) 108, 109
file sharing xii, 25, 60, 95, 96, 125
Fleet Foxes (band) 9, 121-124
   Fleet Foxes (album) 124
   Sun Giant (EP) 123
Foucault, Michel 33, 37-39, 94, 95
   The History of Sexuality 94
Frank, Thomas 57, 119, 121
   The Conquest of Cool 119

Garofalo, Reebee 13n, 16, 115-117
Gittoes, George 185, 186, 188, 189-191
Go Army (website) 17
Green Day 9, 33, 34, 117, 137, 146, 149,
      151, 153-157, 177
   American Idiot (album) 34, 35, 146,
      153-155
Grizzly Bear (band) 9, 121-124
   Horn of Plenty (album) 121, 122
   Yellow House (album) 123
Gunner Palace (film) 187, 191-195, 200,
      203
Guthrie, Woody 57, 62, 118

heavy metal 7, 9, 20, 185-204
   power and 190
   "nu metal" 7
Heavy Metal in Baghdad (film) 187, 190,
      191, 200-204
Hebdige, Dick 135, 146
   Subculture 135
Hendrix, Jimi 40, 120, 175, 194
hip-hop 9, 48n, 69, 72, 107-114, 187, 189,
      192, 193
   Diamond Age of 108, 113
   politics and 9
hipsters 46, 47
Hrasky, Christopher xii-xvi
Hurt Locker, The (film) 187, 195-200, 203,
      204
Hurricane Katrina xi, xiv, 111

Hussein, Saddam 186-188

improvisation 8, 44, 79-89
improvised explosive devices (IED) 8,
    79-89, 190
Indie rock xi, xiii, 129, 146
Internet xii, 6-8, 13-26, 31-33, 40, 48-51,
    59, 86, 96, 98, 110, 144, 145, 148,
    202
iPod 8, 31, 33, 38-42, 46, 49
Iraq xi, 15, 16, 70, 75, 115, 116, 185-204
    United States War in Iraq 8, 9, 15, 34,
        36, 46, 79-89, 93, 94, 99, 107, 124,
        129, 147, 151, 154, 155, 185-204
iTunes xv, 39, 49

Jay-Z 5, 6, 111, 112
    The Black Album (album) 6
    The Blueprint (album) 5, 111
    The Blueprint 3 (album) 112
jazz 8, 79-89
free jazz 44
Jobs, Steve 40, 41
Johnson, Steven 59, 60, 63, 65, 66

Keith, Toby 5, 74, 169
    "Courtesy of the Red, White, and Blue
        (The Angry American)" (song) 5,
        74
Kerry, John 35, 36, 130, 133, 140
Kid Rock 20, 175

bin Laden, Osama 36, 46, 76n
LCD Soundsystem (band) 4, 7
Lennon, John 117, 118, 120, 125, 126
lo-fi 1, 3, 4, 8, 44, 51, 52
Lynn, Loretta 165, 166, 168

MacKaye, Ian 9, 134-136, 139, 141
McCartney, Paul 5, 121
McLuhan, Marshall 58, 59, 66
McTague, Tim (Underoath) 177-181
Messenger, The (film) 187, 195, 198-200,
    203, 204
Metallica 88, 117, 202
Ministry (band) 198, 204
Moore, Michael 182, 185, 186, 204
mp3 files 6, 8, 25, 33, 38, 39, 47, 96, 100

Music Television (MTV) 21, 22, 111, 129,
    130
MySpace 63, 96

Napster (filesharing service) 33, 39, 60, 53,
    95, 96
National Recording Preservation Act of
    2000 6, 7
networks (computing) 31-41, 49, 57-68
New York City 1, 3-5, 41, 57, 69-78, 89,
    107, 112, 147,
    New York City Fire Department 3, 145
The 9/11 Commission Report 2, 3, 20, 72,
    76n, 81
Nine Inch Nails 6, 8, 33, 34 39, 93-103
    The Slip (album) 6, 103
    Year Zero (album) 8, 34, 35, 93-103
NOFX (band) 129, 130, 137, 144, 145,
    177, 179, 180
noise 3, 4, 32, 33, 37, 44-48, 50-52
nostalgia 7, 34, 35, 43-52, 115-126
    technostalgia 43-52

Obama, Barack 110, 111, 113, 140

Palumbo-Liu, David 13, 18
Pentagon 3, 69, 115
Pitchfork (online magazine) xi, 1, 8, 31,
    53, 65, 67, 73
politics xiii, 9, 13, 16, 19, 26, 32-34, 45,
    52, 57, 58, 83, 89, 115-118, 148,
    195
    American politics 4, 110
    biopolitics 93-103
    conservative politics 129-141
    gender politics 146
    musicians as apolitical 47, 87
    musicians and political activism 33-36,
        103, 129, 134, 140
    digital activism 18, 19
    politics of race 107-114
PopMatters (online magazine) 1, 8, 44
Propagandhi (band) 14, 18-20, 23, 25, 26,
    130, 140
    "(America's Army) Die Jugend
        Marschiert" (song) 14, 18, 19
protest music 9, 13, 14, 19, 26, 52, 57, 58,
    61-63, 66, 67, 115-119, 125

anti-War protest music 115, 117
"big tent" protest movements 58, 66
    in post-9/11 context 52, 118
punk rock 9, 129-141, 146-156
    Christianity and 9, 173-182
Punk Voter 129-133, 136, 139-141
    conservatism and 9, 129-141, 180, 181

al Qaeda 32, 33, 71, 72, 80, 73, 88

Rabid, Jack 148, 149, 152, 156
Radiohead 6, 8, 66, 67
    Hail to the Thief (album) 8, 66, 67
    In Rainbows (album) 6, 8, 66, 67
Ramones 64, 133, 135, 140, 142, 143
Reagan, Ronald 77, 133, 136, 139, 175
Reznor, Trent see Nine Inch Nails
Rizzuto, Nick 131-133, 138, 141
Rock Against Bush campaign see 2004
    United States Presidential Election
Rock Against Bush (album) 130, 133, 151
The Rolling Stones 57, 118, 119, 121
    "Street Fighting Man" (song) 118, 119
Roszak, Theodore 37, 38
R.E.M. (band) 35, 117, 121

September 11, 2001 terrorist attacks xi-xiii,
    1-5, 7, 8, 34, 41, 69-81, 89, 109-
    112, 132
    media coverage of 2, 3, 5, 8, 145
    patriotic responses to 5, 9, 94, 95
Sex Pistols (band) 137, 140, 153, 156, 176
Sinatra, Frank 7, 8, 69, 70, 72-75, 77
Skiba, Matt (Alkaline Trio) 150-152
Slayer (band) 5, 7, 188, 189
    "Angel of Death" (song) 188
    God Hates Us All (album) 5
    Reign in Blood (album) 7, 188
Soundtrack to War (film) 185, 187-192,
    194, 195, 200, 201
Springsteen, Bruce 1, 75, 76, 125, 129
    The Rising (album) 1
Stockhausen, Karlheinz 79-81, 89
Strokes, The (band) 3-5
    Is This It (album) 3-5

Taliban Movement 116, 173
    John Walker Lindh and 116

Tea Party Movement 83, 173
Telecommunications Act of 1996 95n, 116,
    168
3 Doors Down 14, 21, 24, 26
    "Citizen/Soldier" (video) 14, 16, 17-26
    as recruitment tool for National
        Guard 20-26
    trauma 69, 72, 76, 107, 151-153, 192, 195,
        198-200
Tucker, Michael 192, 193
2004 United States Presidential Election
    35, 129
    Rock Against Bush campaign 129, 130,
        133, 146, 151

Underoath 9, 173-182
    "In Regards to Myself" (song) 178
Underwood, Carrie 5, 9, 161-166, 169
    "Before He Cheats" (song) 162, 164,
        165, 170
United States military 14, 15, 17-20
    US Army National Guard 14, 16-18,
        20-26
USA Patriot Act 34, 93, 94, 111

Vale, Val 148, 149
Vietnam War 13, 19, 21, 40, 57, 76, 115,
    119, 125, 151, 175
vinyl records xv, 7
    resurgence of vinyl 7
Virilio, Paul 41
Vivian Girls (Brooklyn, NY band) 46, 51,
    52

Waksman, Steve 7, 9, 24
"the war on terror" 13, 14, 17-20, 23, 26,
    70, 74, 108, 116, 145, 148, 150,
    182, 188, 194, 204
Wavves (band) 44, 46, 50, 51, 54
weapons of mass destruction (WMD) 93,
    109, 147
West, Kanye 111
Wilf, Stuart 193-195, 204
Wilkow, Andrew 131, 132, 138, 139
Williams, Nathan see Wavves
Woodstock Festival (1969) 34, 35, 120,
    128, 175, 194

World Trade Center 1, 3, 5, 15, 35, 69-80,
    111, 112, 115, 152, 168, 173
    Ground Zero 79, 89, 112, 152, 168,
       173
       Ground Zero Mosque 112, 152,
          173

YouTube 8, 20, 22, 25, 59

Zizek, Slavoj 2, 3, 13, 16, 77n, 173
    Welcome to the Desert of the Real! 2,
       173